Math in Focus®

Singapore Math®
by Marshall Cavendish

Student Edition

Program Consultant
Dr. Fong Ho Kheong

Marshall Cavendish
Education

U.S. Distributor

Houghton Mifflin Harcourt.
The Learning Company™

Course
3A

Contents

Chapter

2 Exponents

Chapter Opener

How do you represent repeated multiplication of the same factor?

Interpreting the real number system • Adding and subtracting integers
• Multiplying and dividing integers • Finding the square of a whole number
• Finding the cube of a whole number

Activity

Scientific Notation

Chapter Opener

 How do you write very large and very small numbers in a convenient way?

RECALL PRIOR KNOWLEDGE

Multiplying and dividing decimals by positive powers of 10

Activity

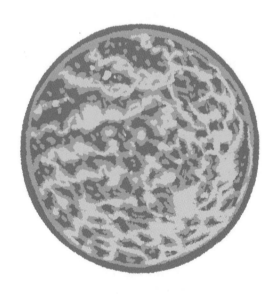

4 Linear Equations and Inequalities

Chapter Opener   157

 **How do you solve for a variable in a linear equation with two variables?**

RECALL PRIOR KNOWLEDGE   158

Identifying equivalent fractions • Expressing the relationship between two quantities with a linear equation • Solving algebraic equations • Representing fractions as repeating decimals • Solving algebraic inequalities

Activity

$x^2 + x - 1 = 0$

5 Lines and Linear Equations

Chapter Opener

How do you write an equation of a linear graph?

RECALL PRIOR KNOWLEDGE

Interpreting direct proportion

▶ Activity

Bike $7 per hour
Baby Seat $8

Systems of Linear Equations

Chapter Opener

 How do you solve two equations involving two variables?

RECALL PRIOR KNOWLEDGE

Graphing linear equations using a table of values • Solving real-world problems algebraically

▶ Activity

Preface

Welcome!

Math in Focus® is a program that puts you at the center of an exciting learning experience! This experience is all about equipping you with critical thinking skills and mathematical strategies, explaining your thinking to deepen your understanding, and helping you to become a skilled and confident problem solver.

What's in your book?

Each chapter in this book begins with a real-world situation of the math topic you are about to learn.

In each chapter, you will encounter the following features:

THINK introduces a problem for the whole section, to stimulate creative and critical thinking and help you hone your problem-solving skills. You may not be able to answer the problem right away but you can revisit it a few times as you build your knowledge through the section.

ENGAGE consists of tasks that link what you already know with what you will be learning next. The tasks allow you to explore and discuss mathematical concepts with your classmates.

LEARN introduces new mathematical concepts through a Concrete-Pictorial-Abstract (C-P-A) approach, using activities and examples.

Activity comprises learning experiences that promote collaboration with your classmates. These activities allow you to reinforce your learning or uncover new mathematical concepts.

TRY supports and reinforces your learning through guided practice.

INDEPENDENT PRACTICE allows you to work on a variety of problems and apply the concepts and skills you have learned to solve these problems on your own.

Additional features include:

RECALL PRIOR KNOWLEDGE	 Math Talk	MATH SHARING	⚠️ Caution, and Math Note
Helps you recall related concepts you learned before, accompanied by practice questions	Invites you to explain your reasoning and communicate your ideas to your classmates and teachers	Encourages you to create strategies, discover methods, and share them with your classmates and teachers using mathematical language	Highlights common errors and misconceptions, as well as provides you with useful hints and reminders
LET'S EXPLORE	**MATH JOURNAL**	**PUT ON YOUR THINKING CAP!**	**CHAPTER WRAP-UP**
Extends your learning through investigative activities	Allows you to reflect on your learning when you write down your thoughts about the mathematical concepts learned	Challenges you to apply the mathematical concepts to solve problems, and also hones your critical thinking skills	Summarizes your learning in a flow chart and helps you to make connections within the chapter
CHAPTER REVIEW	**Assessment Prep**	**PERFORMANCE TASK**	**STEAM**
Provides you with ample practice in the concepts learned	Prepares you for state tests with assessment-type problems	Assesses your learning through problems that allow you to demonstrate your understanding and knowledge	Promotes collaboration with your classmates through interesting projects that allow you to use math in creative ways

Are you ready to experience math the Singapore way? Let's go!

The Real Number System

Have you ever been on a Ferris wheel?

A Ferris wheel revolves around its hub, lifting passengers and carrying them in a circle. You need the number π to calculate the distance traveled in one revolution of a Ferris wheel. Common approximations of π include $\frac{22}{7}$ and 3.14. A closer approximation of π is the calculator value 3.141592654.

Look again at the last digit in the approximation of π. Did you know that the exact value of π does not stop there? π belongs to a group of numbers called irrational numbers.

The real number system comprises irrational numbers and rational numbers. In this chapter, you will learn about the numbers that make up real numbers and how to locate them on a number line.

? **What numbers make up the set of real numbers?**

Name: _____   Date: _____

Expressing rational numbers in $\frac{m}{n}$ form

A rational number is a number that can be written as $\frac{m}{n}$, where m and n are integers with $n \neq 0$.

Integers, fractions, and decimals can all be written as $\frac{m}{n}$.

a $-52 = \dfrac{-52}{1}$

b $7\dfrac{2}{3} = \dfrac{7 \cdot 3}{3} + \dfrac{2}{3}$

$\quad\quad = \dfrac{21}{3} + \dfrac{2}{3}$

$\quad\quad = \dfrac{23}{3}$

c $-1.64 = -1\dfrac{64}{100}$

$\quad\quad\quad = \dfrac{-164}{100}$

$\quad\quad\quad = \dfrac{-41}{25}$

▶ **Quick Check**

Write each number in $\frac{m}{n}$ form, where m and n are integers, with $n \neq 0$.

1 29   **2** $5\dfrac{1}{8}$ **3** -2.37

Locating rational numbers on a number line

To locate the rational numbers $\frac{3}{4}$ and -1.8 on a number line:

STEP 1 Find the integers that each rational number lies between.

$$0 < \frac{3}{4} < 1, -2 < -1.8 < -1$$

STEP 2 Graph a number line and label the integers.

© 2020 Marshall Cavendish Education Pte Ltd

STEP 3 Divide the distance between –2 and –1 into 10 equal segments and the distance between 0 and 1 into 4 equal segments

STEP 4 Use the segments to locate $\frac{3}{4}$ and –1.8.

▶ **Quick Check**

Draw a number line. Then, locate each pair of rational numbers on the number line.

④ $\frac{3}{2}$ and –0.25

⑤ –0.8 and $\frac{1}{5}$

Writing rational numbers as terminating or repeating decimals

Any rational number can be written in decimal form using long division.

To write $\frac{3}{4}$ as a decimal:

```
   0.75      Divide 3 by 4.
4)3.00       Add zeros after the decimal point.
 -2 8
 ‾‾‾‾
   20
  -20
  ‾‾‾
    0        The remainder is 0.
```

So, $\frac{3}{4}$ = 0.75.

0.75 is called a terminating decimal because it has a finite number of nonzero decimal places.

To write $\frac{2}{11}$ as a decimal:

```
        0.181818
   11 ) 2.000000
        1 1
          90
          88
          20
          11
            90
            88
            20
            11
              90
              88
               2
```

Divide 2 by 11.
Add zeros after the decimal point.

The remainder will not terminate with 0.

You can stop dividing when you see the digits continue to repeat themselves.

So, $\frac{2}{11}$ = 0.1818...

0.1818... is called a repeating decimal because it has a group of one or more digits that repeat endlessly.

You write 0.1818... as $0.\overline{18}$ since the digits 1 and 8 repeat.

 Quick Check

Using long division, write each rational number as a terminating decimal.

 6 $\frac{4}{32}$

7 $\frac{77}{25}$

Using long division, write each rational number as a repeating decimal.

8 $\frac{4}{9}$

9 $\frac{31}{6}$

Comparing rational numbers on a number line

It can be easier to compare rational numbers on a number line if you write the rational numbers as decimals.

To compare $\frac{13}{11}$ and $\frac{7}{4}$:

$\frac{13}{11} = 1.1818…$

$\frac{7}{4} = 1.75$

$\quad = 1.\overline{18}$

On a number line, 1.75 lies to the right of $1.\overline{18}$.

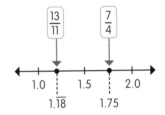

So, $1.75 > 1.\overline{18}$

$\quad \frac{7}{4} > \frac{13}{11}$

To compare $-1\frac{2}{5}$ and $-\frac{19}{10}$:

$-1\frac{2}{5} = -1.4$

$-\frac{19}{10} = -1.9$

You can use the absolute values of $-1\frac{2}{5}$ and $-\frac{19}{10}$ to locate the decimals on a number line.

$|-1.4| = 1.4$

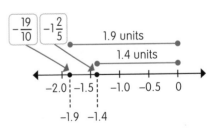

$|-1.9| = 1.9$

On a number line, $-\frac{19}{10}$ lies further left of 0 than $-1\frac{2}{5}$.

So, $-1.9 < -1.4$

$\quad -\frac{19}{10} < -1\frac{2}{5}$

▶ **Quick Check**

Compare each pair of rational numbers using the symbols < or >. Use a number line to help you.

10. $\dfrac{20}{3} \bigcirc \dfrac{5}{2}$

11. $-\dfrac{18}{5} \bigcirc -1\dfrac{7}{10}$

Rounding numbers

When rounding a number to a particular place value, you look at the digit to the right of the given place value to decide whether you have to round up or round down.

For example, to round a number to the nearest tenth you round down if the digit in the hundredths place is less than 5. If the digit in the hundredths place is 5 or more, you round up.

▶ **Quick Check**

Round each decimal to 2 decimal places.

12. 1,356.255
    (2 decimal places)

13. 405.4101
    (2 decimal places)

1 Introducing Irrational Numbers

Learning Objective:
• Use rational approximations of irrational numbers to locate irrational numbers approximately on a number line.

New Vocabulary
irrational number

THINK

The dots on a grid are 1 centimeter apart. On a number line, locate the side length of the square drawn on the grid.

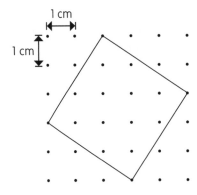

ENGAGE

Find the side length of each square that has the area given.

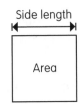
Side length
Area

Area (square units)	1	4	9	16
Side Length (units)				

How does the table of values help you find the side length of a square with an area of 2 square units? How do you use the areas of other squares to locate the value of the side length on a number line? Explain your thinking.

LEARN Locate irrational numbers on a number line using areas of squares

Activity Finding the value of √2 using a square

① Square *ABCD* is made up of 4 smaller squares. The side length of each small square is 1 inch. Find the area of *ABCD*.

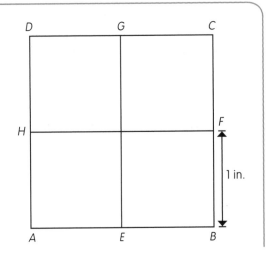

(2) If there are lines joining the points *EF, FG, GH,* and *HE,* state how the areas of squares *ABCD* and *EFGH* are related. Write the area of *EFGH.* Then, express the side length of *EFGH* in exact form.

(3) Use your ruler to measure the length of *EF.* How is this measurement different from the length found in (2)?

(1) An irrational number is a number that cannot be written as $\frac{m}{n}$, where *m* and *n* are integers with $n \neq 0$. When written in decimal form, an irrational number is nonterminating and nonrepeating.

Some examples of irrational numbers are π and $\sqrt{2}$.

$\pi = 3.14159265358979323846264338327950\ldots$

$\sqrt{2} = 1.41421356237309504880168872420969\ldots$

Math Note

Since the term "rational number" means that the number can be expressed as a ratio of two integers, so the term "irrational number" means that the number cannot be expressed as a ratio of two integers.

(2) All rational numbers can be expressed as fractions, and you can locate their exact positions on a number line. Irrational numbers, however, do not have exact values. You estimate the positions of irrational numbers by approximating irrational numbers as rational numbers.

(3) You can use areas of squares to approximate the values of irrational numbers.
Consider $\sqrt{2}$. The area of a square with side length $\sqrt{2}$ units is 2 square units.

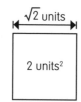

$\sqrt{2}$ units

2 units²

Notice that 2 is more than 1 but less than 4.

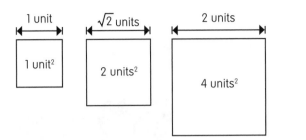

$1 < 2 < 4$

$1 < \sqrt{2} < 2$

To more accurately locate $\sqrt{2}$ on a number line, you need to determine if $\sqrt{2}$ is closer to 1 or 2. Consider another square with side length 1.5 units.
The area of the square is 1.5^2 square units or 2.25 square units.

1.5 units

2.25 units²

$1 < 2 < 2.25$

$1 < \sqrt{2} < 1.5$

Since 2 is very close to 2.25, you can conclude that $\sqrt{2}$ is slightly less than 1.5.

The approximate value of $\sqrt{2}$ is shown on the following number line.

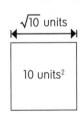

4. Locate $\sqrt{10}$ on a number line using areas of squares.

The area of a square with side length $\sqrt{10}$ units is 10 square units.

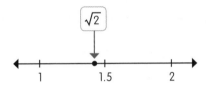

Compare this square with squares of areas 9 square units and 16 square units.

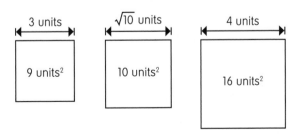

$9 < 10 < 16$

$3 < \sqrt{10} < 4$

Since 10 is very close to 9, you can conclude that $\sqrt{10}$ is slightly greater than 3.
The approximate value of $\sqrt{10}$ is shown on the following number line.

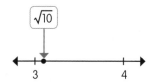

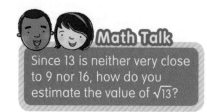

Math Talk

Since 13 is neither very close to 9 nor 16, how do you estimate the value of $\sqrt{13}$?

TRY Practice using areas of squares to locate irrational numbers on a number line

Use areas of squares to locate each irrational number on a number line.

1 $\sqrt{34}$

The area of a square with side length $\sqrt{34}$ units is 34 square units.

_____ < 34 < _____

_____ < $\sqrt{34}$ < _____

Since 34 is very close to _____, you can conclude

that $\sqrt{34}$ is slightly _____ than _____.

The approximate value of $\sqrt{34}$ shown on the number line is:

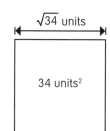

2 $\sqrt{198}$

ENGAGE

Use areas of squares to locate $\sqrt{5}$ on a number line. This method only gives you an approximate value. How do you locate $\sqrt{5}$ more precisely on a number line? Discuss.

LEARN Locate irrational numbers on a number line using a calculator

1 You can use a calculator to locate irrational numbers more precisely on a number line.

2 Locate $\sqrt{5}$ on a number line using a calculator.

STEP 1 Find an approximate value of $\sqrt{5}$ using a calculator, and round the value obtained to 2 decimal places.

$\sqrt{5}$ is 2.24 when rounded to 2 decimal places.

STEP 2 Use the approximate value to identify the numbers, to 1 decimal place, that $\sqrt{5}$ lies between.

$2.2 < 2.24 < 2.3$
$2.2 < \sqrt{5} < 2.3$

STEP 3 Estimate the position of $\sqrt{5}$ in a suitable interval on a number line.

2.24 is about halfway between the interval 2.2 to 2.3 and is closer to 2.2 than 2.3. The approximate value of $\sqrt{5}$ is shown on the following number line.

```
◄──┼─────●──────┼──►
   2.2  √5      2.3
```

3 Locate $-\sqrt{61}$ on a number line using a calculator.

STEP 1 Find an approximate value of $-\sqrt{61}$ using a calculator, and round the value obtained to 2 decimal places.

$-\sqrt{61}$ is -7.81 when rounded to 2 decimal places.

STEP 2 Use the approximate value to identify the numbers, to 1 decimal place, that $-\sqrt{61}$ lies between.

$-7.9 < -7.81 < -7.8$
$-7.9 < -\sqrt{61} < -7.8$

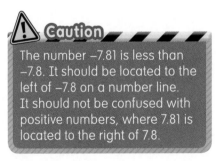

Caution

The number -7.81 is less than -7.8. It should be located to the left of -7.8 on a number line. It should not be confused with positive numbers, where 7.81 is located to the right of 7.8.

STEP 3 Estimate the position of $-\sqrt{61}$ in the interval on a number line.

–7.81 is slightly less than –7.8. The approximate value of $-\sqrt{61}$ is shown on the following number line.

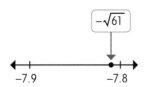

TRY Practice using a calculator to locate irrational numbers on a number line

 Use a calculator to locate each irrational number on a number line.

1 $\sqrt{28}$

$\sqrt{28}$ is 5.29 when rounded to 2 decimal places.

_____ < 5.29 < _____

_____ < $\sqrt{28}$ < _____

5.29 is slightly _____ than _____.

The approximate value of $\sqrt{28}$ shown on following number line is:

2 $-\sqrt{123}$

INDEPENDENT PRACTICE

Draw a number line. Then, locate each irrational number on the number line using areas of squares.

1 $\sqrt{11}$

2 $\sqrt{24}$

3 $\sqrt{50}$

4 $\sqrt{79}$

5 $\sqrt{164}$

6 $\sqrt{200}$

Draw a number line. Then, locate each irrational number on a number line using a calculator.

7 $\sqrt{6}$

8 $\sqrt{12}$

9 $\sqrt{99}$

10 $-\sqrt{22}$

11 $-\sqrt{128}$

12 $-\sqrt{250}$

2 Introducing the Real Number System

Learning Objective:
• Order real numbers.

New Vocabulary
real number

THINK

A piece of paper has a length of 29.7 cm and a width of 21.0 cm. Find the paper's length-to-width ratio. Which of the following numbers is closest to the ratio?

$$\frac{7}{5} \quad \sqrt{2} \quad 1.\overline{41}$$

ENGAGE

Using a calculator, locate $\frac{17}{9}$, 2.56, and $\sqrt{7}$ on a number line.

Now, think of another three numbers of different forms and put them in order.

LEARN Order real numbers

1. The real number system is a combination of the set of rational numbers and the set of irrational numbers.

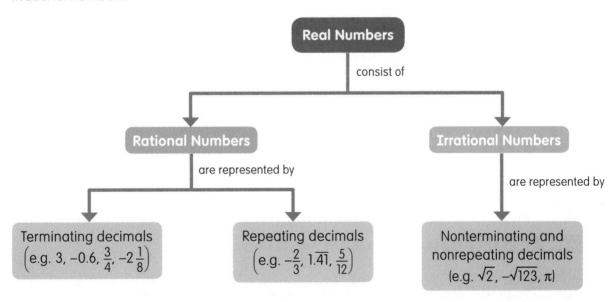

Real Numbers consist of

Rational Numbers are represented by
- Terminating decimals (e.g. 3, −0.6, $\frac{3}{4}$, −2$\frac{1}{8}$)
- Repeating decimals (e.g. −$\frac{2}{3}$, 1.$\overline{41}$, $\frac{5}{12}$)

Irrational Numbers are represented by
- Nonterminating and nonrepeating decimals (e.g. $\sqrt{2}$, −$\sqrt{123}$, π)

2. To compare different forms of real numbers, it is generally easier to convert all numbers to decimal form before comparing.

3 Locate the set of real numbers on a number line, and order them from least to greatest using the symbol <.

$$2\frac{4}{7} \quad -\frac{72}{15} \quad -2.3492 \quad \sqrt{\pi}$$

Express each number in decimal form rounded to at least 3 decimal places where appropriate.

$$2\frac{4}{7} \approx 2.571 \qquad -\frac{72}{15} = -4.8 \qquad -2.3492 \approx -2.349 \qquad \sqrt{\pi} \approx 1.772$$

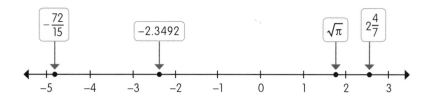

So, $-\frac{72}{15} < -2.3492 < \sqrt{\pi} < 2\frac{4}{7}$.

TRY Practice ordering real numbers

Locate the set of real numbers on a number line, and order them from least to greatest using the symbol <.

1 $\sqrt{10} \qquad -\frac{53}{9} \qquad -\frac{3\pi}{2} \qquad 6.2\overline{86}$

MATH SHARING

Mathematical Habit 6 Use precise mathematical language

Which of the real numbers are rational numbers, and which are irrational numbers? Explain how you arrived at your answer. Represent all the numbers on a number line.

$$2 \qquad -\sqrt{2} \qquad -\pi \qquad \frac{10}{3} \qquad 0.2 \qquad -3$$

INDEPENDENT PRACTICE

Compare each pair of real numbers using the symbol > or <.

1. $\sqrt{15}$ ◯ $\sqrt[3]{30}$

2. -4.38 ◯ $-\sqrt{12}$

3. 5.1543 ◯ $\sqrt{26}$

4. -16.4371 ◯ $-16.43715\ldots$

5. 5.55 ◯ $\dfrac{50}{9}$

6. $-\sqrt{98}$ ◯ $-\pi^2$

7. $\sqrt[3]{432}$ ◯ $7\dfrac{3}{8}$

8. $-\dfrac{1}{15\pi}$ ◯ $-0.0\overline{21}$

Locate each set of real numbers on a number line, and order them from least to greatest using the symbol <.

9 π^2 $\dfrac{43}{9}$ $\sqrt{61}$ $\sqrt[3]{285}$

10 -5^2 $-\pi^3$ $-26\dfrac{12}{13}$ $-\sqrt{800}$

11 $\dfrac{19}{23}$ -7.045 $-\pi^2$ $-\sqrt{75}$

3 Introducing Significant Digits

Learning Objectives:
• Determine the number of significant digits in a number.
• Round a number to a particular number of significant digits.

New Vocabulary
significant digit

THINK

A piece of glass is exactly 0.004512 meters thick. State the thickness rounded to 2 decimal places. Would this rounded figure be meaningful to a contractor? What estimated thickness would be meaningful?

ENGAGE

The length of a ribbon is measured using two different rulers.

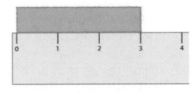

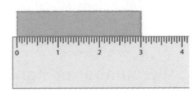

Andy says the length is 3 centimeters. Becky says the length is 3.0 centimeters. What do you think is the difference in the way that both of them have presented their measurements? Explain your thinking.

LEARN Determine the number of significant digits

① When you measure a quantity, the precision of your reading depends on the type of measuring instrument used.

Look at the following measurement.

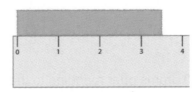

The ruler indicates that the length of the ribbon is between 3 centimeters and 4 centimeters. You see that the length is at least 3 centimeters. So, the digit 3 is certain.

You can estimate that the digit in the first decimal place is 5 because the length seems to be halfway between 3 centimeters and 4 centimeters. So, the approximate length of the ribbon is 3.5 centimeters, where the digit 5 is estimated.

The length 3.5 centimeters has 2 significant digits. In general, the more significant digits there are, the more precise a measurement is.

2 You use five rules to determine which digits in a number are significant.

> **Rule 1:** Any digit that is not zero is significant.
> For example, 3.5612 has 5 significant digits.
>
> **Rule 2:** Zeroes between non-zero digits are significant.
> For example, 60.00103 has 7 significant digits
>
> **Rule 3:** For decimals, all the trailing zeroes are significant.
> For example, 2.500 has 4 significant digits.
>
> **Rule 4:** Zeroes to the left of the first non-zero digit are not significant.
> For example, 0.000482 has 3 significant digits.
>
> **Rule 5:** For whole numbers, the trailing zeroes may or may not be significant.
> For example, 800 has 2 significant digits when rounded to the nearest ten and 1 significant digit when rounded to the nearest hundred.

TRY Practice determining the number of significant digits

Find the number of significant digits in each number.

1 900,045

Refer to Rule 1 and Rule 2.

2 0.0068

3 734.100

Solve.

4 The mass of an object is 5,400 grams after rounding to the nearest 10 grams. State the number of significant digits in the mass.

Recall and discuss the rules of rounding a number to a particular place value. Use specific examples to explain your thinking. Now, how do you round 123,000 to 1 significant digit? Explain.

Discuss what other numbers when rounded to 1 significant digit give you the same answer.

LEARN Round whole numbers to a particular number of significant digits

1. Round 5,632 to 3 significant digits.

   As the fourth significant digit is 2, which is less than 5, you round down.

   So, 5,632 rounded to 3 significant digits is 5,630.

> ⚠️ **Caution**
> When you round 5,632 to 5,630, be sure to replace the last digit with 0. A common mistake is to completely remove the last digit. In this example, the result would be 563, which is much smaller than the original value.

2. Round 345,090 to 4 significant digits.

   As the fifth significant digit is 9, which is 5 or more, you round up.

   So, 345,090 rounded to 4 significant digits is 345,100.

3. Round 669,420 to 2 significant digits.

   As the third significant digit is 9, which is 5 or more, you round up.

   So, 669,420 rounded to 2 significant digits is 670,000.

4. Round 43,540,245 to 7 significant digits.

   As the eighth significant digit is 5 or more, you round up.

   So, 43,540,245 rounded to 7 significant digits is 43,540,250.

> When you round a number to a particular number of significant digits, check that the answer has the same number of significant digits given.

TRY Practice rounding whole numbers to a particular number of significant digits

Round each whole number to the given number of significant digits.

1 627
(2 significant digits)

As the third significant digit is 7, which is 5 or more, you round up.

So, 627 rounded to 2 significant digits is _____.

2 5,030
(2 significant digits)

As the third significant digit is 3, which is less than 5, you round down.

So, 5,030 rounded to 2 significant digits is _____.

3 459,610
(3 significant digits)

4 18,455
(4 significant digits)

ENGAGE

You have learned to round a whole number to a particular number of significant digits. Now, how do you round 0.0123 to 1 significant digit? Explain.

Compare rounding 0.0123 to 1 significant digit and rounding 123,000 to 1 significant digit. How is rounding to a significant digit different in decimals than it is in whole numbers? Discuss.

LEARN Round decimals to a particular number of significant digits

1 Round 0.023461 to 3 significant digits.
As the fourth significant digit is 6, which is 5 or more, you round up.
So, 0.023461 rounded to 3 significant digits is 0.0235.

2 Round 0.0005549 to 2 significant digits.
As the third significant digit is 4, which is less than 5, you round down.
So, 0.0005549 rounded to 2 significant digits is 0.00055.

③ Round 1.00308 to 5 significant digits.

As the sixth significant digit is 8, which is 5 or more, you round up.

So, 1.00308 rounded to 5 significant digits is 1.0031.

④ Round 32.401 to 4 significant digits.

As the fifth significant digit is 1, which is less than 5, you round down.

So, 32.401 rounded to 4 significant digits is 32.40.

Caution

32.401 rounded to 4 significant digits is 32.40 and not 32.4.

⑤ Round 589.54 to 3 significant digits.

As the fourth significant digit is 5 or more, you round up.

So, 589.54 rounded to 3 significant digits is 590.

⑥ The length of a parallelogram is 13.54 centimeters and the height is 8.22 centimeters.

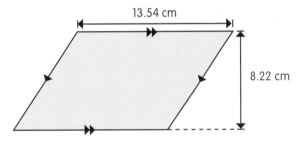

13.54 cm

8.22 cm

a Calculate the area of the parallelogram.

Area of the parallelogram = 13.54 · 8.22
= 111.2988 cm²

Area of a parallelogram = Base · Height

b State the area of the parallelogram to 3 significant digits.

The area of the parallelogram to 3 significant digits is 111 square centimeters.

TRY Practice rounding decimals to a particular number of significant digits

Round each decimal to the given number of significant digits.

① 0.683125
(3 significant digits)

As the fourth significant digit is 1, which is less than 5, you round down.

So, 0.683125 rounded to 3 significant digits is _____.

② 0.00914073
(4 significant digits)

③ 24.00963
(5 significant digits)

④ 32.018
(3 significant digits)

⑤ 2,560.58
(4 significant digits)

 Solve.

⑥ The radius of a circle is 2.53 centimeters.

a Find the area of the circle. Use 3.14 as an approximation for π.

2.53 cm

Area of circle = πr^2

b Find the area of the circle to 3 significant digits.

LET'S EXPLORE

The average distance from Earth to the Sun is about 149,600,000 kilometers.
How many of the trailing zeroes could be significant? Explain.

Name: _____ Date: _____

INDEPENDENT PRACTICE

Find the number of significant digits in each number.

1 7,294

2 56,001

3 0.0700

4 3.008

5 600.0

6 0.0045

7 0.505

8 10.400

Round each whole number to the given number of significant digits.

9 9,591
(2 significant digits)

10 613,256
(4 significant digits)

11 17,447
(3 significant digits)

12 10,300
(2 significant digits)

13 2,490,983
(4 significant digits)

14 350,216
(4 significant digits)

15 75,000
(3 significant digits)

16 675,348
(1 significant digit)

Round each decimal to the given number of significant digits.

17 0.5482
(1 significant digit)

18 1.0023
(2 significant digits)

19 36.82073
(5 significant digits)

20 0.04945
(3 significant digits)

21 830.7
(3 significant digits)

22 5.129
(2 significant digits)

23 3.38049
(4 significant digits)

24 0.0999
(2 significant digits)

Solve.

25 Evaluate $5.68 \times \dfrac{19.3^2}{6.251} - 0.982 \times 41.4$. Give each answer to the given number of significant digits.

   a 1 significant digit

   b 2 significant digits

   c 3 significant digits

   d 5 significant digits

26 The distance between San Antonio and San Diego is 1,100 miles after rounding to the nearest 100 miles. State the number of significant digits in the distance.

27 John measures the volume of a liquid using the measuring cylinder shown. The smallest division in the scale represents 2 milliliters. He recorded his reading as 42.5 milliliters. How would you know that his reading is incorrect?

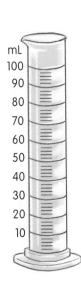

28 The length of a rectangle is 23.46 centimeters and the height is 11.68 centimeters.

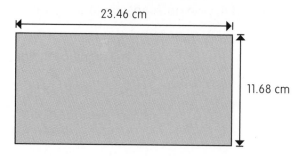

23.46 cm

11.68 cm

a Find the area of the rectangle.

b Find the area of the rectangle to 3 significant digits.

29 How many seconds are in a month of 30 days? Give your answer to 3 significant digits.

Mathematical Habit 7 Make use of structure

Create your own diagram summarizing the relationships among the types of real numbers that you have learned.

Problem Solving with Heuristics

1 **Mathematical Habit 1** **Persevere in solving problems**

Use the decimal representation of $\sqrt{11}$, which is 3.31662479…, to answer the following questions.

a Describe an irrational number, x, that is 0.0001 more or less than $\sqrt{11}$.

b Describe another irrational number, y, which is between $\sqrt{11}$ and x.

c Graph the positions of $\sqrt{11}$, x and y on a real number line.

Describe another irrational number, a, which is between x and y. Graph a on the number line in c.

Next, describe another irrational number, b, which is between x and a. Graph b on the number in c.

d By continuing the pattern, what can you conclude about the irrational numbers on the number line?

2 **Mathematical Habit 6** Use precise mathematical language

In an experiment, Sarah used a ruler to measure the radius of a circular disc, and she measured it at 7.2 centimeters. Using the calculator value of π, she calculated the area of the circular disc as shown.

Area of the circular disc
$= \pi \cdot 7.2^2$
$= \pi \cdot 51.84$
$\approx 162.86 \text{ cm}^2$

How can Sarah write her answer to better reflect the precision of the measuring instrument used during the experiment?

CHAPTER WRAP-UP

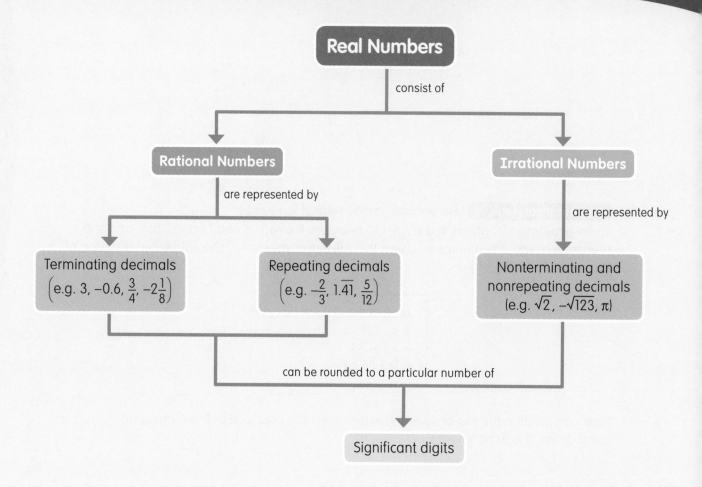

KEY CONCEPTS

- An irrational number is a number that cannot be written as $\frac{m}{n}$, where m and n are integers with $n \neq 0$.

- When written in decimal form, an irrational number is nonterminating and nonrepeating.

- You can make use of areas of squares to approximate the values of irrational numbers and estimate their locations on the number line. You can use a calculator to locate irrational numbers more precisely on a number line.

- The real number system is a combination of the set of rational numbers and the set of irrational numbers.

- To compare different forms of real numbers, it can be easier if you convert any non-decimal to decimal form before comparing.

- You use five rules to determine the number of significant digits in a given number.

Name: _____ Date: _____

Draw a number line. Then, locate each irrational number on the number line.

1 $\sqrt{46}$

2 $-\sqrt{133}$

3 $\sqrt[3]{170}$

4 $-\frac{2}{7}\pi^3$

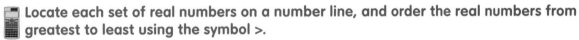

Locate each set of real numbers on a number line, and order the real numbers from greatest to least using the symbol >.

5 -1.2675 $3\sqrt{2}$ $\frac{22}{7}$ $6.\overline{67}$

6 $-\pi$ $5.\overline{3}$ $\sqrt[3]{90}$ $1\frac{3}{17}$ $-\sqrt{28}$

Find the number of significant digits in each number.

7 4.23

8 0.07009

9 8657

10 5.600

Round each number to the given number of significant digits.

11 0.060984
(2 significant digits)

12 0.060984
(3 significant digits)

13 27,345
(1 significant digit)

14 27,345
(3 significant digits)

Solve.

15 Evaluate $\dfrac{38.14}{\sqrt{21} - \pi}$. Give your answer to 3 significant digits.

16 The price of a used car was $8,299 in April. The price of the used car was reduced by 20% one month later in May.
Find the price of the used car in May. Give your answer to 3 significant digits.

17 A metal cube has a mass of 0.2531 kilograms. Express this mass in grams to 2 significant digits.

18 The base and height of a triangle are $\sqrt{2}$ inches and $\sqrt{3}$ inches respectively. Find the area of the triangle to 4 significant digits.

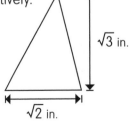

$\sqrt{3}$ in.

$\sqrt{2}$ in.

Assessment Prep

Answer each question.

19 Look at the following decimals.

        3240.0   658.090   0.213   0.004159

Which statements are true about the decimals? Choose **all** that apply.

(A) 3240.0 has 3 significant digits.

(B) 658.090 has 6 significant digits.

(C) 0.213 has 4 significant digits.

(D) 0.004159 has 4 significant digits.

20 Which number is less than 3.142?

(A) $\frac{22}{7}$

(B) π

(C) $3.14\bar{2}$

(D) $3.1\overline{42}$

21 Locate $-\sqrt{17}$ on a number line.
Draw the number line in the space below.

Name: _____ Date: _____

Lighting for Ferris Wheel

1 Kevin, an electrician, was asked to install a rope light cable around the circular rim of a Ferris wheel. He had to estimate the cost of purchasing the total length of the cable based on the following information.

> Diameter of rim of Ferris wheel: 150 meters
> Cost of cable: $50 per meter

150 m

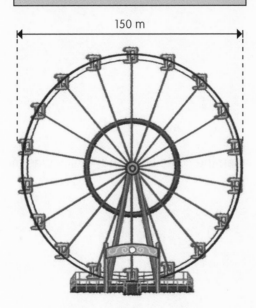

a Kevin calculated the cost using $\frac{22}{7}$ as an approximation for π. Find the cost obtained.

b Based on a suggestion, Kevin worked out the cost again using the calculator value of π. Find the cost obtained.

c Find the difference between the costs obtained. Which was more accurate? Explain.

2 How are $\frac{22}{7}$ and π classified in the real number system? Justify your answer.

Rubric

Point(s)	Level	My Performance
7–8	4	• Most of my answers are correct. • I showed complete understanding of the concepts. • I used effective and efficient strategies to solve the problems. • I explained my answers and mathematical thinking clearly and completely.
5–6	3	• Some of my answers are correct. • I showed adequate understanding of the concepts. • I used effective strategies to solve the problems. • I explained my answers and mathematical thinking clearly.
3–4	2	• A few of my answers are correct. • I showed some understanding of the concepts. • I used some effective strategies to solve the problems. • I explained some of my answers and mathematical thinking clearly.
0–2	1	• A few of my answers are correct. • I showed little understanding of the concepts. • I used limited effective strategies to solve the problems. • I did not explain my answers and mathematical thinking clearly.

Teacher's Comments

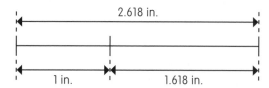

Fibonacci in Nature

Divide a straight line into two parts so that the whole length divided by the long part equals the long part divided by the short part. The result is the Golden Ratio, an irrational number with a value of 1.6180339887. . ., or approximately 1.618.

```
|<--------------- 2.618 in. --------------->|
|                      |                    |
|<----- 1 in. -----> |<----- 1.618 in. --->|
```

In nature, the Golden Ratio manifests itself in many ways. One of the ways it can be demonstrated is through a number pattern called the Fibonacci sequence. The Fibonacci sequence is a series of numbers in which adding two consecutive numbers results in the successive number. The first few numbers of the Fibonacci sequence are 0, 1, 1, 2, 3, 5, 8, 13, 21, 34, 55 … When we divide a number in the sequence with the number preceding it, and continue to do so for other numbers later on in the sequence, we find that the result approximates to the Golden Ratio.

Task

Work in small groups to illustrate the Fibonacci sequence in nature.

1 Investigate how to use numbers in the Fibonacci sequence to draw squares within a rectangle to produce a spiral shape. Draw and label a model.

2 Continue your investigation to find examples of the Fibonacci sequence in the natural world. Create a print or digital collage of examples. Write a brief text to support each example.

Exponents

How loud is loud?

The human ear can hear a range of noises, from a soft whisper to the enormous blast of a rocket being launched into space. The intensity of sound is measured using a scale that involves powers of 10. A general rule of thumb is that if a noise sounds ten times as loud to your ears as another noise, the intensity is 10 decibels greater for the louder noise. In this chapter, you will learn how to use exponents to compare quantities such as the intensities of different noises.

How do you represent repeated multiplication of the same factor?

Name: _____   Date: _____

Interpreting the real number system

The real number system is a combination of the set of rational numbers and the set of irrational numbers.

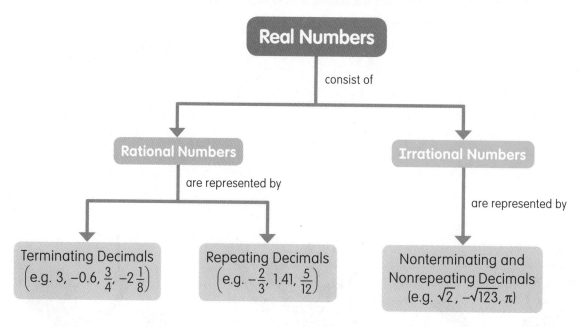

Unlike rational numbers, irrational numbers do not have exact values. You use rational approximations of irrational numbers to compare the size of irrational numbers and locate them approximately on a number line.

▶ **Quick Check**

Locate each irrational number on a number line.

1 $\sqrt[3]{-47}$ **2** $\sqrt{19}$

Adding and subtracting integers

You can use a number line to add and subtract integers. When you add a positive integer, move to the right on the number line. When you add a negative integer, move to the left. You can also use these rules.

Adding or Subtracting Integers	Rule	Expression
Add integers with the same sign.	Add the absolute values and keep the same sign.	$3 + 5 = 8$
Add integers with different signs.	Subtract the absolute values and use the sign of the number with the greater absolute value.	$-5 + 8 = 3$
Subtract two integers.	Add the opposite of the number being subtracted.	$8 - 3$ $= 8 + (-3)$ $= 5$

▶ **Quick Check**

Evaluate each expression.

3 $-3 + (-4)$

4 $-4 - (-2)$

Multiplying and dividing integers

You multiply or divide integers just as you do whole numbers, except that you must keep track of the signs. To multiply or divide integers, always multiply or divide the absolute values, and use these rules to determine the sign of the result.

Multiplying or Dividing Integers	Rule	Expression
Multiply or divide two integers with the same sign.	Multiply or divide the absolute values of the numbers and make the result positive.	$24 \cdot 4 = 96$ $(-24) \div (-4) = 6$
Multiply or divide two integers with different signs.	Multiply or divide the absolute values of the numbers and make the result negative.	$25 \cdot (-5) = -125$ $(-25) \div 5 = -5$

▶ **Quick Check**

Evaluate each expression.

5 $(-7) \cdot (-3)$

6 $(-12) \div 3$

Finding the square of a whole number

5^2 is called the square of 5. The square of a whole number is called a perfect square. Since $5 \times 5 = 25$, 25 is a perfect square.

▶ **Quick Check**

Find the square of each number.

7 9

8 12

Finding the cube of a whole number

4^3 is called the cube of 4. The cube of a whole number is called a perfect cube. Since $4 \times 4 \times 4 = 64$, 64 is a perfect cube.

▶ **Quick Check**

Find the cube of each number.

9 8

10 11

1 Exponential Notation

Learning Objectives:
- Write in exponential notation.
- Expand and evaluate expressions in exponential notation.
- Use exponents to write the prime factorization of a number.

THINK

Lily cut a piece of paper in half and threw away the other half. She continued cutting the remaining paper in half until she had a piece of paper whose area was $\frac{1}{64}$ as large as the area of the original piece of paper. How many cuts did she make? Explain how the number of cuts made is related to the final size of the paper relative to the original size.

ENGAGE

The square of 3 is 3^2. The cube of 2 is 2^3. Which is greater, 3^2 or 2^3? Explain your reasoning.

Now, compare these two numbers.

a $10 \cdot 10 \cdot 10 \cdot 10 \cdot 10$

b $5 \cdot 5 \cdot 5 \cdot 5 \cdot 5 \cdot 5 \cdot 5 \cdot 5 \cdot 5$

Which is greater? How do you know?

LEARN Write numbers in exponential notation

1 On the decibel scale, the smallest audible sound (near total silence) has an intensity of 0 decibel (dB). A lawnmower is 90 dB or 1,000,000,000 times louder than near total silence.

You can use exponential notation to describe this increase in sound intensity.

$$1,000,000,000 = \underbrace{10 \cdot 10 \cdot 10 \cdot 10 \cdot 10 \cdot 10 \cdot 10 \cdot 10 \cdot 10}_{9 \text{ times}}$$
$$= 10^9 \leftarrow \text{exponent}$$
$$\uparrow \text{ base}$$

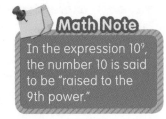

Math Note

In the expression 10^9, the number 10 is said to be "raised to the 9th power."

The expression 10^9 is written in exponential notation to show repeated multiplication of the factor 10. The exponent represents how many times the base is used as a factor.

2 Tell whether the statement $2 \cdot 2 \cdot 2 = 6^2$ is correct. If it is incorrect, state the reason.

The statement is incorrect. The base is 2, not 6, and the exponent is 3, not 2.
So, $2 \cdot 2 \cdot 2 = 2^3$.

③ Write $5 \cdot 5 \cdot 5 \cdot 5$ in exponential notation.

$5 \cdot 5 \cdot 5 \cdot 5 = 5^4$ The base is 5 and the exponent is 4.

④ Write $(-3) \cdot (-3) \cdot (-3) \cdot (-3) \cdot (-3)$ in exponential notation.

$(-3) \cdot (-3) \cdot (-3) \cdot (-3) \cdot (-3) = (-3)^5$ The base is –3 and the exponent is 5.

In the expression $(-3)^5$, the base is –3 because –3 is inside the parentheses.

⑤ Write $\frac{1}{2} \cdot \frac{1}{2} \cdot \frac{1}{2}$ in exponential notation.

$\frac{1}{2} \cdot \frac{1}{2} \cdot \frac{1}{2} = \left(\frac{1}{2}\right)^3$ The base is $\frac{1}{2}$ and the exponent is 3.

TRY Practice writing in exponential notation

Determine whether each statement is correct. If it is incorrect, state the reason.

① $6^3 = 6 \cdot 6 \cdot 6$

② $5 \cdot 5 = 2^5$

Write each expression in exponential notation.

③ $2 \cdot 2 \cdot 2 \cdot 2 \cdot 2 \cdot 2$

$2 \cdot 2 \cdot 2 \cdot 2 \cdot 2 \cdot 2 =$ _____   The base is 2 and the exponent is 6.

④ $(-4) \cdot (-4) \cdot (-4)$

⑤ $\frac{2}{3} \cdot \frac{2}{3} \cdot \frac{2}{3} \cdot \frac{2}{3}$

ENGAGE

Sebastian has a cube-shaped box with edges of length 1.2 feet. Using exponents, write an expression to find the volume of the box. Evaluate your expression.

The volume of another cube-shaped box is 3.375 cubic feet. What is the length of each edge of the box? Explain your thinking.

LEARN Expand and evaluate expressions in exponential notation

1 Expand and evaluate 2.5^3.

$$2.5^3 = 2.5 \cdot 2.5 \cdot 2.5$$
$$= 15.625$$

2 Expand and evaluate $(-4)^2$.

$$(-4)^2 = (-4) \cdot (-4)$$
$$= 16$$

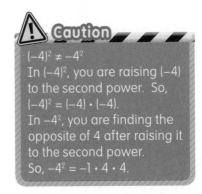

Caution

$(-4)^2 \neq -4^2$
In $(-4)^2$, you are raising (-4) to the second power. So, $(-4)^2 = (-4) \cdot (-4)$.
In -4^2, you are finding the opposite of 4 after raising it to the second power.
So, $-4^2 = -1 \cdot 4 \cdot 4$.

3 Expand and evaluate $\left(\dfrac{2}{3}\right)^5$.

$$\left(\dfrac{2}{3}\right)^5 = \dfrac{2}{3} \cdot \dfrac{2}{3} \cdot \dfrac{2}{3} \cdot \dfrac{2}{3} \cdot \dfrac{2}{3}$$
$$= \dfrac{32}{243}$$

4 Victoria deposits $100 in a bank account that earns 5% interest, compounded yearly. How much will be in her account at the end of 5 years?

> When interest is compounded yearly, a year's interest is deposited in the account at the end of the year. During the next year, interest is earned on this larger balance. Because Victoria's deposit increases to 105% of its value each year, she can use the formula $A = P(1 + r)^n$ to find out how much money she has in her account after n years when she invests a principal of P dollars at an interest rate of r %.

$A = P(1 + r)^n$
$\quad = 100(1 + 0.05)^5$ Substitute 100 for P, 5 for n and 0.05 for r.
$\quad = 100(1.05)^5$ Add within the parentheses.
$\quad \approx 127.63$ Round to the nearest hundredth.

$127.63 will be in her account at the end of 5 years.

Practice expanding and evaluating expressions in exponential notation

Expand and evaluate each expression.

1 3^4

$3^4 =$ _____ · _____ · _____ · _____

$=$ _____

2 $(-5)^3$

3 $\left(\dfrac{3}{4}\right)^3$

 Solve.

4 Zachary, at age 25, has $2,000 in his retirement account. It will earn 6% interest, compounded yearly. How much will be in his account when he retires at age 65? Give your answer to the nearest cent.

> Use the formula $A = P(1 + r)^n$ to find out how much money Zachary has in his account after n years when he invests a principal of P dollars at an interest rate of r %.

ENGAGE

Find all of the factors of 60 and 120. Now, express each number as a product of their prime factors. How do you write them in exponential notation? Share your observations.

1 Any composite number can be written as a product of prime factors. This prime factorization of a number can be expressed using exponents.

You may use the following divisibility rules to help you find the prime factors.

A number is divisible by	if ...
2	the last digit is even (0, 2, 4, 6, or 8).
3	the sum of the digits is divisible by 3.
5	the last digit is 0 or 5.
7	the last digit, when doubled, and then subtracted from the number formed by the remaining digits, gives a result of 0 or a number divisible by 7.

2 Write the prime factorization of 81 in exponential notation.

$81 = 3 \cdot 27$
$= 3 \cdot 3 \cdot 9$
$= \mathbf{3 \cdot 3 \cdot 3 \cdot 3}$
$= 3^4$

```
3 | 81
3 | 27
3 | 9
3 | 3
    1
```

Express 81 as a product of its prime factors.

Math Talk

If the last digit of a number is 0, do you divide the number by 2 or 5 first? Why?

3 Write the prime factorization of 1,470 in exponential notation.

$$1{,}470 = 5 \cdot 294$$
$$= 5 \cdot 2 \cdot 147$$
$$= 5 \cdot 2 \cdot 3 \cdot 49$$
$$= \mathbf{5 \cdot 2 \cdot 3 \cdot 7 \cdot 7}$$
$$= 2 \cdot 3 \cdot 5 \cdot 7^2$$

5	1,470
2	294
3	147
7	49
7	7
	1

For 1,470, 1 + 4 + 7 + 0 = 12.
So, 1,470 is also divisible by 3.

TRY Practice using exponents to write the prime factorization of a number

Write the prime factorization of each number in exponential notation.

1 625

$$625 = 5 \cdot \underline{\hspace{2cm}}$$

$$= 5 \cdot \underline{\hspace{2cm}} \cdot \underline{\hspace{2cm}}$$

$$= 5 \cdot \underline{\hspace{2cm}} \cdot \underline{\hspace{2cm}} \cdot \underline{\hspace{2cm}}$$

$$= \underline{\hspace{2cm}}$$

5	625
5	125
5	25
5	5
	1

2 630

INDEPENDENT PRACTICE

Determine whether each statement is correct. If it is incorrect, state the reason.

1 $24^3 = 2 \cdot 4 \cdot 4 \cdot 4$

2 $(-2)^5 = 2 \cdot 2 \cdot 2 \cdot 2 \cdot 2$

Write each expression in exponential notation.

3 $\dfrac{1}{3} \cdot \dfrac{1}{3}$

4 $5 \cdot 5 \cdot 5 \cdot 5$

5 $(-2) \cdot (-2) \cdot (-2)$

6 $0.12 \cdot 0.12 \cdot 0.12 \cdot 0.12 \cdot 0.12$

Expand and evaluate each expression.

7 2^3

8 $\left(\dfrac{3}{8}\right)^4$

9 10^4

10 -3.4^4

Write the prime factorization of each number in exponential notation.

11 125

12 4,802

 Solve.

13 A bank account has $500 in it. Use the formula $A = P(1 + r)^n$ to find out how much will be in the account in 20 years if it earns 8% interest, compounded yearly. Give your answer to the nearest cents.

2 The Product and the Quotient of Powers

Learning Objectives:
- Use the product of powers property.
- Use the quotient of powers property.

THINK

Jupiter is 10^8 kilometers from the Sun. An asteroid is 100 times this distance from the Sun. How far is the asteroid from the Sun? The dwarf planet Eris is 10^{10} kilometers from the Sun. How many times as far as Jupiter is Eris from the Sun? Write each answer in exponential notation.

ENGAGE

Expand $2^3 \cdot 2^4$. Now, expand 2^7. What do you notice? Expand $10^2 \cdot 10^5$. Now, expand 10^7. What do you notice? Share your observations.

Write a rule for multiplying two numbers with the same base. Create another example in which your rule applies. Discuss your work.

LEARN Use the product of powers property

1 You have learned that

$$10^6 = 10 \cdot 10 \cdot 10 \cdot 10 \cdot 10 \cdot 10$$

and that $10^9 = 10 \cdot 10 \cdot 10 \cdot 10 \cdot 10 \cdot 10 \cdot 10 \cdot 10 \cdot 10$.

$10^6 \cdot 10^9 = \underbrace{(10 \cdot 10 \cdot 10 \cdot 10 \cdot 10 \cdot 10)}_{\text{6 factors}} \cdot \underbrace{(10 \cdot 10 \cdot 10 \cdot 10 \cdot 10 \cdot 10 \cdot 10 \cdot 10 \cdot 10)}_{\text{9 factors}}$

$= \underbrace{10 \cdot 10 \cdot 10 \cdot 10 \cdot 10 \cdot 10 \cdot 10 \cdot 10 \cdot 10 \cdot 10 \cdot 10 \cdot 10 \cdot 10 \cdot 10 \cdot 10}_{\text{15 factors}}$

$= 10^{15}$

So, $10^6 \cdot 10^9 = 10^{6+9}$
$\qquad\qquad = 10^{15}$.

Notice that 10^6 and 10^9 have the same base. You apply the same reasoning to find the product of any powers that have the same base.

$a^4 \cdot a^3 = \underbrace{(a \cdot a \cdot a \cdot a)}_{\text{4 factors}} \cdot \underbrace{(a \cdot a \cdot a)}_{\text{3 factors}}$

$= \underbrace{a \cdot a \cdot a \cdot a \cdot a \cdot a \cdot a}_{\text{7 factors}}$

$= a^7$

So, $a^4 \cdot a^3 = a^{4+3}$
$\qquad\qquad = a^7$.

When you find the product of two algebraic expressions with the same base, you add their exponents and use this exponent with the same base.

$$a^m \cdot a^n = a^{m+n}$$

2 Simplify $(-4)^2 \cdot (-4)^4$. Write your answer in exponential notation.

$(-4)^2 \cdot (-4)^4 = (-4)^{2+4}$ Use the product of powers property.
             $= (-4)^6$ Simplify.

3 Simplify $1.2 \cdot 1.2^4$. Write your answer in exponential notation.

$1.2 \cdot 1.2^4 = 1.2^{1+4}$ Use the product of powers property.
          $= 1.2^5$ Simplify.

When a number or variable does not have an exponent, it means the number or variable is raised to the first power.

Math Talk
Explain why $2^4 \cdot 3^4 \neq (2 \cdot 3)^8$.

4 Simplify $2x^4y^2 \cdot 3x^2y^6$. Write your answer in exponential notation.

$2x^4y^2 \cdot 3x^2y^6 = 2 \cdot x^4 \cdot y^2 \cdot 3 \cdot x^2 \cdot y^6$ Rewrite the product.
               $= 2 \cdot 3 \cdot x^4 \cdot x^2 \cdot y^2 \cdot y^6$ Regroup the numbers, and regroup the factors with the same bases.
               $= 6 \cdot x^{4+2} \cdot y^{2+6}$ Add the exponents of the factors with the same base.
               $= 6x^6y^8$ Simplify.

TRY **Practice using the product of powers property**

Simplify each expression. Write each answer in exponential notation.

1 $(-5) \cdot (-5)^5$

$(-5) \cdot (-5)^5 =$ _____   Use the product of powers property.

            $=$ _____   Simplify.

2 $\left(\dfrac{1}{5}\right)^3 \cdot \left(\dfrac{1}{5}\right)^4$

3 $4s^4t^3 \cdot 5s^4t^6$

ENGAGE

Expand 10^4 and 10^2. What is $10^4 \div 10^2$? Use two methods to solve. Now, use each of your methods to solve $3^6 \div 3^4$. How are these problems the same? How are they different? Discuss.

LEARN Use the quotient of powers property

1 How are the exponents in 5^5 and 5^2 related to the exponent of their quotient?

$$5^5 \div 5^2 = (5 \cdot 5 \cdot 5 \cdot 5 \cdot 5) \div (5 \cdot 5)$$

$$= \dfrac{\overbrace{5 \cdot 5 \cdot 5 \cdot 5 \cdot 5}^{\textbf{5 factors}}}{\underbrace{5 \cdot 5}_{\textbf{2 factors}}}$$

$$= \underbrace{5 \cdot 5 \cdot 5}_{\textbf{3 factors}}$$

$$= 5^3$$

Notice that $5^3 = 5^{5-2}$. You find the exponent of the quotient by subtracting the exponent of the divisor from the exponent of the dividend.

So, $5^5 \div 5^2 = 5^{5-2}$
$ = 5^3$.

$$y^7 \div y^4 = (y \cdot y \cdot y \cdot y \cdot y \cdot y \cdot y) \div (y \cdot y \cdot y \cdot y)$$

$$= \dfrac{\overbrace{y \cdot y \cdot y \cdot y \cdot y \cdot y \cdot y}^{\textbf{7 factors}}}{\underbrace{y \cdot y \cdot y \cdot y}_{\textbf{4 factors}}}$$

$$= \underbrace{y \cdot y \cdot y}_{\textbf{3 factors}}$$

$$= y^3$$

So, $y^7 \div y^4 = y^{7-4}$
$ = y^3$.

When you find the quotient of two algebraic expressions with the same base, you subtract the exponent of the divisor from the exponent of the dividend and use it with the common base.

$$a^m \div a^n = \frac{a^m}{a^n} = a^{m-n}, a \neq 0$$

② Simplify $(-7)^5 \div (-7)$. Write your answer in exponential notation.

$(-7)^5 \div (-7)$
$= (-7)^{5-1}$ Use the quotient of powers property.
$= (-7)^4$ Simplify.

③ Simplify $3.5^8 \div 3.5^6$. Write your answer in exponential notation.

$3.5^8 \div 3.5^6$
$= 3.5^{8-6}$ Use the quotient of powers property.
$= 3.5^2$ Simplify.

Math Talk

Can you use the quotient of powers property to simplify $5^4 \div 3^{20}$? Explain why.

④ Simplify $28m^7n^4 \div 7m^3n^2$. Write your answer in exponential notation.

$28m^7n^4 \div 7m^3n^2$
$= \dfrac{28m^7n^4}{7m^3n^2}$ Write the quotient as a fraction.

$= \dfrac{28}{7} \cdot \dfrac{m^7}{m^3} \cdot \dfrac{n^4}{n^2}$ Rewrite the fraction as a product of three fractions.

$= 4 \cdot m^{7-3} \cdot n^{4-2}$ Use the quotient of powers property.
$= 4m^4n^2$ Simplify.

TRY **Practice using the quotient of powers property**

Simplify each expression. Write each answer in exponential notation.

① $10^8 \div 10^5$

$10^8 \div 10^5 = $ _____   Use the quotient of powers property.

$= $ _____   Simplify.

2 $2.7^9 \div 2.7^6$

3 $63x^9y^7 \div 9x^3y^4$

ENGAGE

Is $a^3 \cdot a \cdot a^2 = a^{3+1+2}$? Is $\dfrac{a^6}{a^3} = a^{6-3}$? Explain your thinking. How do you simplify $\dfrac{a^3 \cdot a \cdot a^2}{a \cdot a \cdot a}$? Discuss.

Create a problem involving multiplying and dividing expressions in exponential notation. Trade with your partner. Simplify the expression. Write your answer in exponential notation.

LEARN Multiply and divide expressions in exponential notation

1 You may have to use both the product of powers and quotient of powers properties together to simplify expressions.

2 Simplify $\dfrac{\left(\frac{1}{4}\right)^3 \cdot \left(\frac{1}{4}\right) \cdot \left(\frac{1}{4}\right)^2}{\left(\frac{1}{4}\right) \cdot \left(\frac{1}{4}\right) \cdot \left(\frac{1}{4}\right)}$. Write your answer in exponential notation.

$$\dfrac{\left(\frac{1}{4}\right)^3 \cdot \left(\frac{1}{4}\right) \cdot \left(\frac{1}{4}\right)^2}{\left(\frac{1}{4}\right) \cdot \left(\frac{1}{4}\right) \cdot \left(\frac{1}{4}\right)} = \dfrac{\left(\frac{1}{4}\right)^{3+1+2}}{\left(\frac{1}{4}\right)^{1+1+1}}$$ Use the product of powers property.

$$= \dfrac{\left(\frac{1}{4}\right)^6}{\left(\frac{1}{4}\right)^3}$$ Simplify.

$$= \left(\frac{1}{4}\right)^{6-3}$$ Use the quotient of powers property.

$$= \left(\frac{1}{4}\right)^3$$ Simplify.

All the numbers in the numerator and denominator have the same base. You use the product of powers property before using the quotient of powers property.

3 Simplify $\dfrac{3x^4 \cdot 5y^5 \cdot 6x^6}{2y \cdot 3x^2 \cdot 5y^3}$. Write your answer in exponential notation.

$$\dfrac{3x^4 \cdot 5y^5 \cdot 6x^6}{2y \cdot 3x^2 \cdot 5y^3} = \dfrac{3 \cdot 5 \cdot 6 \cdot x^4 \cdot x^6 \cdot y^5}{2 \cdot 3 \cdot 5 \cdot x^2 \cdot y \cdot y^3}$$

Regroup the numbers, and regroup the factors with the same bases.

$$= \dfrac{90x^{4+6}y^5}{30x^2y^{1+3}}$$

Use the product of powers property.

$$= \dfrac{3x^{10}y^5}{x^2y^4}$$

Simplify.

$$= 3(x^{10-2})(y^{5-4})$$

Use the quotient of powers property.

$$= 3x^8y$$

Simplify.

TRY Practice multiplying and dividing expressions in exponential notation

Simplify each expression. Write each answer in exponential notation.

1 $\dfrac{7.5^5 \cdot 7.5^3 \cdot 7.5}{7.5^2 \cdot 7.5 \cdot 7.5^4}$

$$\dfrac{7.5^5 \cdot 7.5^3 \cdot 7.5}{7.5^2 \cdot 7.5 \cdot 7.5^4} = \dfrac{7.5^{5+3+1}}{7.5^{2+1+4}}$$

Use the product of powers property.

$$= \dfrac{7.5^9}{7.5^7}$$

Simplify.

$$= \underline{\hspace{3cm}}$$

Use the quotient of powers property.

$$= \underline{\hspace{3cm}}$$

Simplify.

2 $\dfrac{b^5 \cdot 4a^4 \cdot 9a^3}{2a^2 \cdot b^2 \cdot 6a^2}$

INDEPENDENT PRACTICE

Simplify each expression. Write each answer in exponential notation.

1 $(-2)^6 \cdot (-2)^2$

2 $7.2^3 \cdot 7.2^4$

3 $\left(\dfrac{2}{3}\right) \cdot \left(\dfrac{2}{3}\right)^5$

4 $p \cdot p^8$

5 $xy^2 \cdot x^4y^3$

6 $2.5x^3y^6 \cdot 3x^2y^4$

7 $(-3)^4 \div (-3)^2$

8 $\left(-\dfrac{1}{6}\right)^5 \div \left(-\dfrac{1}{6}\right)^2$

9 $h^2k^5 \div hk^4$

10 $64a^8b^5 \div 4a^3b^2$

11 $\dfrac{5^9 \cdot 5^7 \cdot 5^8}{5^3 \cdot 5^2 \cdot 5}$

12 $\dfrac{\left(\frac{4}{9}\right)^6 \cdot \left(\frac{4}{9}\right)^5 \cdot \left(\frac{4}{9}\right)^4}{\left(\frac{4}{9}\right)^3 \cdot \left(\frac{4}{9}\right)^3 \cdot \left(\frac{4}{9}\right)^4}$

13 $\dfrac{a^9 \cdot a^2 \cdot a^3}{a^6 \cdot a^3 \cdot a^4}$

14 $\dfrac{4c^6 \cdot 3b^4 \cdot 9c^5}{b^3 \cdot 6c^3 \cdot 2c^3}$

Name: _____ Date: _____

3 The Power of a Power

Learning Objective:
• Use the power of a power property.

THINK

It is given that $(p \cdot p \cdot p)^2 = a^{12}$ and $(q \cdot q)^2 = a^{12}$. Express p and q in exponential notation in terms of a.
How do you write $(p \cdot q)^2$ in exponential notation in terms of a?

ENGAGE

Show the steps to solve $(2 \cdot 2)^4$. Now, solve $(2^2)^4$. How does the order of operations apply to solving these problems? What pattern can you see?
How can you make use of the pattern to solve $(5^2)^5$? Discuss.

LEARN Use the power of a power property

1 You can use the order of operations to evaluate the expression $(2^4)^3$. First, evaluate the expression inside the parentheses. Then, use 16 as a factor 3 times.

$$(2^4)^3 = (2 \cdot 2 \cdot 2 \cdot 2)^3$$
$$= (16)^3$$
$$= 16 \cdot 16 \cdot 16$$
$$= 4,096$$

You can also evaluate the expression $(2^4)^3$ by using 2 as a factor 12 times.

$$(2^4)^3 = (2 \cdot 2 \cdot 2 \cdot 2)^3$$
$$= \underbrace{(2 \cdot 2 \cdot 2 \cdot 2) \cdot (2 \cdot 2 \cdot 2 \cdot 2) \cdot (2 \cdot 2 \cdot 2 \cdot 2)}_{\textbf{3 groups} \text{ of } \textbf{4 factors}}$$
$$= \underbrace{2^{4 \cdot 3}}_{4 \cdot 3 = \textbf{12} \text{ factors of } \textbf{2}}$$
$$= 2^{12}$$
$$= 4,096$$

You use the same method to evaluate $(n^2)^5$.

$$(n^2)^5 = (n \cdot n)^5$$
$$= \underbrace{(n \cdot n) \cdot (n \cdot n) \cdot (n \cdot n) \cdot (n \cdot n) \cdot (n \cdot n)}_{\textbf{5 groups} \text{ of } \textbf{2 factors}}$$
$$= \underbrace{n^{2 \cdot 5}}_{2 \cdot 5 = \textbf{10} \text{ factors of } \textbf{n}}$$
$$= n^{10}$$

> When you raise a power to a power, keep the base and multiply the exponents.
>
> $$(a^m)^n = a^{m \cdot n} = a^{mn}$$

2 Simplify $(3^4)^2$. Write your answer in exponential notation.

$(3^4)^2 = 3^{4 \cdot 2}$ Use the power of a power property.
      $= 3^8$ Simplify.

3 Simplify $\left[\left(\dfrac{2}{7}\right)^6\right]^4$. Write your answer in exponential notation.

$\left[\left(\dfrac{2}{7}\right)^6\right]^4 = \left(\dfrac{2}{7}\right)^{6 \cdot 4}$ Use the power of a power property.

      $= \left(\dfrac{2}{7}\right)^{24}$ Simplify.

4 Simplify $[(2a)^5]^3$. Write your answer in exponential notation.

$[(2a)^5]^3 = (2a)^{5 \cdot 3}$ Use the power of a power property.
      $= (2a)^{15}$ Simplify.

5 Simplify $[(-x)^4]^3$. Write your answer in exponential notation.

$[(-x)^4]^3 = (-x)^{4 \cdot 3}$ Use the power of a power property.
      $= (-x)^{12}$ Simplify.

Activity **Exploring the power of a power property**

Work in pairs.

In this activity, you and your partner will play a game in which you write and evaluate expressions in the form $(a^m)^n$. You will obtain a point for each expression you write. The person with the greater score wins.

① Take three stacks of five cards, where the cards of each stack are numbered 1 to 5. Shuffle each stack of cards. You and your partner each randomly draws three cards, one from each stack.

(2) **Mathematical Habit 5** **Use tools strategically**

Use your three cards to write an expression in the form $(a^m)^n$. For instance, if you draw 2, 4, and 5, you could write $(2^4)^5$, $(4^2)^5$ or another expression. Write as many expressions as you can. You may want to use a calculator to evaluate your expressions. For instance, to evaluate $(2^4)^5$, use the following keystrokes.

Press  .

(3) Record your expressions and their values. Your partner should also record his or her expressions and their values. Check your partner's work.

(4) Continue the game by replacing the cards you used and shuffling the stacks. Repeat ① to ③ several times. Find each player's score by counting the number of correct expressions that each player has written. The player with the greater score wins.

(5) **Mathematical Habit 8** **Look for patterns**

Is it correct to assume that using the greatest number drawn as the base will give an expression with the greatest possible value? Explain or give an example.

TRY Practice using the power of a power property

Simplify each expression. Write each answer in exponential notation.

1 $(5^3)^4$

$(5^3)^4 = $ _____   Use the power of a power property.

     $ = $ _____   Simplify.

2 $(2.3^4)^2$

$(2.3^4)^2 = $ _____   Use the power of a power property

     $ = $ _____   Simplify.

3 $[(3p)^5]^4$

4 $[(-y)^4]^7$

ENGAGE

Is $3^4 \cdot 3^2 = 3^{4+2}$? Is $(3^6)^5 = 3^{6 \cdot 5}$? Explain your thinking.

How do you simplify $3^4 \cdot 3^2 \cdot (3^6)^5$ and $\dfrac{(3^6)^5}{3^4 \cdot 3^2}$? Discuss.

Create a problem using at least two properties of exponents. Trade with your partner. Simplify the expression. Write your answer in exponential notation.

LEARN Use properties of exponents to simplify expressions

1 You may need to use more than one property of exponents to simplify expressions.

2 Simplify $[(-4)^2 \cdot (-4)^3]^6$. Write your answer in exponential notation.

> Follow the order of operations. First, use the product of powers property within the brackets. Then, use the power of a power property.

$[(-4)^2 \cdot (-4)^3]^6$
$= [(-4)^{2+3}]^6$ Use the product of powers property.
$= [(-4)^5]^6$ Simplify.
$= (-4)^{5 \cdot 6}$ Use the power of a power property.
$= (-4)^{30}$ Simplify.

3 Simplify $(m^5 \cdot m)^3$. Write your answer in exponential notation.

$(m^5 \cdot m)^3$
$= (m^{5+1})^3$ Use the product of powers property.
$= (m^6)^3$ Simplify.
$= m^{6 \cdot 3}$ Use the power of a power property.
$= m^{18}$ Simplify.

4 Simplify $\dfrac{(6^4 \cdot 6^3)^4}{(6^2)^5}$. Write your answer in exponential notation.

$\dfrac{(6^4 \cdot 6^3)^4}{(6^2)^5}$

$= \dfrac{(6^{4+3})^4}{6^{2 \cdot 5}}$ Use the product of powers and the power of a power properties.

$= \dfrac{(6^7)^4}{6^{10}}$ Simplify.

$= \dfrac{6^{7 \cdot 4}}{6^{10}}$ Use the power of a power property.

$= \dfrac{6^{28}}{6^{10}}$ Simplify.

$= 6^{28-10}$ Use the quotient of powers property.

$= 6^{18}$ Simplify.

5 Simplify $(a^4 \cdot a^2)^4 \div 2a^8$. Write your answer in exponential notation.

$[a^4 \cdot a^2]^4 \div 2a^8$
$= (a^{4+2})^4 \div 2a^8$ Use the product of powers property.

$= (a^6)^4 \div 2a^8$ Simplify.
$= a^{6 \cdot 4} \div 2a^8$ Use the power of a power property.
$= a^{24} \div 2a^8$ Simplify.
$= \dfrac{a^{24-8}}{2}$ Use the quotient of powers property.

$= \dfrac{a^{16}}{2}$ Simplify.

**Math Talk**

Suppose a can be any integer in the expression $\dfrac{a^{16}}{2}$. Will the value of the expression be positive or negative? How do you know?

TRY Practice using properties of exponents to simplify expressions

Simplify each expression. Write each answer in exponential notation.

1. $[(-3) \cdot (-3)^6]^2$

   $[(-3) \cdot (-3)^6]^2 =$ _____ Use the product of powers property.

   $=$ _____ Simplify.

   $=$ _____ Use the power of a power property.

   $=$ _____ Simplify.

2. $(p^4 \cdot p^2)^5$

   $(p^4 \cdot p^2)^5 =$ _____ Use the product of powers property.

   $=$ _____ Simplify.

   $=$ _____ Use the power of a power property.

   $=$ _____ Simplify.

3. $(6^3 \cdot 6^3)^7 \div 6^{10}$

4. $\dfrac{(x^8 \cdot x^4)^2}{(x^3)^6}$

Simplify the expressions within each parentheses first.

INDEPENDENT PRACTICE

Simplify each expression. Write each answer in exponential notation.

1 $(2^6)^2$

2 $(3^4)^3$

3 $(25^3)^3$

4 $(x^6)^3$

5 $\left[\left(\dfrac{1}{8}\right)^3\right]^6$

6 $\left[\left(\dfrac{4}{5}\right)^2\right]^4$

7 $[(2y)^3]^8$

8 $[(57p)^4]^4$

9 $[(-6)^4]^3$

10 $[(-p)^2]^{11}$

11 $(5^5 \cdot 5^6)^2$

12 $(p^4 \cdot p^2)^6$

13 $\left[\left(\frac{1}{2}\right) \cdot \left(\frac{1}{2}\right)^3\right]^5$

14 $\left[\left(-\frac{4}{9}\right)^2 \cdot \left(-\frac{4}{9}\right)^3\right]^2$

15 $(2^2 \cdot 2^4)^3 \div 2^8$

16 $(7 \cdot 7^2)^5 \div 7^3$

17 $(s^6 \cdot s)^2 \div s^4$

18 $(t^4 \cdot t^4)^4 \div t^4$

19 $\dfrac{(8^8 \cdot 8^3)^2}{(8^5)^4}$

20 $\dfrac{(3^4 \cdot 3^2)^4}{(3^5)^2}$

21 $\dfrac{(b \cdot b^3)^5}{(b^2)^4}$

22 $\dfrac{(h^6 \cdot h^4)^2}{(h^3)^5}$

23 $(q^5 \cdot q^2)^3 \div 5q^5$

24 $(c^7 \cdot c^3)^4 \div 6c^2$

25 $\dfrac{\left(\dfrac{2}{3}\right)^2 \cdot \left(\dfrac{2}{3}\right)^6}{\left(\dfrac{2^2}{3^2}\right)^3}$

26 $\dfrac{\left(\dfrac{x}{2}\right)^3 \cdot \left(\dfrac{x}{2}\right)^4}{\left(\dfrac{x}{2}\right)^2}$

4 The Power of a Product and the Power of a Quotient

Learning Objectives:
• Use the power of a product property.
• Use the power of a quotient property.

THINK

Write the prime factorization of 54 in exponential notation.

If $\frac{(2^a)^2 \cdot 3^b}{(2 \cdot 3)^a} = 54$, what are the values of a and b?

ENGAGE

Solve $(4 \cdot 5) \cdot (4 \cdot 5) \cdot (4 \cdot 5)$ and $4^3 \cdot 5^3$.

What do you notice about your answers? What can you say about $(4 \cdot 5)^3$ and $4^3 \cdot 5^3$?

How can you use your observations to simplify $2^6 \cdot 5^6$? Discuss.

LEARN Use the power of a product property

1 You can use the order of operations to evaluate the expression $(4 \cdot 5)^3$. First, evaluate the expression inside the parentheses. Then, use 20 as a factor 3 times.

$$(4 \cdot 5)^3 = (20)^3$$
$$= 20 \cdot 20 \cdot 20$$
$$= 8,000$$

You can also evaluate the expression $(4 \cdot 5)^3$ by using $(4 \cdot 5)$ as a factor 3 times.

$$(4 \cdot 5)^3 = (4 \cdot 5) \cdot (4 \cdot 5) \cdot (4 \cdot 5)$$
$$= \underbrace{(4 \cdot 4 \cdot 4)}_{3 \text{ factors of } 4} \cdot \underbrace{(5 \cdot 5 \cdot 5)}_{3 \text{ factors of } 5}$$
$$= 4^3 \cdot 5^3$$
$$= 64 \cdot 125$$
$$= 8,000$$

You can use the same method to evaluate $(h \cdot k)^4$.

$$(h \cdot k)^4 = (h \cdot k) \cdot (h \cdot k) \cdot (h \cdot k) \cdot (h \cdot k)$$
$$= \underbrace{(h \cdot h \cdot h \cdot h)}_{4 \text{ factors of } h} \cdot \underbrace{(k \cdot k \cdot k \cdot k)}_{4 \text{ factors of } k}$$
$$= h^4 \cdot k^4$$

For expressions with the same exponent, you can distribute the exponent to each base.

$$(a \cdot b)^m = a^m \cdot b^m$$

Similarly, to find the product of two algebraic expressions with the same exponent, you can multiply their bases.

$$a^m \cdot b^m = (a \cdot b)^m$$

2 Simplify $3^4 \cdot 7^4$. Write your answer in exponential notation.

$3^4 \cdot 7^4 = (3 \cdot 7)^4$ Use the power of a product property.
$ = 21^4$ Simplify.

3 Simplify $\left(-\frac{1}{3}\right)^5 \cdot \left(-\frac{2}{5}\right)^5$. Write your answer in exponential notation.

$\left(-\frac{1}{3}\right)^5 \cdot \left(-\frac{2}{5}\right)^5 = \left[\left(-\frac{1}{3}\right) \cdot \left(-\frac{2}{5}\right)\right]^5$ Use the power of a product property.

$\phantom{\left(-\frac{1}{3}\right)^5 \cdot \left(-\frac{2}{5}\right)^5} = \left(\frac{2}{15}\right)^5$ Simplify.

4 Simplify $(2r)^5 \cdot (7s)^5$. Write your answer in exponential notation.

$(2r)^5 \cdot (7s)^5 = (2r \cdot 7s)^5$ Use the power of a product property.
$ = (14rs)^5$ Simplify.

TRY Practice using the power of a product property

Simplify each expression. Write each answer in exponential notation.

1 $6^3 \cdot 7^3$

$6^3 \cdot 7^3 = ($_____ $\cdot$ _____$)^3$ Use the power of a product property.

$ = $ _____   Simplify.

2 $\left(-\frac{5}{6}\right)^4 \cdot \left(-\frac{1}{4}\right)^4$

3 $(3a)^4 \cdot (4b)^4$

Solve $\frac{2}{3} \cdot \frac{2}{3} \cdot \frac{2}{3} \cdot \frac{2}{3} \cdot \frac{2}{3}$ and $\frac{2^5}{3^5}$.

What do you notice about your answers? What can you say about $\left(\frac{2}{3}\right)^5$ and $\frac{2^5}{3^5}$?

How can you use your observations to simplify $8^6 \div 4^6$? Discuss.

LEARN Use the power of a quotient property

1. You can evaluate the expression $\left(\frac{2}{3}\right)^5$ by using $\frac{2}{3}$ as a factor 5 times.

$$\left(\frac{2}{3}\right)^5 = \frac{2}{3} \cdot \frac{2}{3} \cdot \frac{2}{3} \cdot \frac{2}{3} \cdot \frac{2}{3}$$

5 factors of 2

$$= \frac{\overbrace{2 \cdot 2 \cdot 2 \cdot 2 \cdot 2}}{\underbrace{3 \cdot 3 \cdot 3 \cdot 3 \cdot 3}}$$

5 factors of 3

$$= \frac{2^5}{3^5}$$

$$= \frac{32}{243}$$

You can use the same method to evaluate $\left(\frac{s}{t}\right)^4$.

$$\left(\frac{s}{t}\right)^4 = \frac{s}{t} \cdot \frac{s}{t} \cdot \frac{s}{t} \cdot \frac{s}{t}$$

4 factors of s

$$= \frac{\overbrace{s \cdot s \cdot s \cdot s}}{\underbrace{t \cdot t \cdot t \cdot t}}$$

4 factors of t

$$= \frac{s^4}{t^4}$$

For expressions with the same exponent, you can distribute the exponent to each base.

$$\left(\frac{a}{b}\right)^m = \frac{a^m}{b^m}, \; b \neq 0$$

Similarly, to find the quotient of two algebraic expressions with the same exponent, you can divide their bases.

$$\frac{a^m}{b^m} = \left(\frac{a}{b}\right)^m, \; b \neq 0$$

You can use this property to simplify algebraic expressions like the one shown below.

$$\left(\frac{2m}{6n}\right)^3 = \frac{(2m)^3}{(6n)^3}$$
$$= \frac{8m^3}{216n^3}$$
$$= \frac{m^3}{27n^3}$$

Reduce fractions to the simplest form when possible.

2 Simplify $2^4 \div 6^4$. Write your answer in exponential notation.

$2^4 \div 6^4 = \left(\frac{2}{6}\right)^4$ Use the power of a quotient property.

$ = \left(\frac{1}{3}\right)^4$ Simplify.

3 Simplify $(-8)^5 \div (-2)^5$. Write your answer in exponential notation.

$(-8)^5 \div (-2)^5 = \left(\frac{-8}{-2}\right)^5$ Use the power of a quotient property.

$ = 4^5$ Simplify.

4 Simplify $(5x)^9 \div (4y)^9$. Write your answer in exponential notation.

$(5x)^9 \div (4y)^9 = \left(\frac{5x}{4y}\right)^9$ Use the power of a quotient property.

TRY Practice using the power of a quotient property

Simplify each expression. Write each answer in exponential notation.

1 $2^5 \div 4^5$

$2^5 \div 4^5 = \left(\frac{}{}\right)^5$ Use the power of a quotient property.

$ = \left(\frac{}{}\right)^5$ Simplify.

2 $(-9)^3 \div (-3)^3$

3 $(8p)^5 \div (3q)^5$

What properties of exponents are required to simplify $\frac{6^3 \cdot 6^2}{3^2 \cdot 3^3}$?

List the properties you used in the order they were needed. Explain your thinking.

Can you do it in another way? Discuss.

LEARN Use properties of exponents to simplify more expressions

1 Simplify $\frac{4^5 \cdot 4^3}{2^2 \cdot 2^6}$. Write your answer in exponential notation.

$$\frac{4^5 \cdot 4^3}{2^2 \cdot 2^6} = \frac{4^{5+3}}{2^{2+6}}$$ Use the product of powers property.

$$= \frac{4^8}{2^8}$$ Simplify.

$$= \left(\frac{4}{2}\right)^8$$ Use the power of a quotient property.

$$= 2^8$$ Simplify.

2 Simplify $\frac{5^5 \cdot 2^9 \cdot 5^4}{10^3}$. Write your answer in exponential notation.

$$\frac{5^5 \cdot 2^9 \cdot 5^4}{10^3} = \frac{5^{5+4} \cdot 2^9}{10^3}$$ Use the product of powers property.

$$= \frac{5^9 \cdot 2^9}{10^3}$$ Simplify.

$$= \frac{(5 \cdot 2)^9}{10^3}$$ Use the power of a product property.

$$= \frac{10^9}{10^3}$$ Simplify.

$$= 10^{9-3}$$ Use the quotient of powers property.

$$= 10^6$$ Simplify.

3 Simplify $\frac{(7^2)^3 \cdot 4^6}{2^6}$. Write your answer in exponential notation.

$$\frac{(7^2)^3 \cdot 4^6}{2^6} = \frac{7^{2 \cdot 3} \cdot 4^6}{2^6}$$ Use the power of a power property.

$$= \frac{7^6 \cdot 4^6}{2^6}$$ Simplify.

$$= \frac{(7 \cdot 4)^6}{2^6}$$ Use the power of a product property.

$$= \frac{28^6}{2^6}$$ Simplify.

$$= \left(\frac{28}{2}\right)^6$$ Use the power of a quotient property.

$$= 14^6$$ Simplify.

Simplify each expression. Write each answer in exponential notation.

1. $\dfrac{6^4 \cdot 6^3}{3^2 \cdot 3^5}$

   $\dfrac{6^4 \cdot 6^3}{3^2 \cdot 3^5} = \dfrac{6^{4+3}}{3^{2+5}}$ Use the product of powers property.

   $\qquad = \dfrac{6^7}{3^7}$ Simplify.

   $\qquad = \left(\dfrac{6}{3}\right)^7$ Use the power of a quotient property.

   $\qquad = \underline{\hspace{2cm}}$ Simplify.

2. $\dfrac{4^6 \cdot 3^8 \cdot 4^2}{12^5}$

You use the properties of exponents to first simplify the numerator and denominator. Look for more than one property of exponents to use.

3. $\dfrac{(25^3)^2 \cdot 7^6}{5^6}$

INDEPENDENT PRACTICE

Simplify each expression. Write each answer in exponential notation.

1 $5^4 \cdot 6^4$

2 $5.4^3 \cdot 4.5^3$

3 $(2x)^5 \cdot (3y)^5$

4 $(2.5a)^6 \cdot (1.6b)^6$

5 $9^2 \div 3^2$

6 $2.8^7 \div 0.7^7$

7 $(3.3x)^9 \div (1.1y)^9$

8 $(3a)^6 \div (2b)^6$

9 $\left(\dfrac{32m^6}{4n^4}\right)^2$

10 $\dfrac{9^2 \cdot 9^7}{3^5 \cdot 3^4}$

11 $\dfrac{6^5 \cdot 2^3 \cdot 6^4}{12^3}$

12 $\dfrac{(5^4)^2 \cdot 6^8}{10^8}$

13 $\dfrac{24^9}{4^3 \cdot 6^2 \cdot 4^6}$

14 $\dfrac{9^{12}}{(3^3)^3 \cdot 3^3}$

5 Zero and Negative Exponents

Learning Objectives:
• Simplify expressions involving the zero exponent.
• Simplify expressions involving negative exponents.

THINK

Write two expressions in exponential notation that are equivalent to $\frac{x^{-8}}{x^0}$, where x is any number except zero.

ENGAGE

Use one of the properties of exponents to simplify $2^4 \div 2^2$ and $2^4 \div 2^3$.
How do you use the same property to simplify $2^4 \div 2^4$? Explain your thinking.
Discuss whether $2^0 = 1$. Create an example to justify your reasoning.

Now, choose a nonzero number. Raise it to the zero power. What is the answer? Will you have same answer if you choose other base numbers? Explain your thinking.

LEARN Simplify expressions involving the zero exponent

 Understanding the zero exponent

Work in pairs.

1. Use the quotient of powers property to simplify each expression. Write each answer in exponential notation.

Expression	Exponential Notation
$\frac{3^5}{3^2}$	3^3
$\frac{3^5}{3^3}$	
$\frac{3^5}{3^4}$	
$\frac{3^5}{3^5}$	

What expression did you write for $\frac{3^5}{3^5}$? What exponent did you obtain?

② In factored form, the quotient $\frac{3^5}{3^5}$ is $\frac{3 \cdot 3 \cdot 3 \cdot 3 \cdot 3}{3 \cdot 3 \cdot 3 \cdot 3 \cdot 3}$. If you divide out all the common factors in the numerator and denominator, what is the value of $\frac{3^5}{3^5}$?

③ Based on your findings, what can you conclude about the value of 3^0?

④ **Mathematical Habit 5 Use tools strategically**
Make a prediction about the value of any nonzero number raised to the zero power. Then, use a calculator to check your prediction for several numbers. For example, to raise the number −2 to the zero power, use the following keystrokes.

Press .

Does your prediction hold true?

① You have seen that when a number such as 3 is raised to the zero power, its value is 1. In fact, any number except 0 raised to the zero power is equal to 1.

A nonzero number raised to the zero power is equal to 1.

$$a^0 = 1, a \neq 0$$

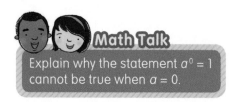
Math Talk
Explain why the statement $a^0 = 1$ cannot be true when $a = 0$.

© 2020 Marshall Cavendish Education Pte Ltd

2 Simplify and evaluate $7^3 \cdot 7^0$.

$$7^3 \cdot 7^0 = 7^3 \cdot 1 \qquad \text{Raise to the zero power.}$$
$$ = 7^3 \qquad \text{Simplify.}$$
$$ = 343 \qquad \text{Evaluate.}$$

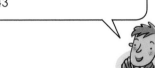

In this case, you can also use the product of powers property to solve.

$$7^3 \cdot 7^0 = 7^{3+0}$$
$$ = 7^3$$
$$ = 343$$

3 Simplify and evaluate $1 \cdot 10^2 + 2 \cdot 10^1 + 3 \cdot 10^0$.

$$1 \cdot 10^2 + 2 \cdot 10^1 + 3 \cdot 10^0$$
$$= 1 \cdot 100 + 2 \cdot 10 + 3 \cdot 1 \qquad \text{Raise to the zero power.}$$
$$= 100 + 20 + 3 \qquad \text{Simplify.}$$
$$= 123 \qquad \text{Evaluate.}$$

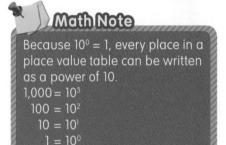

Math Note

Because $10^0 = 1$, every place in a place value table can be written as a power of 10.
$$1{,}000 = 10^3$$
$$100 = 10^2$$
$$10 = 10^1$$
$$1 = 10^0$$

4 Simplify and evaluate $\dfrac{4^2 \cdot 4^6}{4^8}$.

$$\frac{4^2 \cdot 4^6}{4^8} = \frac{4^{2+6}}{4^8} \qquad \text{Use the product of powers property.}$$
$$\phantom{\frac{4^2 \cdot 4^6}{4^8}} = \frac{4^8}{4^8} \qquad \text{Simplify.}$$
$$\phantom{\frac{4^2 \cdot 4^6}{4^8}} = 4^{8-8} \qquad \text{Use the quotient of powers property.}$$
$$\phantom{\frac{4^2 \cdot 4^6}{4^8}} = 4^0 \qquad \text{Simplify.}$$
$$\phantom{\frac{4^2 \cdot 4^6}{4^8}} = 1 \qquad \text{Evaluate.}$$

5 Simplify $(a^4 \div a^0) \cdot a^3$.

$$(a^4 \div a^0) \cdot a^3 = (a^4 \div 1) \cdot a^3 \qquad \text{Raise to the zero power.}$$
$$ = a^4 \cdot a^3 \qquad \text{Simplify.}$$
$$ = a^{4+3} \qquad \text{Use the product of powers property.}$$
$$ = a^7 \qquad \text{Simplify.}$$

TRY Practice simplifying expressions involving the zero exponent

Simplify each expression and evaluate where applicable.

1 $1.6^0 \div 0.4^2$

$$1.6^0 \div 0.4^2 = \underline{} \div 0.4^2 \qquad \text{Raise to the zero power.}$$

$$= \frac{}{} \qquad \text{Write the division as a fraction.}$$

$$= \underline{} \qquad \text{Evaluate.}$$

2 $2 \cdot 10^3 + 1 \cdot 10^2 + 4 \cdot 10^0$

$2 \cdot 10^3 + 1 \cdot 10^2 + 4 \cdot 10^0$

$= 2 \cdot \underline{\hspace{2cm}} + 1 \cdot \underline{\hspace{2cm}} + 4 \cdot \underline{\hspace{2cm}}$

$= \underline{\hspace{2cm}} + \underline{\hspace{2cm}} + \underline{\hspace{2cm}}$

$= \underline{\hspace{2cm}}$

3 $\dfrac{3 \cdot 3^9}{3^{10}}$
                                        2 $(t^0 \cdot t^7) \div t^5$

ENGAGE

How do you express $\dfrac{2 \cdot 2}{2 \cdot 2 \cdot 2}$ and $\dfrac{2 \cdot 2}{2 \cdot 2 \cdot 2 \cdot 2}$ in similar equivalent forms? Explain your thinking.

LEARN Simplify expressions involving negative exponents

Activity Understanding negative exponents

Work in pairs.

① Use the quotient of powers property to simplify each expression.
Write each answer in exponential notation.

Expression	Exponential Notation
$\dfrac{4^5}{4^3}$	4^2
$\dfrac{4^5}{4^4}$	
$\dfrac{4^5}{4^5}$	
$\dfrac{4^5}{4^6}$	
$\dfrac{4^5}{4^7}$	

What expression did you write for $\frac{4^5}{4^6}$? What exponent did you obtain?

2 In factored form, the quotient $\frac{4^5}{4^6}$ is $\frac{4 \cdot 4 \cdot 4 \cdot 4 \cdot 4}{4 \cdot 4 \cdot 4 \cdot 4 \cdot 4 \cdot 4}$. If you divide out all the common factors in the numerator and denominator, what is the value of $\frac{4^5}{4^6}$?

3 Repeat 2 for $\frac{4^5}{4^7}$. What is the value of $\frac{4^5}{4^7}$?

4 **Mathematical Habit 8 Look for patterns**
Suppose a represents any nonzero number. How would you write a^{-3} using a positive exponent?

1 For any nonzero number that has a negative exponent, you can write it using a positive exponent.

> For any nonzero real number a and any integer n,
> $$a^{-n} = \frac{1}{a^n}, \, a \neq 0$$

2 Simplify $13^{-7} \cdot 13^4$. Write your answer using a positive exponent.

$$13^{-7} \cdot 13^4 = 13^{(-7)+4} \qquad \text{Use the product of powers property.}$$
$$= 13^{-3} \qquad \text{Simplify.}$$
$$= \frac{1}{13^3} \qquad \text{Write using a positive exponent.}$$

3 Simplify $9m^{-2} \div 3m$. Write your answer using a positive exponent.

$9m^{-2} \div 3m$

$= \dfrac{9m^{-2}}{3m}$ Write the division as a fraction.

$= \dfrac{9}{3} \cdot \dfrac{m^{-2}}{m}$ Rewrite the fraction as the product of two fractions.

$= 3 \cdot m^{(-2)-1}$ Use the quotient of powers property.

$= 3 \cdot m^{-3}$ Simplify.

$= 3 \cdot \dfrac{1}{m^3}$ Write using a positive exponent.

$= \dfrac{3}{m^3}$ Simplify.

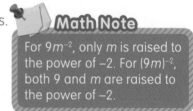

Math Note

For $9m^{-2}$, only m is raised to the power of -2. For $(9m)^{-2}$, both 9 and m are raised to the power of -2.

TRY Practice simplifying expressions involving negative exponents

Simplify each expression. Write each answer using a positive exponent.

1 $2.5^{-7} \div 2.5^{-4}$

$2.5^{-7} \div 2.5^{-4} =$ _____   Use the quotient of powers property.

$=$ _____   Simplify.

$= \dfrac{1}{\rule{1.5cm}{0.4pt}}$ Write using a positive exponent.

2 $14a^{-5} \div (7a \cdot 2a^{-4})$

Usually you write your answer using a positive exponent unless asked to use a negative exponent.

INDEPENDENT PRACTICE

Simplify and evaluate each expression.

1 $8^3 \cdot 8^0$

2 $5^4 \cdot (-5)^0$

3 $\left(\dfrac{1}{3}\right)^4 \cdot \left(\dfrac{1}{3}\right)^0$

4 $7 \cdot 10^3 + 4^2 \cdot 10^2 + 5 \cdot 10^0$

5 $2.3 \cdot 10^2 + 5 \cdot 10^1 + 1 \cdot 10^0$

6 $\dfrac{7^4 \cdot 7^5}{7^9}$

7 $(9^{-3})^0 \cdot 5^2$

8 $\dfrac{(6^{-3})^{-2} \cdot 8^6}{48^6}$

Simplify each expression. Write each answer using a negative exponent.

9 $7^3 \cdot 7^{-4}$

10 $\dfrac{(-5)^{-2}}{(-5)^3}$

11 $\left(\dfrac{3}{4}\right) \div \left[\left(\dfrac{3}{4}\right)^0 \cdot \left(\dfrac{3}{4}\right)^2\right]$

12 $\left(\dfrac{2}{5}\right)^{-4} \cdot \left(\dfrac{2}{5}\right)^{-1} \div \left(\dfrac{2}{5}\right)^{-3}$

13 $\dfrac{x^0}{x^2 \cdot x^3}$

14 $\dfrac{2h^{-5} \cdot 3h^{-2}}{6h^{-3}}$

Evaluate each expression. Write each answer using a positive exponent

15. $1.2^0 \div 1.8^2$

16. $5.2^{-3} \div 2.6^{-3}$

17. $\dfrac{(-3)^{-4}}{(-3)^2}$

18. $\left(\dfrac{5}{6}\right)^{-4} \cdot \left(\dfrac{5}{6}\right)^{-2} \div \left(\dfrac{5}{6}\right)^{-3}$

19. $\dfrac{9k^{-1} \cdot 2k^{-3}}{27k^{-6}}$

20. $\dfrac{c^{-4} \cdot c^{12}}{c^{-7}}$

Simplify each expression and evaluate where applicable.

21 $\dfrac{7^{-2} \cdot 7^0}{8^3 \cdot 8^{-5}}$

22 $\dfrac{(7^{-2})^2 \cdot 9^{-4}}{21^{-4}}$

23 $\dfrac{10^0}{2^{-2} \cdot (5^{-1})^2}$

24 $\dfrac{(3^6)^{-2}}{6^{-9}(-2^{10})}$

25 $\left(\dfrac{7m^3}{-49m^0}\right)^{-1}$

26 $\dfrac{8r^2 s}{4s^{-3}r^4}$

6 Squares, Square Roots, Cubes, and Cube Roots

Learning Objectives:
- Evaluate square roots and cube roots of positive real numbers.
- Solve an equation involving a variable that is squared or cubed.
- Solve real-world problems that use equations involving variables that are squared or cubed.

New Vocabulary
square root
cube root

THINK

Use each of the numbers 1 to 9 exactly once to replace the question marks shown.

$$\frac{3^{?-?} \cdot (?+?)^{?-?}}{\sqrt{?+?}} = 3^{?}$$

ENGAGE

Draw a square with a side length of 4 units. Write an expression to find the area of the square. Now, draw a square with an area of 16 square units. Write an expression to find the side length. What is the relationship between the two expressions you wrote? Can you say the same relationship exists when using the negative square root of a number? Why or why not?

LEARN Find the square roots of a number

1. When you multiply a number by itself, you are squaring that number or raising it to the second power. For example, $3^2 = 9$ and $(-3)^2 = 9$.

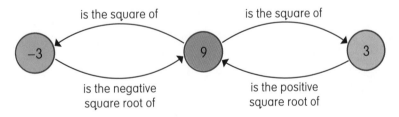

You use $\sqrt{9} = 3$ to indicate the positive square root of 9 and $-\sqrt{9} = -3$ to indicate the negative square root of 9.

Not every number has a square root. For example, -9 has no square root as there are no two identical factors of -9. Both $(-3)^2$ and 3^2 are equal to 9.

2. Find the two square roots of 49.

$\sqrt{49} = 7$ 7 is the positive square root of 49 since $7 \cdot 7 = 49$.

$-\sqrt{49} = -7$ -7 is the negative square root of 49 since $(-7) \cdot (-7) = 49$.

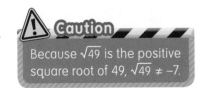

Caution
Because $\sqrt{49}$ is the positive square root of 49, $\sqrt{49} \neq -7$.

TRY Practice finding the square roots of a number

Solve.

1. Find the two square roots of 169.

ENGAGE

Sketch a cube with an edge length of 5 units. Write an expression to find the volume of the cube. Now, sketch a cube with a volume of 125 cubic units. Write an expression to find the edge length of the cube. Does this type of expression work with all rectangular prisms? Why or why not?

LEARN Find the cube root of a number

1. When you use a number as a factor three times, you are cubing that number or raising it to the third power. For example, $4^3 = 64$.

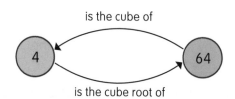

is the cube of

is the cube root of

Table of Cubes									
x	1	2	3	4	5	6	7	8	9	10
x³	1	8	27	64	125	216	343	512	729	1,000

$\sqrt[3]{64} = 4$ because $4 \cdot 4 \cdot 4 = 64$. So, 4 is the cube root of 64.

Notice that −4 is not a cube root of 64, because $(-4)^3 = -64$. −4 is a cube root of −64. So every number, positive, negative, or 0, has exactly one cube root.

2. Find the cube root of 343.

$$\sqrt[3]{343} = \sqrt[3]{7^3} \quad \text{7 is a cube root of 343 since } 7 \cdot 7 \cdot 7 = 343.$$
$$= 7 \quad \text{Simplify.}$$

Solve.

1 Find the cube root of $\frac{1}{729}$.

ENGAGE

When you solve an algebraic equation, what rules do you follow to keep the equation "balanced"? Use specific examples to explain your thinking. By making a systematic list, show how you can solve the equations $x^2 = 9$ and $y^3 = 8$.

LEARN Solve an equation involving a variable that is squared or cubed

1 To solve equations like $x^2 = 25$ and $y^3 = 125$, you need to find the value or values of the variable that make each equation a true statement. You do that by finding the square root or the cube root of both sides of the equation.

2 Solve $x^2 = 4.41$.

$x^2 = 4.41$
$x^2 = 2.1^2$ or $(-2.1)^2$ $4.41 = 2.1 \cdot 2.1$ and $4.41 = (-2.1) \cdot (-2.1)$.
$x = 2.1$ or -2.1 Show both the positive and negative square roots.

> Since $4 = 2^2$, use a guess-and-check strategy to find the square root of 4.41, starting with 2.1, 2.2, and so on.

3 Solve $x^3 = 1,000$.

$x^3 = 1,000$

$x^3 = 10^3$

$\sqrt[3]{x^3} = \sqrt[3]{10^3}$ Solve for x by taking the cube root of both sides.

$x = 10$ Show the cube root.

TRY Practice solving an equation involving a variable that is squared or cubed

Solve.

1 $x^2 = 2.25$

$x^2 = 2.25$

$x^2 = $ _____ or _____ $2.25 = 1.5 \cdot 1.5$ and $2.25 = (-1.5) \cdot (-1.5)$.

$x = $ _____ or _____   Show both the positive and negative square roots.

2 $x^3 = \dfrac{1}{8}$

ENGAGE

Suppose an artist makes a cube-shaped sculpture. The area of one face of the sculpture is 121 square inches and the volume of the sculpture is 1,331 cubic inches.

How do you find the edge length of the cube? Justify your answer.

Area = 121 in²

Volume = 1,331 in³

LEARN Solve real-world problems involving squares or cubes of unknowns

1 You can use equations that involve squares and cubes to solve real-world problems. Sometimes, only one of the square root solutions makes sense for the problem.

2 Theresa wants to put a piece of carpet on the floor of her living room. The floor is a square with an area of 182.25 square feet. How long should the piece of carpet be on each side?

STEP 1 Understand the problem.

What is the area of the floor?
What do I need to find?

STEP 2 Think of a plan.
I can form an algebraic equation.

STEP 3 Carry out the plan.

Let the length of each side of the square carpet be x feet.

$x^2 = 182.25$ Translate into an equation.
$\sqrt{x^2} = \sqrt{182.25}$ Solve for x by taking the positive square root of both sides.
$x = 13.5$ Use a calculator to find the square root.

The length of each side of the carpet is 13.5 feet.

STEP 4 Check the answer.
I can use the value found to find the area of the floor to check if my answer is correct.

$13.5 \cdot 13.5 = 182.25$
My answer is correct.

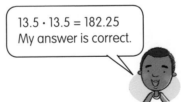

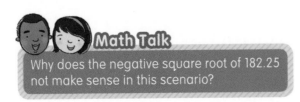

Math Talk
Why does the negative square root of 182.25 not make sense in this scenario?

3 The volume of an ice cube is 1.728 cubic meters. What is the surface area of the ice cube?

Let the length of one side of the ice cube be x meters.

$x^3 = 1.728$ Translate into an equation.

$\sqrt[3]{x^3} = \sqrt[3]{1.728}$ Solve for x by taking the cube root of both sides.

$x = 1.2$ Use a calculator to find the cube root.

Surface area of the ice cube $= 6 \cdot 1.2 \cdot 1.2$
$$= 8.64 \text{ m}^2$$

The surface area of the ice cube is 8.64 square meters.

TRY **Practice solving real-world problems involving squares or cubes of unknowns**

 Solve.

1 A square field has an area of 98.01 square meters. Find the length of each side of the field.
Let the length of each side of the field be x meters.

$x^2 = $ _____   Translate into an equation.

$\sqrt{x^2} = $ _____   Solve for x by taking the square root of both sides.

$x = $ _____   Use a calculator to find the square root.

The length of each side of the field is _____ meters.

2 Richard bought a crystal cube that has a volume of 1,331 cubic centimeters. Find the length of a side of the crystal cube.

INDEPENDENT PRACTICE

Find the two square roots of each number. Round each answer to the nearest tenth where applicable.

 1 25

 2 64

 3 80

4 120

Find the cube root of each number. Round each answer to the nearest tenth where applicable.

5 512

6 1,000

 7 999

8 $\dfrac{64}{343}$

Solve each equation. Round each answer to the nearest tenth where applicable.

9 $a^2 = 46.24$

10 $n^2 = 350$

11 $x^3 = 74.088$

12 $x^3 = \dfrac{216}{729}$

 Solve.

13 An orchard planted on a square plot of land has 3,136 apple trees. If each tree requires an area of 4 square meters to grow, find the length of each side of the plot of land.

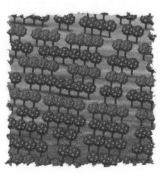

14 The volume of a cube-shaped box is 2,197 cubic centimeters. Find the area of a side of the box.

Mathematical Habit 2 **Use mathematical reasoning**

Jacob thinks that 57^2 is greater than 39^6 ? Is he correct? Why?

Problem Solving with Heuristics

1 **Mathematical Habit** **1** **Persevere in solving problems**

Evaluate $\dfrac{4^3 \cdot 10^4}{5^2}$ without using a calculator.

2 **Mathematical Habit** **1** **Persevere in solving problems**

Find the values of x and y that make the equation $\dfrac{81x^4 \cdot 16y^4}{[(2y)^2]^2} = 1{,}296$ true.

© 2020 Marshall Cavendish Education Pte Ltd

CHAPTER WRAP-UP

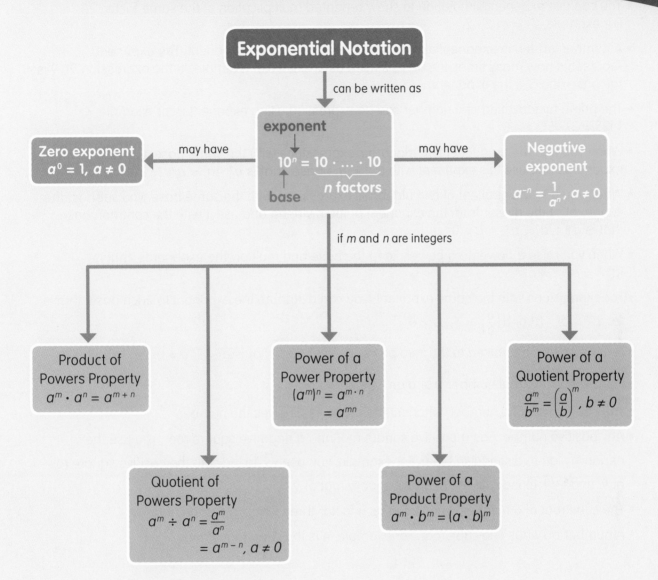

Exponential Notation

can be written as

exponent

$$10^n = \underbrace{10 \cdot \ldots \cdot 10}_{n \text{ factors}}$$

base

may have

Zero exponent
$a^0 = 1, a \neq 0$

may have

Negative exponent
$a^{-n} = \dfrac{1}{a^n}, a \neq 0$

if m and n are integers

Product of Powers Property
$a^m \cdot a^n = a^{m+n}$

Power of a Power Property
$(a^m)^n = a^{m \cdot n}$
$\qquad = a^{mn}$

Power of a Quotient Property
$\dfrac{a^m}{b^m} = \left(\dfrac{a}{b}\right)^m, b \neq 0$

Quotient of Powers Property
$a^m \div a^n = \dfrac{a^m}{a^n}$
$\qquad = a^{m-n}, a \neq 0$

Power of a Product Property
$a^m \cdot b^m = (a \cdot b)^m$

KEY CONCEPTS

- You can use exponential notation to show repeated multiplication of the same factor. For example, $2^3 = 2 \cdot 2 \cdot 2$.

- A number written in exponential notation has a base and an exponent. The exponent represents how many times the base is used as a factor. For example, in the expression 9^5, 9 is the base and 5 is the exponent.

- The prime factorization of a number can be expressed using exponents. For example, $1{,}125 = 3^2 \cdot 5^3$.

- When you find the product of two algebraic expressions with the same base, you add their exponents and use this exponent with the same base, that is $a^m \cdot a^n = a^{m+n}$.

- When you find the quotient of two algebraic expressions with the same base, you subtract the exponent of the divisor from the exponent of the dividend and use it with the common base, that is $a^m \div a^n = a^{m-n}$, $a \neq 0$.

- When you raise a power to a power, keep the base and multiply the exponents, that is $(a^m)^n = a^{m \cdot n} = a^{mn}$.

- For expressions with the same exponent, you can distribute the exponent to each base, that is $(a \cdot b)^3 = a^3 \cdot b^3$ and $\left(\dfrac{a}{b}\right)^3 = \dfrac{a^3}{b^3}$, $b \neq 0$.

- A nonzero number raised to the zero power is equal to 1, that is $a^0 = 1$, $a \neq 0$.

- For any nonzero real number a and any integer n, $a^{-n} = \dfrac{1}{a^n}$.

- The square root of a number, when multiplied by itself, gives the number.

- Any positive number has a positive square root and a negative square root. You use the negative sign to distinguish them. For example, you use $\sqrt{9}$ to indicate the positive square root of 9, and $-\sqrt{9}$ to indicate the negative square root of 9.

- The cube root of a number, when used as a factor three times, gives the number.

- A number only has one cube root. For example, 4 is the cube root of 64.

Determine whether each statement is correct. If it is incorrect, state the reason.

1 $0.7^3 = 0.7 \cdot 0.7 \cdot 0.7$

2 $5^{-4} = (-5) \cdot (-5) \cdot (-5) \cdot (-5)$

Write each expression in exponential notation.

3 $2 \cdot 2 \cdot 2 \cdot 2$

4 $4.8 \cdot 4.8$

5 $\frac{1}{2} \cdot \frac{1}{2} \cdot \frac{1}{2}$

6 $(-1.2)(-1.2)(-1.2)(-1.2)$

Expand and evaluate each expression.

7 $(-6)^2$

8 1.1^2

9 10^5

10 $\left(\frac{2}{3}\right)^3$

Write the prime factorization of each number in exponential notation.

(11) 3,780

(12) 27,720

Simplify each expression. Write each answer in exponential notation.

(13) $\left(\dfrac{5}{6}\right)^4 \cdot \left(\dfrac{5}{6}\right)^3$

(14) $5m^3n^4 \cdot 4m^5n^2$

15 $\left(\dfrac{7}{8}\right)^3 \div \left(\dfrac{7}{8}\right)$

16 $(-h)^{15} \div (-h)^9$

Simplify and evaluate each expression.

17 $\left[\left(\dfrac{2}{3}\right)^2 \cdot \left(\dfrac{2}{3}\right)^{-1}\right]^3$

18 $\dfrac{(9^{-2})^{-2} \cdot 2^2}{9^2}$

19 $(-4)^4 \cdot (-0.5)^4$

20 $\dfrac{6^7 \cdot 56^2}{6^5 \cdot 7^2}$

Simplify each expression. Write each answer using a positive exponent.

21) $\dfrac{6^3 \cdot 15^3}{(7^0)^3}$

22) $x^8 z^5 \div x^3 z^9$

23) $25p^6 q^9 \div 45p^8 q^4$

24) $40c^5 d^3 \div 10c^9 d^2$

Simplify and evaluate each expression.

25) $\dfrac{(3^5 \cdot 3^4)^2}{(3^3)^6}$

26) $\dfrac{42^{-1}}{(2^0)^{12} \cdot 21^{-1}}$

Solve.

27 Find the two square roots of 256.

28 Find the cube root of 32.768.

Solve each equation.

29 $c^2 = \dfrac{121}{169}$

30 $t^3 = -\dfrac{27}{343}$

Solve.

31 The floor of an elevator shaft is a square with an area of 42.25 square feet. Find the length of a side of the floor.

32 The volume of a model of a puzzle cube is 110,592 cubic inches. It is made up of 27 smaller cubes. What is the length of one side of each smaller cube?

Assessment Prep

Answer each question.

33 Which statement best describes the value of $\sqrt{18}$?

Ⓐ The value of $\sqrt{18}$ is between 3 and 3.5.

Ⓑ The value of $\sqrt{18}$ is between 3.5 and 4.

Ⓒ The value of $\sqrt{18}$ is between 4 and 4.5.

Ⓓ The value of $\sqrt{18}$ is between 4.5 and 5.

34 Which equation has both 5 and −5 as possible values of m?

Ⓐ $m^2 = 10$

Ⓑ $m^3 = 15$

Ⓒ $m^2 = 25$

Ⓓ $m^3 = 125$

35 Which expressions are equivalent to $\frac{2^{-14}}{2^{-7}}$? Choose **all** that apply.

Ⓐ 2^{-21}

Ⓑ 2^{-7}

Ⓒ 2^2

Ⓓ $\frac{1}{2^2}$

Ⓔ $\frac{1}{2^7}$

Ⓕ $\frac{1}{2^{21}}$

Name: _____ Date: _____

Intensity of Sound

1. Intensity of sound is the power of sound in watts divided by area covered in square meters. Loudness is the relative intensity of sound, above the threshold of hearing, that is perceived by a human ear. It is measured in decibels (dB). The intensity of the threshold of human hearing is about 10^{-12} watts per square meter (watts/m^2), corresponding to 0 dB.

The table shows the intensity and the corresponding decibels of some common sources of sound.

Source of Sound	Intensity (watts/m²)	Loudness (dB)
Rustle of leaves	10^{-11}	10
Quiet library	10^{-8}	40
Busy street traffic	10^{-5}	70
Rock band	1	120
Jet engine, 30 m away	10^2	140

a Consider the sound of a quiet library and of busy street traffic. How many times is the increase in the sound intensity from 40 dB to 70 dB?

b The pain threshold of a human ear is 120 dB. Which two sources of sound in the table on page 107 should you avoid?

2 As the distance, d metres, from the source of a sound increases, the loudness, L dB, decreases according to the formula $\frac{L_1}{L_2} = \left(\frac{d_2}{d_1}\right)^2$. Sophia, who is standing 10 meters away from the loud speakers of a rock band, finds the noise unbearable. How far does she need to stand away from the loud speakers so that the noise reduces to 90 dB? Round your answer to the nearest tenth.

Rubric

Point(s)	Level	My Performance
7–8	4	• Most of my answers are correct. • I showed complete understanding of the concepts. • I used effective and efficient strategies to solve the problems. • I explained my answers and mathematical thinking clearly and completely.
5–6	3	• Some of my answers are correct. • I showed adequate understanding of the concepts. • I used effective strategies to solve the problems. • I explained my answers and mathematical thinking clearly.
3–4	2	• A few of my answers are correct. • I showed some understanding of the concepts. • I used some effective strategies to solve the problems. • I explained some of my answers and mathematical thinking clearly.
0–2	1	• A few of my answers are correct. • I showed little understanding of the concepts. • I used limited effective strategies to solve the problems. • I did not explain my answers and mathematical thinking clearly.

Teacher's Comments

STEAM

School Is Noisy

What comes to mind when you think of noise in your daily life? Voices on a school bus? A hallway crowded with students on the move? The school band's practice room? The volume on music players and phones? These noises definitely contribute to every day's noise pollution.

Builders often install acoustic insulation to reduce unwanted or excessive sound in public buildings, such as schools, restaurants, and event centers. Likewise, some people also install soundproofing products in their homes and apartments.

Engineers evaluate the effectiveness of soundproofing products and assign each product a Noise Reduction Coefficient (NRC) rating. A product with an NRC of 0 absorbs no sound, while a product with an NRC of 1 absorbs all sound.

Task

Work in small groups to investigate the costs of acoustic insulation.

1. Download a free noise app for your smart phone. Use the noise meter to measure and record the decibel levels of common daily activities in your classroom and school.

2. Calculate how many times greater the intensity of the sound with the highest decibel reading is than the sound with the lowest dB reading. Share your results with the class.

3. Investigate the acoustic insulation products available to consumers. Compare NRCs and prices. Then measure the dimensions of your classroom ceiling and determine the cost of replacing existing ceiling tiles with the best product currently available on the market.

Scientific Notation

How far away are the stars?

When you look at the stars through a telescope, you are seeing light that has traveled an enormous distance. Proxima Centauri, the star that is closest to Earth after the Sun, is 39,900,000,000,000 kilometers from Earth. Many numbers like this are so large that scientists have invented a method called scientific notation to write them. In this chapter, you will use scientific notation to describe and compare very large and very small numbers.

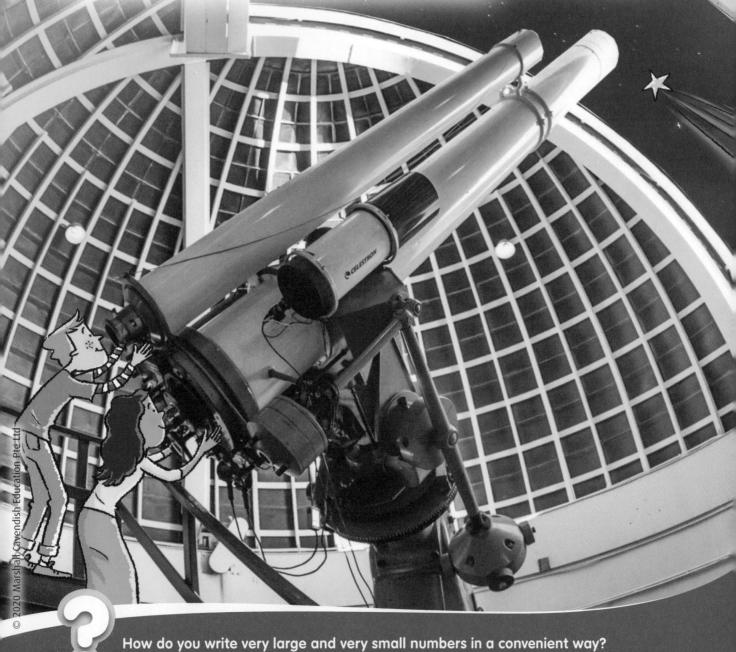

How do you write very large and very small numbers in a convenient way?

Name: _____   Date: _____

Multiplying and dividing decimals by positive powers of 10

When you multiply a decimal by a positive power of 10, the decimal point moves to the right.

Examples:

$1.47 \cdot 10 = 14.7$ Multiply by 10^1.

$1.47 \cdot 100 = 147$ Multiply by 10^2.

$-1.47 \cdot 100 = -147$ Multiply by 10^2.

When you divide a decimal by a positive power of 10, the decimal point moves to the left.

Examples:

$1.2 \div 10 = 0.12$ Divide by 10^1.

$1.2 \div 100 = 0.12$ Divide by 10^2.

$-1.2 \div 100 = -0.012$ Divide by 10^2.

▶ Quick Check

Evaluate each expression.

1 $1.8 \cdot 100$

2 $-0.28 \cdot 10^3$

3 $1.3 \cdot 10^4$

4 $74.5 \div 1,000$

5 $-3.8 \div 10$

6 $2.81 \div 10^2$

Understanding Scientific Notation

Learning Objectives:
- Write numbers in scientific notation or in standard form.
- Compare numbers in scientific notation.

> **New Vocabulary**
> scientific notation
> coefficient
> standard form

THINK

When visible light passes through a prism, the light waves refract, or bend, and the colors that make up the light can be seen. Each color has a different wavelength, as shown in the table.

Color	Wavelength
Green	$5.1 \cdot 10^{-7}$ m
Orange	$5.9 \cdot 10^{-5}$ cm
Red	0.00065 mm
Blue	$4.7 \cdot 10^{-10}$ km

a Shorter wavelengths refract more than longer wavelengths. Which color of light wave shows the most refraction? Which color of light wave shows the least refraction?

b The frequency of a light wave is the number of waves that travel a given distance in a given amount of time. The shorter the wavelength, the greater the frequency. List the colors of light wave, in order of their frequencies, from least to greatest.

ENGAGE

Consider the following form of each expression.
$1,000 = 10^x$ and $90,000 = 9 \cdot 10^y$
How do you find the values of x and y?

How do you write the number 90,000,000,000,000 in a similar form? How do you write 0.0000000009? Explain your thinking.

LEARN Write numbers in scientific notation

1 Astronomers have to work with very large and very small numbers. For instance, the average distance from Earth to the moon is 380,000,000 meters.

Light from the moon travels to Earth at a speed of 300,000,000 meters per second. This means that light travels 1 meter in about 0.00000000333… seconds. It is not easy to keep track of all the zeros in such numbers. For this reason, scientists use scientific notation to represent very large and very small numbers.

2 You can write a very large number or a very small number as the product of a number between 1 and 10, inclusive of 1, and an integer power of ten.

$$300,000,000 = 3 \cdot 100,000,000$$
$$= 3 \cdot 10^8$$

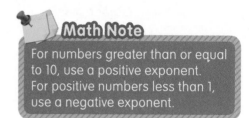

Math Note

For numbers greater than or equal to 10, use a positive exponent. For positive numbers less than 1, use a negative exponent.

$$0.00000000333 = 3.33 \cdot \frac{1}{1,000,000,000}$$
$$= 3.33 \cdot 10^{-9}$$

Numbers written this way are said to be in scientific notation.

Any number can be written in scientific notation by expressing it in two parts: a coefficient A where $1 \le A < 10$, and a power of 10 where the exponent n is an integer.

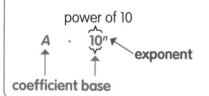

power of 10

$A \cdot 10^n$ ← exponent

coefficient base

You can also write it as $A \times 10^n$.

3 The wavelength of infrared light is $0.01 \cdot 10^{-5}$ meter. $0.01 \cdot 10^{-5}$ is not in scientific notation as the coefficient 0.01 is less than 1. It needs to be greater than or equal to 1.

4 A field is 10×10^1 yards long. 10×10^1 is not in scientific notation as the coefficient is not less than 10.

5 Write 427.7 in scientific notation.

$$427.7 = 4.277 \cdot 100 \quad \text{Move the decimal point 2 places to the left and multiply by 100.}$$
$$= 4.277 \cdot 10^2 \quad \text{Rewrite 100 as a power of 10.}$$

6 Write 0.007 in scientific notation.

$$0.007 = 7 \cdot \frac{1}{1,000} \quad \text{Move the decimal point 3 places to the right and multiply by } \frac{1}{1,000}.$$
$$= 7 \cdot \frac{1}{10^3} \quad \text{Rewrite } \frac{1}{1,000} \text{ as } \frac{1}{10^3}.$$
$$= 7 \cdot 10^{-3} \quad \text{Rewrite } \frac{1}{10^3} \text{ as a power of 10.}$$

10^{-3} has a negative exponent. You have learned that 10^{-3} can be written with a positive exponent as $\frac{1}{1,000}$.

TRY Practice writing numbers in scientific notation

Tell whether each number is written correctly in scientific notation. If it is incorrectly written, state the reason.

1 A Brazilian gold frog is $9.6 \cdot 10^0$ millimeters long.

> When written in scientific notation, the coefficient should be at least 1 and less than 10.

2 Mars is $0.228 \cdot 10^7$ kilometers from the Sun.

Write each number in scientific notation.

3 856.2

$856.2 = $ _____ $\cdot$ _____   Move the decimal point 2 places to the left and multiply by 100.

$\quad\quad\;\; = $ _____ $\cdot$ _____   Rewrite 100 as a power of 10.

4 0.06

ENGAGE

Every second, 2 million red blood cells are produced in your body. How many red blood cells are produced in one minute? Express your answer in scientific notation.

A normal white blood cell count has a maximum of $1.08 \cdot 10^4$ cells per cubic millimeter of blood. What is another way to express this number? Explain your answer.

LEARN Write numbers in scientific notation to standard form

1 You can use what you know about writing numbers in scientific notation to write them in standard form.

2 Write $7.1 \cdot 10^3$ in standard form.

$7.1 \cdot 10^3 = 7.1 \cdot 1,000$ Evaluate the power.

$\quad\quad\quad\;\; = 7,100$ Multiply by 1,000.

③ Write $8.12 \cdot 10^{-3}$ in standard form.

$8.12 \cdot 10^{-3} = 8.12 \cdot \dfrac{1}{1,000}$ Evaluate the power.

$\phantom{8.12 \cdot 10^{-3}} = 0.00812$ Divide by 1,000.

TRY Practice writing numbers in standard form

Write each number in standard form.

① $9 \cdot 10^4$

$9 \cdot 10^4 =$ _____ $\cdot$ _____   Evaluate the power.

$ =$ _____   Multiply by 10,000.

② $2.5 \cdot 10^{-2}$

ENGAGE

John wrote the expression: $43 \cdot 10^2 > 5.2 \cdot 10^3$. Is he correct? Justify your thinking.

Create two expressions in scientific notation with the same powers. Trade with your partner. Explain which number is greater. Now, create two expressions in scientific notation with different powers. Trade with your partner. Explain which number is lesser.

LEARN Compare numbers in scientific notation

① You can compare numbers easily by writing them in scientific notation. Compare the powers of 10 to determine which number is greater. If the powers are equal, compare the coefficients.

② Identify the greater number in the pair of numbers $5.6 \cdot 10^2$ and $2.1 \cdot 10^3$.

$10^3 > 10^2$ Compare the exponents.
$2.1 \cdot 10^3 > 5.6 \cdot 10^2$

So, $2.1 \cdot 10^3$ is the greater number.

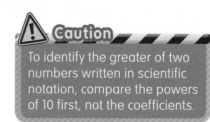

Caution

To identify the greater of two numbers written in scientific notation, compare the powers of 10 first, not the coefficients.

③ Identify the greater number in the pair of numbers $3.4 \cdot 10^{-1}$ and $1.1 \cdot 10^{-1}$.

Because the exponents are the same, compare the coefficients.

$3.4 > 1.1$ Compare the coefficients.

$3.4 \cdot 10^{-1} > 1.1 \cdot 10^{-1}$

So, $3.4 \cdot 10^{-1}$ is the greater number.

④ In 2000, Americans consumed an average of 47.2 pounds of potatoes and $5.936 \cdot 10^2$ pounds of dairy products per person. Did Americans consume more potatoes or dairy products?

▶ **Method 1**
Write the numbers in standard form and then compare the numbers.

> Write the amount of dairy products consumed in standard form. Then, compare the two amounts.

$5.936 \cdot 10^2 = 593.6$

$593.6 > 47.2$

So, Americans consumed more dairy products.

▶ **Method 2**
Write the numbers in scientific notation and then compare the numbers.

> Write the amount of potatoes consumed in scientific notation. Then, compare the two amounts.

$47.2 = 4.72 \cdot 10^1$

Compare $4.72 \cdot 10^1$ and $5.936 \cdot 10^2$.

$10^2 > 10^1$

$5.936 \cdot 10^2 > 4.72 \cdot 10^1$

So, Americans consumed more dairy products.

TRY Practice comparing numbers in scientific notation

Identify the lesser number in each pair of numbers.

1 $4.2 \cdot 10^2$ and $6.5 \cdot 10^1$

_____ < _____   Compare the exponents.

_____ < _____

So, _____ is the lesser number.

2 $3.6 \cdot 10^{-3}$ and $8.4 \cdot 10^{-3}$

Solve.

3 An actor has 75,126 fans on a social network. A musician has $8.58 \cdot 10^4$ fans. By writing both numbers in scientific notation or in standard form, find who has more fans on the social network.

MATH SHARING

Mathematical Habit 6 Use precise mathematical language

What are some other examples of very large and very small numbers? Express these numbers in scientific notation.

INDEPENDENT PRACTICE

Tell whether each number is written correctly in scientific notation. If it is incorrectly written, state the reason.

1 $71 \cdot 10^{22}$

2 $8 \cdot 10^{-2}$

3 $0.99 \cdot 10^{-3}$

4 $1.2 \cdot 10^{4}$

Write each number in scientific notation.

5 $533{,}000$

6 327.8

7 0.0034

8 0.00000728

Write each number in standard form.

9 $7.36 \cdot 10^{3}$

10 $2.431 \cdot 10^{4}$

⑪ $5.27 \cdot 10^{-2}$

⑫ $4.01 \cdot 10^{-4}$

Identify the lesser number in each pair of numbers.

⑬ $8.7 \cdot 10^6$ and $5.9 \cdot 10^3$

⑭ $4.8 \cdot 10^3$ and $9.6 \cdot 10^7$

⑮ $3.1 \cdot 10^{-5}$ and $7.5 \cdot 10^{-5}$

⑯ $6.9 \cdot 10^{-3}$ and $4.3 \cdot 10^{-3}$

Solve.

⑰ The table shows the populations of some countries. Write each population in scientific notation.

Country	Population
Brazil	208,000,000
Fiji	899,000
Monaco	38,000
Singapore	5,600,000

(18) A caterpillar is 76 millimeters long. A praying mantis is 15 centimeters long.

a Write both lengths in millimeters in scientific notation.

b Write both lengths in centimeters in scientific notation.

c How does writing the numbers using the same unit help us compare them?

19 A technician recorded the air pressure from several pressure gauges. The table shows each air pressure reading in pascals (Pa).

Pressure Gauge	Air Pressure (Pa)
A	210,000
B	$5.2 \cdot 10^5$
C	170,000

A pascal is a unit used to measure the amount of force applied on a given area by air or other gases.

a Which pressure gauge showed the highest reading?

b Which pressure gauge showed the lowest reading?

c The atmospheric pressure when these readings were made was $1.1 \cdot 10^5$ pascals. Which gauge(s) showed a reading greater than the atmospheric pressure?

Name: _____   Date: _____

2 Adding and Subtracting in Scientific Notation

Learning Objectives:
- Add and subtract numbers in scientific notation.
- Use the prefix system.

 THINK

Express each population in scientific notation.
Then find the difference between the populations
of any two countries. Show your findings in a table.

Country	Population
Mexico	130,000,000
Haiti	11,100,000
Costa Rica	4,950,000
United States	327,000,000

ENGAGE

Factor $3y + 3x$. How do you use what you know about factoring to simplify the expression
$2.11 \cdot 10^5 + 3.5 \cdot 10^5$? Explain your thinking.

LEARN Add and subtract numbers in scientific notation with the same power of 10

1. A popular social networking site has most of its members between the ages of 15 and 28.
Within this age group, there are $5.11 \cdot 10^7$ student members and $9.55 \cdot 10^7$ nonstudent
members. What is the total number of members in this age group? Write the answer in
scientific notation.

$5.11 \cdot 10^7 + 9.55 \cdot 10^7$
$= (5.11 + 9.55) \cdot 10^7$ Factor 10^7 from each term.
$= 14.66 \cdot 10^7$ Add within parentheses.
$= 1.466 \cdot 10^1 \cdot 10^7$ Write 14.66 in scientific notation.
$= 1.466 \cdot 10^{1+7}$ Use the product of powers property.
$= 1.466 \cdot 10^8$ Write in scientific notation.

> When the powers of 10 are the same, the distributive property can be applied to the sum or difference.

So, the total number of members in this age group is $1.466 \cdot 10^8$.

If you want to find how many more nonstudent members than student members,
you subtract.

$9.55 \cdot 10^7 - 5.11 \cdot 10^7$
$= (9.55 - 5.11) \cdot 10^7$ Factor 10^7 from each term.
$= 4.44 \cdot 10^7$ Subtract within parentheses.

Add and subtract numbers in
scientific notation with the same
power of 10

So, there are $4.44 \cdot 10^7$ more nonstudent members than student members.

> To add or subtract numbers in scientific notation, the powers
> of 10 must be the same.

2 The thickness of a compact disc (CD) is $1.2 \cdot 10^{-3}$ meter.
A slim CD case is $5.3 \cdot 10^{-3}$ meter thick.

a The CD is placed on top of the CD case.
What is the total thickness of the CD and CD case?
Write the answer in scientific notation.

$1.2 \cdot 10^{-3} + 5.3 \cdot 10^{-3}$
$= (1.2 + 5.3) \cdot 10^{-3}$ Factor 10^{-3} from each term.
$= 6.5 \cdot 10^{-3}$ Add within parentheses.

The total thickness of the CD and CD case is $6.5 \cdot 10^{-3}$ meter.

b How much thicker is the CD case than the CD? Write the answer in scientific notation.

$5.3 \cdot 10^{-3} - 1.2 \cdot 10^{-3}$
$= (5.3 - 1.2) \cdot 10^{-3}$ Factor 10^{-3} from each term.
$= 4.1 \cdot 10^{-3}$ Subtract within parentheses.

The CD case is $4.1 \cdot 10^{-3}$ meter thicker than the CD.

TRY Practice adding and subtracting numbers in scientific notation with the same power of 10

Solve.

1 The population of Washington, D.C., is $6.9 \cdot 10^5$.
South Dakota has a population of $8.8 \cdot 10^5$.

 Washington, D.C.
 South Dakota

a Find the sum of the populations.
Write the answer in scientific notation.

$6.9 \cdot 10^5 + 8.8 \cdot 10^5$

Population: $6.9 \cdot 10^5$ Population: $8.8 \cdot 10^5$

$= (6.9 + 8.8) \cdot$ _____   Factor 10^5 from each term.

$= 15.7 \cdot$ _____   Add within parentheses.

$=$ _____ $\cdot$ _____ $\cdot$ _____   Write 15.7 in scientific notation.

$=$ _____ $\cdot$ _____   Use the product of powers property.

$=$ _____ $\cdot$ _____   Write in scientific notation.

The sum of the populations is _____.

b Find the difference between the populations. Write the answer in scientific notation.

$8.8 \cdot 10^5 - 6.9 \cdot 10^5$

= (_____ − _____) · 10^5 Factor 10^5 from each term.

= _____ · 10^5 Subtract within parentheses.

The difference between the populations is _____.

---

2 The length of the smallest salamander is $1.7 \cdot 10^{-2}$ meter. The smallest lizard is $1.6 \cdot 10^{-2}$ meter long.

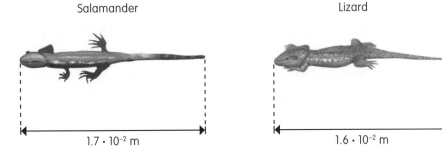

Salamander   Lizard

$1.7 \cdot 10^{-2}$ m $1.6 \cdot 10^{-2}$ m

a Find the sum of the lengths. Write your answer in scientific notation.

b Find the difference between the lengths. Write your answer in scientific notation.

ENGAGE

In order to add or subtract numbers in scientific notation by factoring, what can you say about the powers of 10? Using your answer, explain how you would add $3.2 \cdot 10^7 + 4.5 \cdot 10^9$ by factoring. Share your methods with your partner. What are the similarities and difference between your methods?

LEARN Add and subtract numbers in scientific notation with different powers of 10

1. When you add or subtract numbers written in scientific notation, first check to make sure the numbers have the same power of 10. If they do not, you rewrite one or more numbers so that all the numbers have the same power of 10.

2. The area of the Pacific Ocean is $6.4 \cdot 10^7$ square miles. The area of the Arctic Ocean is $5.4 \cdot 10^6$ square miles.

   a Find the sum of the areas of the two oceans. Write the answer in scientific notation.

   > Rewrite one number so that the two numbers have the same power of 10 as a factor.

   $6.4 \cdot 10^7 + 5.4 \cdot 10^6$
   $= 64 \cdot 10^6 + 5.4 \cdot 10^6$ Rewrite $6.4 \cdot 10^7$ as $64 \cdot 10^6$.
   $= (64 + 5.4) \cdot 10^6$ Factor 10^6 from each term.
   $= 69.4 \cdot 10^6$ Add within parentheses.
   $= 6.94 \cdot 10^1 \cdot 10^6$ Write 69.4 in scientific notation.
   $= 6.94 \cdot 10^{1+6}$ Use the product of powers property.
   $= 6.94 \cdot 10^7$ Write in scientific notation.

   The sum of the areas of the two oceans is $6.94 \cdot 10^7$ square miles.

   b How much larger is the area of the Pacific Ocean than the area of the Arctic Ocean? Write the answer in scientific notation.

   $6.4 \cdot 10^7 - 5.4 \cdot 10^6$
   $= 64 \cdot 10^6 - 5.4 \cdot 10^6$ Rewrite $6.4 \cdot 10^7$ as $64 \cdot 10^6$.
   $= (64 - 5.4) \cdot 10^6$ Factor 10^6 from each term.
   $= 58.6 \cdot 10^6$ Subtract within parentheses.
   $= 5.86 \cdot 10^1 \cdot 10^6$ Write 58.6 in scientific notation.
   $= 5.86 \cdot 10^{1+6}$ Use the product of powers property.
   $= 5.86 \cdot 10^7$ Write in scientific notation.

   The area of the Pacific Ocean is $5.86 \cdot 10^7$ square miles larger than the area of the Arctic Ocean.

   > You can check that you have factored the terms correctly by multiplying again. For example, you obtain $64 \cdot 10^6 - 5.4 \cdot 10^6$ when you multiply $(64 - 5.4)$ and 10^6.

Math Talk

Can you obtain the same answer by rewriting $5.4 \cdot 10^6$ so that it has the same power of 10 as $6.4 \cdot 10^7$? Justify your answer.

3 A CD is $1.2 \cdot 10^{-3}$ meter thick. A thin coating which is added on the CD is $7.0 \cdot 10^{-8}$ meter thick.

a How thick is the CD with the coating added? Write the answer in scientific notation.

$1.2 \cdot 10^{-3} + 7.0 \cdot 10^{-8}$
$= 1.2 \cdot 10^{-3} + 0.00007 \cdot 10^{-3}$ Rewrite $7.0 \cdot 10^{-8}$ as $0.00007 \cdot 10^{-3}$.
$= (1.2 + 0.00007) \cdot 10^{-3}$ Factor 10^{-3} from each term.
$= 1.20007 \cdot 10^{-3}$ Add within parentheses.

> Choose one of the thickness measures and rewrite it so that it has the same power of 10 as the other thickness measure. In this example, the thickness of the coating is rewritten to have a power of 10^{-3}.

The total thickness of the CD and coating is $1.20007 \cdot 10^{-3}$ meter.

b How much thicker is the CD than the coating? Write the answer in scientific notation.
$1.2 \cdot 10^{-3} - 7.0 \cdot 10^{-8}$
$= 1.2 \cdot 10^{-3} - 0.00007 \cdot 10^{-3}$ Rewrite $7.0 \cdot 10^{-8}$ as $0.00007 \cdot 10^{-3}$.
$= (1.2 - 0.00007) \cdot 10^{-3}$ Factor 10^{-3} from each term.
$= 1.19993 \cdot 10^{-3}$ Add within parentheses.

The CD is $1.19993 \cdot 10^{-3}$ meter thicker than the coating.

TRY **Practice adding and subtracting numbers in scientific notation with different powers of 10**

Solve.

1 The area of the continent of Australia is $9 \cdot 10^6$ square kilometers. The area of the continent of Antarctica is $1.37 \cdot 10^7$ square kilometers.

a Find the sum of the land areas of the two continents. Write the answer in scientific notation.

$9 \cdot 10^6 + 1.37 \cdot 10^7$
$= 9 \cdot 10^6 + 13.7 \cdot 10^6$ Rewrite $1.37 \cdot 10^7$ as $13.7 \cdot 10^6$.

$= (9 + 13.7) \cdot$ _____   Factor 10^6 from each term.

$= 22.7 \cdot$ _____   Add within parentheses.

$=$ _____ $\cdot$ _____ $\cdot$ _____   Write 22.7 in scientific notation.

$=$ _____ $\cdot$ _____   Use the product of powers property.

$=$ _____ $\cdot$ _____   Write in scientific notation.

The sum of the land areas of the two continents is _____ square kilometers.

b Find the difference between the land areas. Write the answer in scientific notation.

$1.37 \cdot 10^7 - 9 \cdot 10^6$
$= 13.7 \cdot 10^6 - 9 \cdot 10^6$ Rewrite $1.37 \cdot 10^7$ as $13.7 \cdot 10^6$.

$= (13.7 - 9) \cdot$ _____   Factor 10^6 from each term.

$=$ _____ $\cdot$ _____   Subtract within parentheses.

The difference between the land areas is _____ square kilometers.

2 An invitation card is $2.54 \cdot 10^{-4}$ meter thick. A tissue paper insert is $6.0 \cdot 10^{-6}$ meter thick.

  a The invitation card is placed inside the tissue paper insert. What is the total thickness? Write the answer in scientific notation.

b How much thicker is the invitation card than the tissue paper insert? Write the answer in scientific notation.

ENGAGE

1,000 meters = 1 kilometer and 0.000001 meters = 1 micrometer.

Using scientific notation, how do you express 54,600 meters in terms of kilometers? How do you express 0.000546 meters in micrometers? What pattern do you notice? Describe it to your partner.

LEARN Use the prefix system

1 A prefix that precedes a basic unit of measure indicates a fraction or multiple of the unit. The table shows some of the common prefixes.

Prefix	Symbol	10^n	Standard Form	Term
Tera	T	10^{12}	1,000,000,000,000	Trillion
Giga	G	10^9	1,000,000,000	Billion
Mega	M	10^6	1,000,000	Million
kilo	k	10^3	1,000	Thousand
–	–	10^0	1	One
milli	m	10^{-3}	0.001	Thousandth
micro	μ	10^{-6}	0.000001	Millionth
nano	n	10^{-9}	0.000000001	Billionth
pico	p	10^{-12}	0.000000000001	Trillionth

The width of a human hair can be expressed as $1.76 \cdot 10^{-4}$ meters. Using the prefixes shown in the table, you can also express this measure as

$1.76 \cdot 10^{-7}$ kilometers,
$1.76 \cdot 10^{-1}$ millimeters or
$1.76 \cdot 10^2$ micrometers.

2 A blue whale has a mass of 190,000,000 grams. The mass of a whale shark is $2.6 \cdot 10^4$ kilograms. What is the sum of the masses of the blue whale and whale shark? Write the answer in scientific notation in terms of kilograms.

$$190{,}000{,}000 \text{ g} = 1.9 \cdot 10^8 \text{ g}$$
$$= 1.9 \cdot 10^5 \text{ kg}$$

Rewrite one mass so that the two masses are in kilograms.

$1.9 \cdot 10^5 + 2.6 \cdot 10^4$
$= 19 \cdot 10^4 + 2.6 \cdot 10^4$ Rewrite $1.9 \cdot 10^5$ as $19 \cdot 10^4$.
$= (19 + 2.6) \cdot 10^4$ Factor 10^4 from each term.
$= 21.6 \cdot 10^4$ Add within parentheses.
$= 2.16 \cdot 10^1 \cdot 10^4$ Write 21.6 in scientific notation.
$= 2.16 \cdot 10^{1+4}$ Use the product of powers property.
$= 2.16 \cdot 10^5$ Write in scientific notation.

The sum of the masses of the blue whale and whale shark is $2.16 \cdot 10^5$ kilograms.

TRY Practice using the prefix system

Solve.

1 On average, Jupiter orbits the Sun at a distance of 778.3 gigameters. Mars' average distance from the Sun is $2.273 \cdot 10^8$ kilometers.

Which of the two planets is farther from the Sun? How much farther? Write the answer in scientific notation in terms of kilometers.

INDEPENDENT PRACTICE

Evaluate each expression. Write each answer in scientific notation.

1 $6.3 \cdot 10^{-2} + 4.9 \cdot 10^{-2}$

2 $7.2 \cdot 10^2 - 3.5 \cdot 10^2$

3 $3.8 \cdot 10^3 + 5.2 \cdot 10^4$

4 $8.1 \cdot 10^5 - 2.8 \cdot 10^4$

Solve.

5 The table shows the amounts of energy, in calories, contained in various foods.

   a Find the total energy in chicken breast and cabbage. Write the answer in scientific notation.

Food (per 100 g)	Energy (Cal)
Chicken breast	$1.71 \cdot 10^5$
Raw potato	$7.7 \cdot 10$
Cabbage	$2.5 \cdot 10^4$
Salmon	$1.67 \cdot 10^5$

b Find the total energy in cabbage and raw potato. Write the answer in scientific notation.

c How many more calories are in salmon than in cabbage? Write the answer in scientific notation.

6 A flight from Singapore to New York includes a stopover at Hawaii. The distance between Singapore and Hawaii is $6.7 \cdot 10^3$ miles. The distance between New York and Hawaii is $4.9 \cdot 10^3$ miles.

a Find the total distance of the flight. Write the answer in scientific notation.

b Find the difference in distance between the two flights. Write the answer in scientific notation.

7 Factories A and B produce potato chips. They use the basic ingredients of potatoes, oil, and salt. Last year, each factory used different amounts of these ingredients, as shown in the table.

Ingredient	Factory A Amount Used (lb)	Factory B Amount Used (lb)
Potato	$4.87 \cdot 10^6$	3,309,000
Oil	356,000	$5.61 \cdot 10^5$
Salt	$2.87 \cdot 10^5$	193,500

a Which factory used more potatoes? How many more pounds of potatoes did it use? Write the answer in scientific notation.

b Which factory used more oil? How much more oil did it use? Write the answer in scientific notation.

c Find the total weight of the ingredients used by each factory. Write the answer in scientific notation.

8 Angora wool, obtained from rabbits, has fibers with a width of $1 \cdot 10^{-6}$ meter. Cashmere, obtained from goats, has fibers with a width of $1.45 \cdot 10^{-5}$ meter.

a Find the total width of the two types of fiber. Write the answer in the appropriate unit in prefix form.

b How much wider is the cashmere fiber than the angora fiber? Write the answer in the appropriate unit in prefix form.

3 Multiplying and Dividing in Scientific Notation

Learning Objective:

• Multiply and divide numbers in scientific notation.

 THINK

Emma wrote the following.

$$\frac{4.6 \cdot 10^8 \cdot 3.8 \cdot 10^{-4}}{2 \cdot 10^{-2}} = \frac{4.6 \cdot 3.8 \cdot 10^8 \cdot 10^{-4}}{2 \cdot 10^{-2}}$$

$$= \frac{17.48 \cdot 10^{12}}{2 \cdot 10^{-2}}$$

$$= \frac{17.48}{2} \cdot \frac{10^{12}}{10^{-2}}$$

$$= 8.74 \cdot 10^{14}$$

What mistake did she make?

ENGAGE

What is $10^3 \cdot 10^{-2}$? Next, given that $(a \cdot b) \cdot (c \cdot d) = a \cdot c \cdot b \cdot d$, how would you solve $(3 \cdot 10^3) \cdot (3.2 \cdot 10^2)$?

Write another pair of numbers in scientific notation, one with a positive exponent and another with a negative exponent. Trade your numbers with your partner and multiply them. Share your working.

LEARN Multiply numbers in scientific notation

① A rectangular swimming pool is $5 \cdot 10^1$ meters long and $2.5 \cdot 10^1$ meters wide. Find the area of the water surface.

Area of water surface $= 5 \cdot 10^1 \cdot 2.5 \cdot 10^1$

$\qquad\qquad\qquad\quad = 5 \cdot 2.5 \cdot 10^1 \cdot 10^1$ Use the commutative property.

$\qquad\qquad\qquad\quad = 12.5 \cdot 10^1 \cdot 10^1$ Multiply the coefficients.

$\qquad\qquad\qquad\quad = 1.25 \cdot 10^1 \cdot 10^1 \cdot 10^1$ Write 12.5 in scientific notation.

$\qquad\qquad\qquad\quad = 1.25 \cdot 10^{1+1+1}$ Use the product of powers property.

$\qquad\qquad\qquad\quad = 1.25 \cdot 10^3 \text{ m}^2$ Write in scientific notation.

The area of the water surface is $1.25 \cdot 10^3$ square meters.

Multiplication of numbers is commutative.

3 A rectangular field is $1.05 \cdot 10^2$ meters long and $6.8 \cdot 10^1$ meters wide. Find the area of the field. Write the answer in scientific notation.

Area of field $= 1.05 \cdot 10^2 \cdot 6.8 \cdot 10^1$

$\qquad\quad\; = 1.05 \cdot 6.8 \cdot 10^2 \cdot 10^1$ Use the commutative property.

$\qquad\quad\; = 7.14 \cdot 10^2 \cdot 10^1$ Multiply the coefficients.

$\qquad\quad\; = 7.14 \cdot 10^{2+1}$ Use the product of powers property.

$\qquad\quad\; = 7.14 \cdot 10^3 \; m^2$ Write in scientific notation.

The area of the field is $7.14 \cdot 10^3$ square meters.

TRY Practice multiplying numbers in scientific notation

Solve.

1 In the 19th century, the Law Courts of Brussels was the largest building ever built. Its rectangular base measures $1.6 \cdot 10^2$ meters by $1.5 \cdot 10^2$ meters. Find the base area of the building. Write the answer in scientific notation.

Base area

$= 1.6 \cdot 10^2 \cdot$ _____ $\cdot$ _____

$=$ _____ $\cdot$ _____ $\cdot$ _____ $\cdot$ _____   Use the commutative property.

$=$ _____ $\cdot$ _____ $\cdot$ _____   Multiply the coefficients.

$=$ _____ $\cdot$ _____   Use the product of powers property.

$=$ _____ $\cdot$ _____ m^2 Write in scientific notation.

The base area of the building is _____ square meters.

2 The outer wall of Angkor Wat, a World Heritage site in Cambodia, encloses a rectangular area of $1.02 \cdot 10^3$ meters by $8.02 \cdot 10^2$ meters. Find the area enclosed by the outer wall. Write the answer in scientific notation.

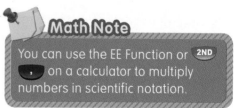

Math Note

You can use the EE Function or **2ND** ⬛ on a calculator to multiply numbers in scientific notation.

ENGAGE

What is $\frac{10^4}{10^2}$? Next, given that $\frac{a \cdot b}{c \cdot d} = \frac{a}{c} \cdot \frac{b}{d}$, how would you solve $\frac{5.4 \cdot 10^4}{2.7 \cdot 10^2}$?

Write another pair of numbers in scientific notation, one with a positive exponent and another with a negative exponent. Trade your numbers with your partner and divide one number by the other. Share your working.

LEARN Divide numbers in scientific notation

1. The planet Mercury has a mass of $3.3 \cdot 10^{23}$ kilograms. Mars has a mass of $6.4 \cdot 10^{23}$ kilograms. How many times as great as the mass of Mercury is the mass of Mars? Round the answer to the nearest tenth.

$$\frac{6.4 \cdot 10^{23}}{3.3 \cdot 10^{23}}$$
$$= \frac{6.4}{33} \cdot \frac{10^{23}}{10^{23}} \qquad \text{Divide the coefficients and divide the powers of 10.}$$
$$\approx 1.9 \cdot 10^{23-23} \qquad \text{Round the coefficient and use the quotient of powers property.}$$
$$= 1.9 \cdot 10^0$$
$$= 1.9 \qquad \text{Write in standard form.}$$

Mars has a mass that is approximately 1.9 times as great as the mass of Mercury.

2. The mass of an oxygen atom is $2.7 \cdot 10^{-26}$ kilograms. The mass of a silver atom is $1.8 \cdot 10^{-25}$ kilograms. How many times as great as the mass of an oxygen atom is the mass of a silver atom? Round the answer to the nearest tenth.

$$\frac{1.8 \cdot 10^{-25}}{2.7 \cdot 10^{-26}}$$
$$= \frac{1.8}{2.7} \cdot \frac{10^{-25}}{10^{-26}} \qquad \text{Divide the coefficients and divide the powers of 10.}$$
$$\approx 0.67 \cdot 10^{-25-(-26)} \qquad \text{Round the coefficient and use the quotient of powers property.}$$
$$= 0.67 \cdot 10^1$$
$$= 6.7 \qquad \text{Write in standard form.}$$

The mass of a silver atom is approximately 6.7 times as great as the mass of an oxygen atom.

You may use the EE function on a graphing calculator to enter numbers in scientific notation.

TRY Practice dividing numbers in scientific notation

Solve.

1. The Jean-Luc Lagardère plant in France is one of the largest buildings in the world. It has a volume of $5.6 \cdot 10^6$ cubic meters. The NASA vehicle assembly building in Florida has a volume of $3.7 \cdot 10^6$ cubic meters. How many times as great as the volume of the NASA vehicle assembly building is the volume of the Jean-Luc Lagardère plant? Round the answer to the nearest tenth.

$$\frac{5.6 \cdot 10^6}{}$$

$$= \frac{}{} \cdot \frac{}{} \qquad \text{Divide the coefficients and divide the powers of 10.}$$

$$\approx \underline{} \cdot \underline{} \qquad \text{Round the coefficient and use the quotient of powers property.}$$

$$= \underline{} \cdot \underline{}$$

$$= \underline{} \qquad \text{Write in standard form.}$$

The volume of the Jean-Luc Lagardère plant is approximately _____ times as great as the volume of the NASA vehicle assembly building.

2. The Abraj Al-Bait towers in Saudi Arabia has a floor area of $1.5 \cdot 10^6$ square meters. The Palazzo in Las Vegas has a floor area of $6.5 \cdot 10^5$ square meters. How many times as great as the floor area of the Palazzo is the floor area of the Abraj Al-Bait towers? Round the answer to the nearest tenth.

LET'S EXPLORE

Most calculators can only handle powers of 10 ranging from -99 to 99. How do you compute $(5 \cdot 10^{111})^2$?

INDEPENDENT PRACTICE

Evaluate each expression. Write each answer in scientific notation and round the coefficient to the nearest tenth where applicable.

1 $7.45 \cdot 10^6 \cdot 5.4 \cdot 10^{-6}$

2 $6.84 \cdot 10^{-5} \cdot 4.7 \cdot 10^{10}$

3 $5.75 \cdot 10^{-5} \div (7.15 \cdot 10^7)$

4 $8.45 \cdot 10^{11} \div (1.69 \cdot 10^{-8})$

Solve.

5 The table shows the volumes of some planets.

    a How many times as great as the volume of Mars is the volume of Venus? Round your answer to the nearest tenth.

Planets	Volume (km³)
Venus	$9.4 \cdot 10^{11}$
Earth	$1.1 \cdot 10^{12}$
Mars	$1.6 \cdot 10^{11}$

b How many times as great as the volume of Mars is the volume of Earth? Round your answer to the nearest tenth.

c How many times as great as the volume of Venus is the volume of Earth? Round your answer to the nearest tenth.

6 Sara's digital camera has a resolution of 2,560 · 1,920 pixels. David's digital camera has a resolution of 3,264 · 2,448 pixels.

a Express the resolution of each digital camera in prefix form to the nearest whole unit. Use the most appropriate unit.

b Whose camera has a higher resolution?

7 Blake downloaded pictures of a cruise ship and a ski run from the internet. The file size of the cruise ship is 794 kilobytes while the file size of the ski run is 2.6 megabytes.

a What is the total file size, in megabytes and in kilobytes, of the two pictures?

b Calculate the difference between the two file sizes, in megabytes and in kilobytes.

c To the nearest tenth, how many times as great as the file size of the ski run picture is the file size of the cruise ship picture?

d Blake saved the two pictures on a USB stick with a capacity of 256 megabytes. Find the remaining free capacity of the USB stick to the nearest tenth megabyte after Blake saved the two pictures in it.

8 A rectangular aquarium is $2.63 \cdot 10^3$ inches long, $1.26 \cdot 10^2$ inches wide, and $3 \cdot 10^1$ inches deep. Find its volume. Write the answer in scientific notation.

9 The time light takes to travel one meter in a vacuum is 3.3 nanoseconds. To travel one mile it takes 5.4 microseconds. How many times longer, to the nearest tenth, does it take light to travel one mile than one meter?

Mathematical Habit 7 **Make use of structure**

The table shows some numbers written in standard form and in the equivalent scientific notation. Describe the relationship between each pair of variables.

Standard Form	Scientific Notation
0.0007	$7 \cdot 10^{-4}$
0.00182	$1.82 \cdot 10^{-3}$
1,280,000,000	$1.28 \cdot 10^{9}$
7,100	$7.1 \cdot 10^{3}$
427.7	$4.277 \cdot 10^{2}$

a The value of the positive number in standard form and the sign of the exponent when expressed in scientific notation.

b The sign of the exponent when expressed in scientific notation and the direction the decimal point moves to express the number in standard form.

Problem Solving with Heuristics

1 **Mathematical Habit** **1** **Persevere in solving problems**
Find the cube root of $2.7 \cdot 10^{10}$.

2 **Mathematical Habit** **1** **Persevere in solving problems**
Given that $a = 3 \cdot 10^3$ and $b = 4 \cdot 10^2$, find the value of each expression.

a $2a + b$

b $\dfrac{2a}{b}$

3 Solve each of the following. Write your answer in scientific notation using the basic unit.

a 80 micrograms + 200 nanograms

b 3 gigameters – 700 megameters

CHAPTER WRAP-UP

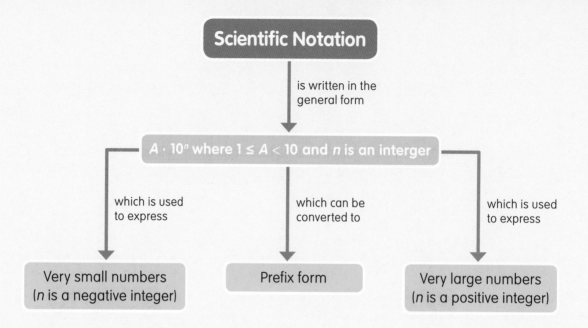

KEY CONCEPTS

- Scientific notation is a convenient way of writing very large or very small numbers.

- The general form of a number in scientific notation is $A \cdot 10^n$, where the coefficient A is at least 1 but less than 10, and the exponent n is any integer.

- To compare two numbers in scientific notation, first compare the powers of 10. If they are the same, then compare the coefficients.

- To add or subtract numbers in scientific notation, the numbers must be expressed using the same power of 10 before applying the distributive property.

- To multiply or divide numbers in scientific notation, multiply or divide the coefficients before multiplying or dividing the powers of 10 using properties of exponents.

- A prefix that precedes a basic unit of measure indicates a fraction or multiple of the unit. Each prefix has a unique symbol that is placed in front of the unit symbol.

Name: _____ Date: _____

Tell whether each number is written correctly in scientific notation. If it is incorrectly written, state the reason.

1 $10 \cdot 10^2$

2 $0.99 \cdot 10^{12}$

3 $1.4 \cdot 10^2$

4 $0.4 \cdot 10^{25}$

Write each number in scientific notation.

5 714,000

6 0.00087

Write each number in standard form.

7 $3.46 \cdot 10^2$

8 $5.4 \cdot 10^4$

Identify the greater number in each pair of numbers.

9 $7.8 \cdot 10^{-5}$ and $5.4 \cdot 10^{-7}$

10 $1.4 \cdot 10^{-5}$ and $6 \cdot 10^{-4}$

⑪ $6.5 \cdot 10^{-15}$ and $9.3 \cdot 10^{-12}$

⑫ $3.5 \cdot 10^{-2}$ and $4 \cdot 10^{-3}$

Evaluate each expression. Write each answer in scientific notation.

⑬ $2.44 \cdot 10^3 + 1.9 \cdot 10^5$

⑭ $3.12 \cdot 10^{-3} - 3 \cdot 10^{-3}$

⑮ $2.4 \cdot 10^{-2} \cdot 5 \cdot 10^{-1}$

⑯ $3.2 \cdot 10^8 \div (1.6 \cdot 10^4)$

Express each expression in prefix form. Choose the most appropriate unit

⑰ $2.8 \cdot 10^3$ meters

⑱ $1.5 \cdot 10^{-6}$ meters

Solve.

19 Organism A, an eriophyid mite, is 250 micrometers long. Organism B, a patiriella parvivipara, is 5 millimeters long.

a Which organism is longer?

b Express the length of the eriophyid mite in millimeters. Write the answer in scientific notation.

c Write each length in scientific notation using the basic unit.

20 The top five materials used in the automotive industry in the United States in a particular year are as shown in the table.

Material	Total Consumption (T)
Plastic	46,240
Aluminium	11,320
Steel	$9.894 \cdot 10^7$
Glass	5,417,000
Rubber	$2.86 \cdot 10^6$

a How much more plastic was used than aluminium? Write the answer in scientific notation and round the coefficient to the nearest tenth.

b How much more steel was used than glass? Write the answer in scientific notation and round the coefficient to the nearest tenth.

c Find the total consumption of these materials used by the automotive industry in that year. Write the answer in scientific notation and round the coefficient to the nearest tenth.

21 The table shows the weights of some animals.

Animal	Weight (lb)
African bush elephant	$2.706 \cdot 10^4$
Hippopotamus	$9.9 \cdot 10^3$
Walrus	$4.4 \cdot 10^3$

African bush elephant

weight $2.706 \cdot 10^4$ lb

Hippopotamus

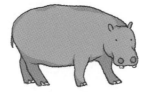

weight $9.9 \cdot 10^3$ lb

Walrus

weight $4.4 \cdot 10^3$ lb

a How many times as heavy as the walrus is the hippopotamus? Round your answer to the nearest tenth.

b How many times as heavy as the hippopotamus is the African bush elephant? Round your answer to the nearest tenth.

Assessment Prep
Answer each question.

22 A company earns $475,000,000 in one year. What is 475,000,000 written in scientific notation?

Ⓐ $4.75 \cdot 10^5$

Ⓑ $4.75 \cdot 10^8$

Ⓒ $4.75 \cdot 10^9$

Ⓓ $4.75 \cdot 10^{11}$

23 The area of California is approximately $1.64 \cdot 10^6$ square miles. What is $1.64 \cdot 10^6$ written in standard form?

Ⓐ 16,400,000

Ⓑ 1,640,000

Ⓒ 164,000

Ⓓ 16,400

24 An atom of oxygen has a mass of $2.7 \cdot 10^{-26}$ kilograms. A gas syringe contains $9 \cdot 10^{20}$ atoms of oxygen. Find the total mass, in kilograms, of the atoms of oxygen in the gas syringe. Write the answer in scientific notation. Write your answer in the space below.

The Solar System

1 The table shows the average distance of each planet from the Sun.

Planet	Average Distance From the Sun (miles)
Mercury	$3.68 \cdot 10^7$
Venus	$6.72 \cdot 10^7$
Earth	$9.3 \cdot 10^7$
Mars	$1.416 \cdot 10^8$
Jupiter	$4.836 \cdot 10^8$
Saturn	$8.865 \cdot 10^8$
Uranus	$1.7837 \cdot 10^9$
Neptune	$2.7952 \cdot 10^9$

a Jack and Rachel want to present the planets in the solar system on a poster. They want to space out all the planets evenly. Show whether the students are correct.

b Rachel wants to calculate the distances of the planets from the Sun in Astronomical Units (au), a unit of length that measures the distance from Earth to the Sun. If Earth's distance from the Sun is 1 au, which planet is about 5 au from the Sun?

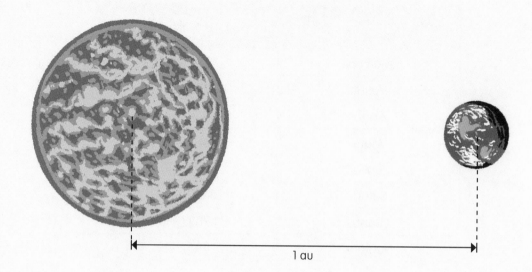

1 au

c Jack observed that to find the distance to and from Venus and the Sun in scientific notation, you would need to multiply the coefficient by 2, move the decimal point one place to the left and increase the exponent by 1. Does this strategy apply to all cases? Justify your reasoning. Use the table below to help you.

Planet	Average Distance From the Sun (miles)	Distance to and from the Sun (miles)	Application of Julio's Strategy (miles)	Does the Strategy Work?
Venus	$6.72 \cdot 10^7$	$6.72 \cdot 10^7 \cdot 2$ $= 13.44 \cdot 10^7$ $= 1.344 \cdot 10^8$	$1.344 \cdot 10^8$	Yes

Rubric

Point(s)	Level	My Performance
7–8	4	• Most of my answers are correct. • I showed complete understanding of the concepts. • I used effective and efficient strategies to solve the problems. • I explained my answers and mathematical thinking clearly and completely.
5–6	3	• Some of my answers are correct. • I showed adequate understanding of the concepts. • I used effective strategies to solve the problems. • I explained my answers and mathematical thinking clearly.
3–4	2	• A few of my answers are correct. • I showed some understanding of the concepts. • I used some effective strategies to solve the problems. • I explained some of my answers and mathematical thinking clearly.
0–2	1	• A few of my answers are correct. • I showed little understanding of the concepts. • I used limited effective strategies to solve the problems. • I did not explain my answers and mathematical thinking clearly.

Teacher's Comments

Linear Equations and Inequalities

Who wants to go bowling?

You and three friends want to go bowling. The bowling alley charges $3.25 for each pair of shoes you rent and $4.75 per game. All four of you need to rent shoes and you are not sure yet how many games you will play. What will be your group's total cost? In this situation, there are two quantities that can vary: the number of games your group plays and the group's total cost. In this chapter, you will learn how to write linear equations to represent situations in which there are two variables.

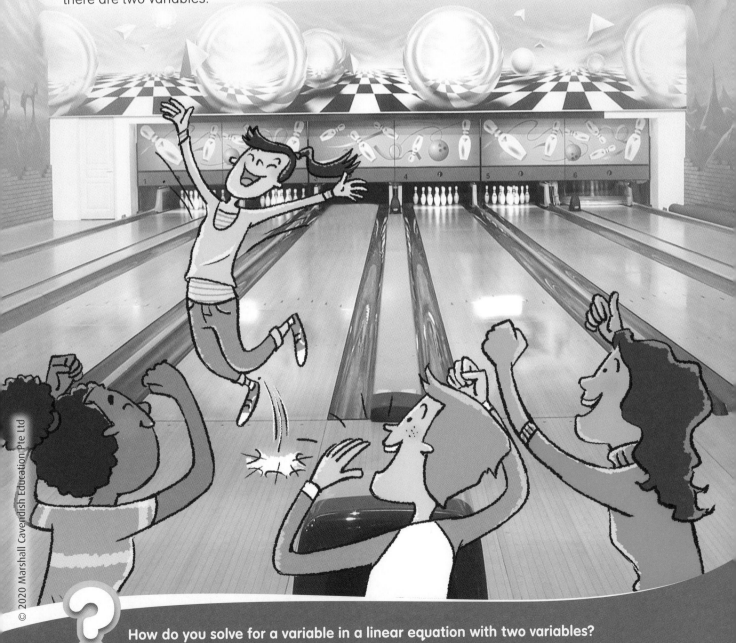

How do you solve for a variable in a linear equation with two variables?

Identifying equivalent equations

Equivalent equations are equations that have the same solution. Performing the same operation on both sides of an equation produces an equivalent equation.

For example, $x = 8$ and $x - 2 = 6$ are equivalent equations. If you subtract 2 from both sides of $x = 8$, you obtain $x - 2 = 6$. The solution to both equations is $x = 8$.

▶ **Quick Check**

Determine whether each pair of equations is equivalent. Justify each answer.

1 $x + 4 = 10$ and $x - 1 = 3$

2 $\frac{1}{5}x = 4$ and $x = 20$

3 $0.5x + 1 = 1.5$ and $2x = 2$

4 $2(x + 9) = 14$ and $2(x - 7) = -18$

© 2020 Marshall Cavendish Education Pte Ltd

Expressing the relationship between two quantities with a linear equation

A wall has width w feet and length $2w$ feet. The perimeter, P feet, of the wall is $2w + 2w + w + w = 6w$ feet.

You can express the relationship between the perimeter and the width of the wall with the linear equation $P = 6w$. In the equation, w is the independent variable and P is the dependent variable because the value of P depends on the value of w.

▶ **Quick Check**

Write a linear equation for each situation. State the independent and dependent variables for each equation.

5 A manufacturer produces beverages in small and large bottles. Each small bottle contains s liters of beverage. Each large bottle contains t liters, which is 1 more liter than the quantity in the small bottle. Express t in terms of s.

6 Hunter is 4 years younger than Alex. Express Alex's age, a, in terms of Hunter's age, h.

7 A bouquet of lavender costs $12. Find the cost, C dollars, of n bouquets of lavender.

8 The distance traveled by a bus, d miles, is 40 times the time, t hours, of the journey. Find d in terms of t.

Solving algebraic equations

To solve an equation, you isolate the variable on one side of the equation. To do this, you add, subtract, multiply or divide both sides of the equation by the same nonzero number.

$$4x + 7 = 15$$
$$4x + 7 - \mathbf{7} = 15 - \mathbf{7} \qquad \text{Subtract 7 from both sides.}$$
$$4x = 8 \qquad \text{Simplify.}$$
$$\frac{4x}{\mathbf{4}} = \frac{8}{\mathbf{4}} \qquad \text{Divide both sides by 4.}$$
$$x = 2 \qquad \text{Simplify.}$$

Remember to keep an equation balanced by performing the same operation on both sides.

When solving the equation $5x + 3(x - 2) = 50$, which includes an expression with parentheses, you need to use the distributive property.

$$5x + 3(x - 2) = 50$$
$$5x + 3x - 6 = 50 \qquad \text{Use the distributive property.}$$
$$8x - 6 = 50 \qquad \text{Combine like items.}$$
$$8x - 6 + \mathbf{6} = 50 + \mathbf{6} \qquad \text{Add 6 to both sides.}$$
$$8x = 56 \qquad \text{Simplify.}$$
$$\frac{8x}{\mathbf{8}} = \frac{56}{\mathbf{8}} \qquad \text{Divide both sides by 8.}$$
$$x = 7 \qquad \text{Simplify.}$$

▶ **Quick Check**

Solve each equation.

⑨ $4x - 2 = 14$

⑩ $\frac{1}{3}v + 9 = 2$

⑪ $c + 2(1 - c) = 10$

⑫ $3(2 + 3x) - 1 = 32$

Representing fractions as repeating decimals

A repeating decimal has a group of one or more digits that repeat endlessly. You use bar notation to show the digits that repeat.

To write $\frac{40}{33}$ as a decimal:

$$\begin{array}{r} 1.2121 \\ 33\overline{)40.0000} \\ \underline{33} \\ 70 \\ \underline{66} \\ 40 \\ \underline{33} \\ 70 \\ \underline{66} \\ 40 \\ \underline{33} \\ 7 \end{array}$$

Divide until the remainders start repeating.

So, $\frac{40}{33} = 1.2121\ldots = 1.\overline{21}$.

▶ **Quick Check**

Write the decimal for each fraction. Use bar notation.

 13 $\frac{3}{18}$ **14** $\frac{16}{99}$

Solving algebraic inequalities

The process of solving an algebraic inequality is the same as solving an algebraic equation, except that you have to reverse the direction of the inequality symbol when you multiply or divide both sides by a negative number.

$$3(3 - 4x) - 1 \leq 20$$

$9 - 12x - 1 \leq 20$ Use the distributive property.

$-12x + 8 \leq 20$ Simplify.

$-12x + 8 - \mathbf{8} \leq 20 - \mathbf{8}$ Subtract 8 from both sides.

$-12x \leq 12$ Simplify.

$\dfrac{-12x}{-12} \geq \dfrac{12}{-12}$ Divide both sides by −12 and reverse the inequality symbol.

$x \geq -1$ Simplify.

The solution set is represented on a number line as shown.

You use a shaded circle above −1 to indicate that −1 is a solution of the inequality $3(3 - 4x) - 1 \leq 20$.

The solution set $x > 4$ of another equality is represented on a number line as shown.

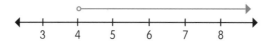

You use an empty circle above 4 to indicate that 4 is not a solution of the inequality.

▶ **Quick Check**

Solve each inequality and graph the solution set on a number line.

15 $x - 6 \leq 9$ **16** $3 - 5(x - 1) < 18$

1 Solving Linear Equations With One Variable

Learning Objectives:
- Solve linear equations with one variable.
- Solve real-world problems involving linear equations with one variable.

THINK

Hailey was told that the length of a rectangle was 2.5 inches longer than its width, and that the perimeter of the rectangle was 75.4 inches. She found the length and width algebraically. How could she use estimation to check if her answers were reasonable?

ENGAGE

Draw a bar model to represent $5x - 2$. Now use that model to solve the equation $5x - 2 = 3x + 3$. Discuss your methods with your partner and discuss if there is another way to solve this equation.

LEARN Solve linear equations with one variable

1. To solve an equation, you add, subtract, multiply or divide both sides of the equation by the same nonzero number. You keep the equation "balanced" by performing the same operation on both sides. This method is also used to solve an equation with variables on both sides.

2. Solve the equation $4x + 7 = x + 13$.

$$4x + 7 = x + 13$$
$$4x + 7 - x = x + 13 - x \quad \text{Subtract } x \text{ from both sides.}$$
$$3x + 7 = 13 \quad \text{Simplify.}$$
$$3x + 7 - 7 = 13 - 7 \quad \text{Subtract 7 from both sides.}$$
$$3x = 6 \quad \text{Simplify.}$$
$$\frac{3x}{3} = \frac{6}{3} \quad \text{Divide both sides by 3.}$$
$$x = 2 \quad \text{Simplify.}$$

 Isolating the variable on either side of the equation will give us the same solution.

3. Solve the equation $x = 44 - 0.1x$.

$$x = 44 - 0.1x$$
$$x + 0.1x = 44 - 0.1x + 0.1x \quad \text{Add } 0.1x \text{ to both sides.}$$
$$1.1x = 44 \quad \text{Simplify.}$$
$$\frac{1.1x}{1.1} = \frac{44}{1.1} \quad \text{Divide both sides by 1.1.}$$
$$x = 40 \quad \text{Simplify.}$$

4 Solve the equation $2(x + 11) = 8 - 5x$.

$$
\begin{array}{ll}
2(x + 11) = 8 - 5x & \\
2x + 22 = 8 - 5x & \text{Use the distributive property.} \\
2x + 22 + 5x = 8 - 5x + 5x & \text{Add } 5x \text{ to both sides.} \\
7x + 22 = 8 & \text{Simplify.} \\
7x + 22 - 22 = 8 - 22 & \text{Subtract 22 from both sides.} \\
7x = -14 & \text{Simplify.} \\
\dfrac{7x}{7} = \dfrac{-14}{7} & \text{Divide both sides by 7.} \\
x = -2 & \text{Simplify.}
\end{array}
$$

5 Solve the equation $\dfrac{3x}{4} = \dfrac{2x + 1}{4} - 1.5$.

$$
\begin{array}{ll}
\dfrac{3x}{4} = \dfrac{2x + 1}{4} - 1.5 & \\[2mm]
\dfrac{3x}{4} - \dfrac{2x + 1}{4} = \dfrac{2x + 1}{4} - 1.5 - \dfrac{2x + 1}{4} & \text{Subtract } \dfrac{2x + 1}{4} \text{ from both sides.} \\[2mm]
\dfrac{3x}{4} - \dfrac{2x + 1}{4} = -1.5 & \text{Simplify.} \\[2mm]
\dfrac{3x - (2x + 1)}{4} = -1.5 & \text{Rewrite the left side as a single fraction.} \\[2mm]
\dfrac{3x - 2x - 1}{4} = -1.5 & \text{Use the distributive property.} \\[2mm]
\dfrac{x - 1}{4} = -1.5 & \text{Simplify the numerator.} \\[2mm]
\dfrac{x - 1}{4} \cdot 4 = -1.5 \cdot 4 & \text{Multiply both sides by 4.} \\[2mm]
x - 1 = -6 & \text{Simplify.} \\
x - 1 + 1 = -6 + 1 & \text{Add 1 to both sides.} \\
x = -5 & \text{Simplify.}
\end{array}
$$

> **Math Note**
>
> Notice that $2x + 1$ is placed in parentheses, because the fraction bar acts as a grouping symbol.
> So, $-\dfrac{2x + 1}{4}$ can be written as $\dfrac{-(2x + 1)}{4}$.

TRY Practice solving linear equations with one variable

Solve each linear equation.

1 $x + 16 = 11 - 4x$

$$
\begin{array}{ll}
x + 16 = 11 - 4x & \\
x + 16 + 4x = 11 - 4x + 4x & \text{Add } 4x \text{ to both sides.} \\
\underline{} + 16 = 11 & \text{Simplify.} \\
\underline{} + 16 - 16 = 11 - 16 & \text{Subtract 16 from both sides.} \\
\underline{} = -5 & \text{Simplify.} \\
\dfrac{}{} = \dfrac{}{} & \text{Divide both sides by 5.} \\
x = \underline{} & \text{Simplify.}
\end{array}
$$

2 $0.6x + 11 = 0.6 + 0.2x$

Subtract 0.2x or 0.6x from both sides of the equation first.

3 $2(3x + 1) = 14 + 2x$

4 $\dfrac{3x}{5} = \dfrac{2}{15} - \dfrac{x-1}{3}$

ENGAGE

How do you write 0.83 as a fraction?

What is $1 \cdot 0.8\overline{3}$? What is $10 \cdot 0.8\overline{3}$?
How does knowing the above help you find $9 \cdot 0.8\overline{3}$?
How do you write $0.8\overline{3}$ as a fraction? Discuss.

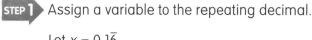 **LEARN** Write repeating decimals as fractions

1 Write the repeating decimal $0.1\overline{6}$ as a fraction.

> **STEP 1** Assign a variable to the repeating decimal.
>
> Let $x = 0.1\overline{6}$.
> $$x = 0.166666\ldots$$
> $$10x = 1.666666\ldots$$

 **Math Note**

When you multiply both sides of the equation $x = 0.1\overline{6}$ by 10, the infinite number of repeating digits does not change. So, you can subtract one equation from the other to eliminate the infinite string of digits.

> **STEP 2** Subtract x from $10x$ to obtain a terminating decimal.
>
> $$10x - x = 1.666666\ldots - 0.166666\ldots$$
> $$9x = 1.5$$

> **STEP 3** Solve for x.
>
> $\dfrac{9x}{9} = \dfrac{1.5}{9}$ Divide both sides by 9.
>
> $x = \dfrac{1}{6}$ Simplify.
>
> So, $0.1\overline{6} = \dfrac{1}{6}$.

$$\frac{1.5}{9} = \frac{3}{18} = \frac{1}{6}$$

Math Talk

If a decimal has two digits that repeat instead of one, what number do you multiply the decimal by before subtracting? Explain.

TRY Practice writing repeating decimals as fractions

Write each repeating decimal as a fraction.

1 $0.\overline{09}$

2 $0.\overline{8}$

A belt costs $30 less than a pair of jeans. The ratio of the cost of the jeans to the cost of a shirt is 2 : 1. The total cost of the three items is $75.50. You can represent the costs using a bar model as shown.

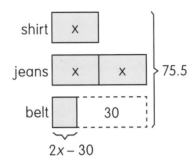

How much does a shirt cost? Solve using the bar model.
Now, write an algebraic equation to represent the bar model. Solve the equation. What does the value of the variable represent?

LEARN Solve real-world problems involving linear equations with one variable

1 Juan's bathroom walls are $91\frac{1}{4}$ inches tall. He wants to mount a mirror with a height of $28\frac{1}{4}$ inches on the wall. The distance from the top of the mirror to the ceiling should be $\frac{1}{2}$ the distance from the bottom of the mirror to the floor. Find the distance of the mirror from the floor.

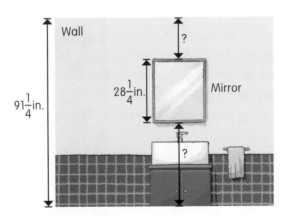

Let the distance of the mirror from the floor be x inches.

So, the distance of the mirror from the ceiling is $\frac{1}{2}x$ inches.

$$x + 28\frac{1}{4} + \frac{1}{2}x = 91\frac{1}{4} \qquad \text{Write an equation.}$$

$$\frac{3}{2}x + 28\frac{1}{4} = 91\frac{1}{4} \qquad \text{Add like terms.}$$

$$\frac{3}{2}x + 28\frac{1}{4} - \mathbf{28\frac{1}{4}} = 91\frac{1}{4} - \mathbf{28\frac{1}{4}} \qquad \text{Subtract } 28\frac{1}{4} \text{ from both sides.}$$

$$\frac{3}{2}x = 63 \qquad \text{Simplify.}$$

$$\frac{3}{2}x \cdot \mathbf{\frac{2}{3}} = 63 \cdot \mathbf{\frac{2}{3}} \qquad \text{Multiply both sides by } \frac{2}{3}.$$

$$x = 42 \qquad \text{Simplify.}$$

The distance of the mirror from the floor is 42 inches.

> The wall's height is about 90 inches and the mirror's height is about 30 inches. So, the total distance above and below the mirror is about 60 inches. $\frac{2}{3}$ of 60 inches is 40 inches. The answer is reasonable.

TRY **Practice solving real-world problems involving linear equations with one variable**

Solve the problem algebraically.

1 Jocelyn wants to add a circular pond to her backyard. The backyard is $20\frac{1}{2}$ yards long and the pond will be $6\frac{1}{4}$ yards across. The distance from the pond to the back fence will be half the distance from the pond to the back of the house. How far will the pond be from the back of the house?

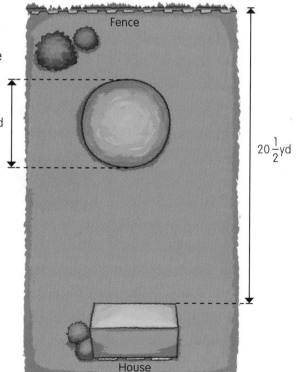

Fence

$6\frac{1}{4}$yd

$20\frac{1}{2}$yd

House

INDEPENDENT PRACTICE

Solve each linear equation.

1 $4x - 10 = 10 - x$

2 $3x - 2 = 5.6 - 0.8x$

3 $2(x - 1) - 6 = 10(1 - x) + 6$

4 $6 + \frac{1}{3}(x - 9) = \frac{1}{2}(2 - x)$

5 $\frac{3x - 2}{8} + \frac{1}{2} = -\frac{2 - x}{4}$

6 $\frac{4(2x + 3)}{5} = \frac{x + 1}{4} + \frac{31}{5}$

Write each repeating decimal as a fraction.

7 $0.8\overline{3}$

8 $0.0\overline{45}$

Solve each problem algebraically.

9 Diego saves $5.50 in dimes and quarters over a week. He has 20 more dimes than quarters. Find the number of dimes and quarters he saves.

10 Aiden earns $2\frac{1}{2}$ times as much as Evan in a day. Jake earns $18 more than Evan in a day. If the total daily salary of all three people is $306, find Aiden's daily salary.

Identifying the Number of Solutions to a Linear Equation

Learning Objective:
• Identify linear equations with no solution, one solution, or infinitely many solutions.

New Vocabulary
inconsistent equation
consistent equation
identity

THINK

Consider the following equations.

$$3x - 2 = -3\left(\frac{2}{3} - x\right)$$

$$3x + 6 = -2\left(\frac{3}{2} - x\right)$$

$$\frac{1}{4}(2x - 1) = \frac{1}{2}x + \frac{3}{8}$$

Identify the equation with one solution, the equation with no solution, and the equation with an infinite number of solutions. Explain your answer.

ENGAGE

Solve the equation $x + 3 = 5$. What is the solution?
Now, consider the equation $x + 3 = x$. What is the solution?
What do you notice? Share your observations. Discuss what the solution shows.

LEARN Identify a linear equation with no solution

① Not all linear equations have one solution.

Consider the equation $x + 4 = x$.

$$x + 4 = x$$
$$x + 4 - x = x - x \quad \text{Subtract } x \text{ from both sides.}$$
$$4 = 0 \quad \text{Simplify.}$$

The variable x has disappeared. 4 is not equal to 0.
Since the solution ends with a false statement,
the equation has no solution.

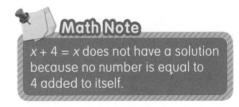

Math Note
$x + 4 = x$ does not have a solution because no number is equal to 4 added to itself.

An inconsistent equation is an equation with no solution.

2 Determine whether the equation $5(x + 3) = 5x + 3$ is an inconsistent equation.

$$5(x + 3) = 5x + 3$$
$$5x + 15 = 5x + 3 \quad \text{Use the distributive property.}$$
$$5x + 15 - \textbf{5x} = 5x + 3 - \textbf{5x} \quad \text{Subtract } 5x \text{ from both sides.}$$
$$15 = 3 \quad \text{Simplify.}$$

> Since 15 is not equal to 3, the equation has no solution.

The equation has no solution. The equation is an inconsistent equation.

3 Determine whether the equation $3(x - 4) = 2(x - 1)$ is an inconsistent equation.

$$3(x - 4) = 2(x - 1)$$
$$3x - 12 = 2x - 2 \quad \text{Use the distributive property.}$$
$$3x - 12 - \textbf{2x} = 2x - 2 - \textbf{2x} \quad \text{Subtract } 2x \text{ from both sides.}$$
$$x - 12 = -2 \quad \text{Simplify.}$$
$$x - 12 + \textbf{12} = -2 + \textbf{12} \quad \text{Add 12 to both sides.}$$
$$x = 10 \quad \text{Simplify.}$$

> The equation has one solution, that is $x = 10$.

The equation has one solution. The equation is a consistent equation.

TRY Practice identifying a linear equation with no solution

Determine whether each equation is a consistent equation or an inconsistent equation.

1 $5\left(x + \dfrac{1}{5}\right) = 5x + 3$

2 $x + \dfrac{1}{4} = -\dfrac{1}{4}(4x - 1)$

Consider the equation $2x - 7 + 4 = 3x - 3 - x$. What could be a solution to the problem?. Discuss what the solution shows.

Create another problem where your solution would be true. Discuss your work.

LEARN **Identify a linear equation with infinitely many solutions**

1 Try solving the equation $3x + 5 = x + 2x + 5$.

$3x + 5 = x + 2x + 5$	
$3x + 5 = 3x + 5$	Combine like terms.
$3x + 5 - \mathbf{3x} = 3x + 5 - \mathbf{3x}$	Subtract $3x$ from both sides.
$5 = 5$	Simplify.

⚠️ **Caution**
$5 = 5$ does not mean that $x = 5$.

An identity is an equation that is true for all values of the variable.

2 Determine whether the equation $7x - 10 = 3(x - 2) + 4(x - 1)$ is an identity.

$7x - 10 = 3(x - 2) + 4(x - 1)$	
$7x - 10 = 3x - 6 + 4x - 4$	Use the distributive property.
$7x - 10 = 7x - 10$	Combine like terms.
$7x - 10 - \mathbf{7x} = 7x - 10 - \mathbf{7x}$	Subtract $7x$ from both sides.
$-10 = -10$	Simplify.

Since $-10 = -10$ is always true no matter what the value of x is, the equation has infinitely many solutions.

The equation has infinitely many solutions. The equation is an identity.

3 Determine whether the equation $\frac{x}{3} + \frac{2(2x + 1)}{5} = \frac{1}{3}$ is an identity.

$$\frac{x}{3} + \frac{2(2x + 1)}{5} = \frac{1}{3}$$

$$\frac{5x}{15} + \frac{6(2x + 1)}{15} = \frac{1}{3}$$ Write equivalent fractions using the LCD, 15.

$$\frac{5x + 6(2x + 1)}{15} = \frac{1}{3}$$ Rewrite the left side as a single fraction.

$$\frac{5x + 12x + 6}{15} = \frac{1}{3}$$ Use the distributive property.

$$\frac{17x + 6}{15} = \frac{1}{3}$$ Combine like terms.

$$\frac{17x + 6}{15} \cdot \mathbf{15} = \frac{1}{3} \cdot \mathbf{15}$$ Multiply both sides by 15.

$$17x + 6 = 5 \qquad \text{Simplify.}$$
$$17x + 6 - 6 = 5 - 6 \qquad \text{Subtract 6 from both sides.}$$
$$17x = -1 \qquad \text{Simplify.}$$
$$\frac{17x}{17} = \frac{-1}{17} \qquad \text{Divide both sides by 17.}$$
$$x = \frac{-1}{17} \qquad \text{Simplify.}$$

The equation has one solution, that is $x = -\dfrac{1}{17}$.

The equation has one solution. The equation is not an identity.

TRY Practice identifying a linear equation with infinitely many solutions

Determine whether each equation is an identity.

1. $2(x - 1) + 3 = 2x + 1$

2. $6(x + 5) - 10 = 3(2x - 3)$

You can try substituting some values of x into each equation. If you find that the left side is always equal to the right side, the equation is an identity.

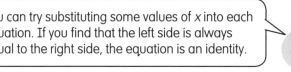

INDEPENDENT PRACTICE

Determine whether each equation is a consistent equation, an inconsistent equation or an identity.

1 $3x - 3 = -2\left(\dfrac{3}{2} - x\right)$

2 $2x + 5 = -4\left(\dfrac{3}{2} - x\right)$

3 $3x + 5 = 2x - 7$

4 $5y + (86 - y) = 86 + 4y$

5 $0.5(6x - 3) = 3(1 + x)$

6 $4(18a - 7) + 40 = 3(4 + 24a)$

7 $\frac{1}{7}(7x - 21) = 8x + 7x - 24$

8 $\frac{1}{6}(12x - 18) = 2\left(x - \frac{3}{2}\right)$

9 $7 - 0.75x = -7\left(\frac{3}{28}x + 1\right)$

10 $6 + 0.5y = -2\left(3 - \frac{1}{4}y\right)$

11 $\frac{x - 3}{4} = 0.25x - 0.75$

12 $\frac{1}{3}x + 5 = \frac{1}{6}(2x - 5)$

Solve.

13 Cabinet A is 5 inches taller than Cabinet B. Cabinet C is 3 inches taller than Cabinet B. The height of Cabinet B is x inches.

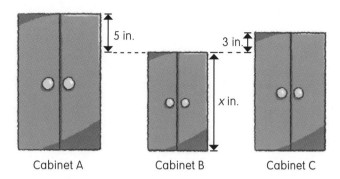

a Write algebraic expressions for the heights of cabinets A and C.

b If the total height of the three cabinets is $(3x + 8)$ inches, can you solve for the height of Cabinet B? Explain.

14 The floor of a room is y meters long. The width is 5 meters shorter. If the perimeter of the floor is $(4y + 1)$ meters, can you solve for its length? Explain.

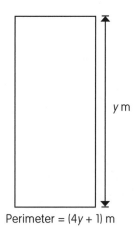

y m

Perimeter = $(4y + 1)$ m

15 **Mathematical Habit 2 Use mathematical reasoning**
Grace gave her sister the following riddle.
I have a number x. I add 15 to twice of x to obtain A. I subtract 4 from x to obtain B. I multiply B by 3 to obtain C. A is equal to C.

Grace's sister said the riddle cannot be solved but Grace thought otherwise. Who is right? Explain.

3 Understanding Linear Equations with Two Variables

Learning Objectives:
- Express a linear relationship between two variables.
- Represent a linear relationship using a table of values.

THINK

Owen sells blood pressure monitors. He earns a monthly salary that includes a basic amount of $750 and $4 for each monitor sold. Write a linear equation for his monthly salary, M dollars, in terms of the number, n, of monitors sold. Think about what kind of restrictions the variables should have, then deduce if it is possible for Owen to earn a monthly salary of $832.

ENGAGE

Michael is 5 years younger than Daniel. Create a table to show their possible ages. What are the variables involved? How are the variables related to each other? Explain your answer.

LEARN Express a linear relationship between two variables

1. The table shows the ages of Diana and Brian over five years.

	2008	2009	2010	2011	2012
Brian's Age	1	2	3	4	5
Diana's Age	4	5	6	7	8

> Look for a pattern between the values for Brian's age and the values for Diana's age.

Notice that Diana's age is always 3 years more than Brian's age. You can represent the relationship between their ages using a linear equation with two variables.

If Brian is x years old and Diana is y years old, the variables x and y are related by the linear equation $y = x + 3$.

Math Talk

What expression can you write to express Brian's age in terms of Diana's age? What equation can you write using this expression? Is the equation equivalent to $y = x + 3$? Explain.

2 Write a linear equation for the relationship between hours, h, and minutes, m.

An hour has 60 minutes.

A linear equation for m in terms of h is $m = 60h$.

> You can also write the equation $h = \dfrac{m}{60}$ to represent the relationship between h and m. The equations $m = 60h$ and $h = \dfrac{m}{60}$ are equivalent.

3 Kaitlyn heated a liquid and measured its temperature. She recorded the results in the following table.

Time (t minute)	0	1	2	3	4
Temperature (T °C)	25	30	35	40	45

Write a linear equation for T in terms of t.

The initial temperature was 25°C. After that, the temperature rose by 5°C every minute.

t	T
0	$25 = 25 + 0\ = 25 + 5 \cdot 0$
1	$30 = 25 + 5\ = 25 + 5 \cdot 1$
2	$35 = 25 + 10 = 25 + 5 \cdot 2$
3	$40 = 25 + 15 = 25 + 5 \cdot 3$
4	$45 = 25 + 20 = 25 + 5 \cdot 4$

Observe that the expressions for T follow a pattern. They also contain a varying number that has the same value as t. You can replace the varying number by t to obtain the general expression $25 + 5t$ for T.

A linear equation for T in terms of t is $T = 25 + 5t$.

TRY Practice expressing a linear relationship between two variables

Write a linear equation for the relationship between the given quantities.

1. days, d, and weeks, w

   A week has _____ days.

   A linear equation for d in terms of w is _____.

Solve.

2. Samuel rented a car from a company for a week. The table shows the rental charges.

Distance (d miles)	0	1	2	3	4
Rental Charge (C dollar)	100	100.10	100.20	100.30	100.40

Write a linear equation for C in terms of d.

ENGAGE

The sum of the measures of the angles in a polygon is related to the number of sides that a polygon has. Think of three shapes and the sum of the measure of their angles. How can you display this information? Share and discuss your answer with your partner.

Name of Shape	Number of Sides (n)	Sum of Angles, in Degrees (S)
Triangle	3	
		360°
	5	
		1,080°

3 Understanding Linear Equations with Two Variables   **181**

© 2020 Marshall Cavendish Education Pte Ltd

LEARN Represent a linear relationship using a table of values

1 Find the value of y when $x = 7$ in the equation $y = \dfrac{x-5}{2}$.

$y = \dfrac{7-5}{2}$ Substitute 7 for x.

$y = \dfrac{2}{2}$ Subtract.

$y = 1$ Simplify.

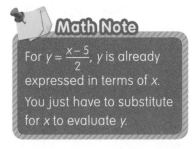

Math Note

For $y = \dfrac{x-5}{2}$, y is already expressed in terms of x. You just have to substitute for x to evaluate y.

2 Find the value of y when $x = 7$ in the equation $3y + 4 = 2x$.

$3y + 4 = 2(7)$ Substitute 7 for x.

$3y + 4 - \mathbf{4} = 14 - \mathbf{4}$ Subtract 4 from both sides.

$3y = 10$

$\dfrac{3y}{\mathbf{3}} = \dfrac{10}{\mathbf{3}}$ Divide both sides by 3.

$y = 3\dfrac{1}{3}$ Simplify.

3 Find the value of y when $x = 7$ in the equation $\dfrac{9}{2}y - x = 15.5$.

$\dfrac{9}{2}y - 7 = 15.5$ Substitute 7 for x.

$\dfrac{9}{2}y - 7 + \mathbf{7} = 15.5 + \mathbf{7}$ Add 7 to both sides.

$\dfrac{9}{2}y = 22.5$ Simplify.

$\dfrac{9}{2}y \cdot \mathbf{2} = 22.5 \cdot \mathbf{2}$ Multiply both sides by 2.

$9y = 45$ Simplify.

$9y \div \mathbf{9} = 45 \div \mathbf{9}$ Divide both sides by 9.

$y = 5$ Simplify.

Math Note

For $3y + 4 = 2x$ and $\dfrac{9}{2}y - x = 15.5$, when you substitute a value for x, you obtain an equation with one variable y. You have to solve this one-variable equation to find the value of y.

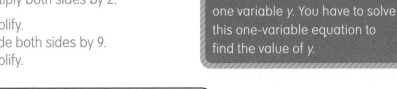

Another way to find the value of y is to express y in terms of x before substituting the value of x into the expression for y. You will learn how to do this in the next lesson.

4 Create a table of *x*- and *y*-values for the equation $\frac{y}{2} = \frac{3}{2}x + 2$.

Use integer values of *x* from –1 to 1.

Substitute –1 for *x* into the equation.

$\frac{y}{2} = \frac{3}{2}(-1) + 2$

$\frac{y}{2} = \frac{1}{2}$ Simplify.

$\frac{y}{2} \cdot \mathbf{2} = \frac{1}{2} \cdot \mathbf{2}$ Multiply both sides by 2.

$y = 1$ Simplify.

Substitute 0 for *x* into the equation.

$\frac{y}{2} = \frac{3}{2}(0) + 2$

$\frac{y}{2} = 2$ Simplify.

$\frac{y}{2} \cdot \mathbf{2} = 2 \cdot \mathbf{2}$ Multiply both sides by 2.

$y = 4$ Simplify.

Substitute 1 for *x* into the equation.

$\frac{y}{2} = \frac{3}{2}(1) + 2$

$\frac{y}{2} = \frac{7}{2}$ Simplify.

$\frac{y}{2} \cdot \mathbf{2} = \frac{7}{2} \cdot \mathbf{2}$ Multiply both sides by 2.

$y = 7$ Simplify.

So, you have the following table of values.

x	–1	0	1
y	1	4	7

When solving a linear equation in two variables, you know that each *x*-value has a corresponding *y*-value. So, the equation has an infinite number of solutions. One way to represent some of these solutions is with a table of values.

⑤ Complete the table of values for the equation $8y = 5(x - 4)$.

x	2	?	6
y	?	0	?

Substitute 2 for x into the equation.

$$8y = 5(2 - 4)$$
$$8y = -10 \qquad \text{Simplify.}$$
$$8y \div 8 = -10 \div 8 \qquad \text{Divide both sides by 8.}$$
$$y = -1.25 \qquad \text{Simplify.}$$

Substitute 0 for y into the equation.

$$0 = 5(x - 4)$$
$$0 \div 5 = 5(x - 4) \div 5 \qquad \text{Divide both sides by 5.}$$
$$0 = x - 4 \qquad \text{Simplify.}$$
$$0 + 4 = x - 4 + 4 \qquad \text{Add 4 to both sides.}$$
$$4 = x \qquad \text{Simplify.}$$

To solve the equation $0 = 5(x - 4)$, you should be able to observe that $x - 4$ is 0 because any number multiplied by 0 equals 0.

Substitute 6 for x into the equation.

$$8y = 5(6 - 4)$$
$$8y = 10 \qquad \text{Simplify.}$$
$$8y \div 8 = 10 \div 8 \qquad \text{Divide both sides by 8.}$$
$$y = 1.25 \qquad \text{Simplify.}$$

So, you have the following table of values.

x	2	4	6
y	−1.25	0	1.25

Using a graphing calculator to create tables of values for
linear equations with two variables

Mathematical Habit 5 Use tools strategically

Work in pairs.

① Enter the equation $y = \dfrac{x}{\pi}$ using the equation screen of a graphing calculator.

② Set the table function to use values of x starting at 0, with increments of 1.

③ Display the table. It will be in two columns as shown.

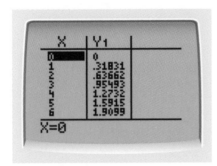

④ Repeat ① to ③ for the equation $y = -2x + \sqrt{2}$.

Caution

For ④, use the (−) key for
the negative coefficient, −2.

TRY Practice representing a linear relationship using a table of values

Find the value of y when $x = -4$.

① $y = 7 + 3x$

$y = 7 + 3(\underline{\hspace{2cm}})$ Substitute −4 for x.

$y = 7 - \underline{\hspace{2cm}}$ Simplify.

$y = \underline{\hspace{2cm}}$

> Since y is already expressed in terms of x, you just have to substitute for x to evaluate y.

② $\dfrac{1}{3}y = 2\left(x - \dfrac{1}{6}\right)$

③ $-6x - y = 17.75$

Create a table of *x*- and *y*-values for each equation. Use integer values of *x* from 1 to 3.

4. $2y = 1.2x + 1$

5. $4y - 11x = 6$

Fill in the table of values for each equation.

6. $\dfrac{y-2}{3} = x$

x		0	1
y	−1		

7. $3(x + 1) - 2y = 0$

x			
y	9	$16\frac{1}{2}$	24

INDEPENDENT PRACTICE

Write a linear equation for the relationship between the given quantities.

1 meters, m, and centimeters, c

2 hours, h, and seconds, s

3 feet, f, and inches, i

4 dollars, d, and cents, c

Find the value of y when $x = 2$.

5 $2x - 1 = y + 4$

6 $y = \frac{1}{7}(x + 5)$

7 $3x - 11 = 2(y - 4)$

8 $4y = 5(x - 1)$

Find the value of x when y = –7.

(9) $2(3x - 7) = 9y$

(10) $\dfrac{2x - 1}{5} = 2(y + 7)$

(11) $2x + y = 0.1(y + 3)$

(12) $2y - 5x = 26$

Create a table of x- and y-values for each equation. Use integer values of x from 1 to 3.

(13) $y = \dfrac{1}{4}(8 - x)$

(14) $x + 7 = \dfrac{1}{2}(y - 5)$

15 $-4y = 2x + 5$

16 $\frac{1}{2}(x + 4) = \frac{1}{3}(y + 1)$

Fill in the table of values for each equation.

17 $y = 5(x + 3)$

x	0	1	2
y			

18 $\frac{x}{4} + y = 1$

x	2		
y		0	−0.5

19 $3x - 4y = \dfrac{5}{3}$

x		-2	-1
y	$-2\dfrac{2}{3}$		

20 $5(y + 4) = 8x$

x			
y	-4	12	28

Solve.

21 A research student recorded the distance traveled by a car for every gallon of gasoline used. He recorded the results in the table. Write a linear equation for the distance traveled, *d* miles, in terms of the amount of gasoline used, *g* gallons.

Amount of Gasoline Used (*g* gallons)	1	2	3	4
Distance Traveled (*d* miles)	40.5	81	121.5	162

4 Solving for a Variable in a Two-Variable Linear Equation

Learning Objective:
• Solve for a variable in a two-variable linear equation.

THINK

Leah's train will leave her local train station in 24 minutes. She is y miles from the station. To catch the train, she walks at a speed of 4 miles per hour and later runs at a speed of 8 miles per hour.

a Write an equation in terms of y for the distance, w miles, Leah has to walk to reach the station in 24 minutes.

b Solve for y in terms of w. How far is Leah from the station if she has to walk 1 mile to reach the station on time?

c Why do the values of y have to be between 1.6 and 3.2?

ENGAGE

You can convert yards (y) to feet (t) using the formula $t = 3y$.
Write an equation to convert feet to yards.
Use three different values for feet to show that your equation is equivalent to the one given.

LEARN Solve for a variable in a two-variable linear equation

1 Given the formula $P = 4\ell$, you can use this formula to find the value of ℓ when you know the value of P. For example, if $P = 18$, you find the value of ℓ by substituting the value of P into the equation and solving for ℓ.

$P = 4\ell$

$18 = 4\ell$ Substitute 18 for P.

$\dfrac{18}{4} = \dfrac{4\ell}{4}$ Divide both sides by 4.

$4.5 = \ell$ Simplify.

If you are given many values of P and asked to find the corresponding values of ℓ, you may want to solve the equation for ℓ first. That is, you express ℓ in terms of P before substituting values of P. To solve the equation for ℓ, you carry out the following steps.

$P = 4\ell$

$\dfrac{P}{4} = \dfrac{4\ell}{4}$ Divide both sides by 4.

$\dfrac{P}{4} = \ell$ Simplify.

Evaluate ℓ when $P = 18$ again.

$\ell = \dfrac{P}{4}$

$\ell = \dfrac{18}{4}$ Substitute 18 to P.

$\ell = 4.5$ Simplify.

> Using either method, you obtain the same value for ℓ.

2 Express F in terms of C for the equation $C = \dfrac{5}{9}(F - 32)$. Find the value of F when $C = 10$.

$C = \dfrac{5}{9}(F - 32)$

$C \cdot \dfrac{9}{5} = \dfrac{5}{9}(F - 32) \cdot \dfrac{9}{5}$ Multiply both sides by $\dfrac{9}{5}$.

$\dfrac{9}{5}C = F - 32$ Simplify.

$\dfrac{9}{5}C + 32 = F - 32 + 32$ Add 32 to both sides.

$\dfrac{9}{5}C + 32 = F$ Simplify.

> To solve the equation for F, you have to isolate F on one side of the equation.

Math Note

Notice that the equation of F in terms of C and the equation of C in terms of F are both linear. If an equation with two variables is linear, expressing either variable in terms of the other produces an equivalent linear equation.

Substitute 10 for C into the equation $F = \dfrac{9}{5}C + 32$.

$F = \dfrac{9}{5}(10) + 32$

$ = 50$

Math Talk

Do you think it is easier to find the value of F by expressing F in terms of C first? Why?

3 In a right isosceles triangle, the lengths of the sides can be expressed as s units, s units, and $s\sqrt{2}$ units. So, its perimeter, P units, is given by $P = s + s + s\sqrt{2}$.

Math Note

The expression $s\sqrt{2}$ means s times the square root of 2.

a Express s in terms of P.

$$P = s + s + s\sqrt{2}$$

$$P = 2s + s\sqrt{2} \qquad \text{Simplify.}$$

$$P = (2 + \sqrt{2})s \qquad \text{Factor the right side.}$$

$$\frac{P}{2 + \sqrt{2}} = \frac{(2 + \sqrt{2})s}{2 + \sqrt{2}} \qquad \text{Divide both sides by } 2 + \sqrt{2}.$$

$$\frac{P}{2 + \sqrt{2}} = s \qquad \text{Simplify.}$$

$\dfrac{P}{2 + \sqrt{2}} = s$ is a linear equation that is equivalent to $P = s + s + s\sqrt{2}$.

b Create a table of values for P and s when $P = 4, 6, 8,$ and 10. Round the values of s to 2 decimal places.

Substitute 4, 6, 8, and 10 for P into the equation $s = \dfrac{P}{2 + \sqrt{2}}$.

$$s = \frac{4}{2 + \sqrt{2}} \approx 1.17$$

$$s = \frac{6}{2 + \sqrt{2}} \approx 1.76$$

$$s = \frac{8}{2 + \sqrt{2}} \approx 2.34$$

$$s = \frac{10}{2 + \sqrt{2}} \approx 2.93$$

So, you have the following table of values.

P	4	6	8	10
s	1.17	1.76	2.34	2.93

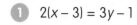

Express *x* in terms of *y*. Find the value of *x* when *y* = 3.

1 $2(x - 3) = 3y - 1$

> To solve the equation for *x*, isolate *x* on one side of the equation.

Solve.

2 The formula for finding the mean, *M*, of the numbers x, $x\sqrt{3}$, and 2 is $M = \frac{x + x\sqrt{3} + 2}{3}$.

   a Express *x* in terms of *M*.

   b Create a table of values for *M* and *x* when *M* = 0, 1, 2, and 3. Round each *x*-value to the nearest hundredth.

INDEPENDENT PRACTICE

Express y in terms of x. Find the value of y when x = –1.

① $5 - y = 3x$

② $-3(x + 2) = 5y$

③ $6(x - y) = 19$

④ $4x - 3 = 0.4x - 2y$

⑤ $\frac{1}{6}x + \frac{3}{4}y = 4$

⑥ $0.5y - 2 = 0.25x$

Express *x* in terms of *y*. Find the value of *x* when *y* = 5.

7 $5x - y = 3(x + y)$

8 $3(x + 2y) = 2x + 5y$

9 $1.5(x - y) = 1$

10 $2y + 8 = \frac{1}{4}x$

11 $\frac{2(x - 3)}{y} = 5$

12 $\frac{1}{3}(6x - 1) = \frac{6y}{5}$

Solve.

13 The perimeter, P inches, of a semicircle of diameter, d inches, is represented by $P = 0.5\pi d + d$.

  a Express d in terms of P.

  b Find the diameter if the perimeter is 36 inches. Use $\frac{22}{7}$ as an approximation for π.

14 The horizontal distance, X inches, and vertical distance, Y inches, of each step of a staircase are related by the linear equation $X = \frac{1}{2}(20 + Y)$.

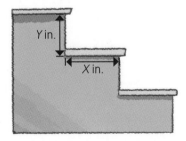

Y in.

X in.

  a Express Y in terms of X.

b Fill in the table.

X		16			19
Y	10		14	16	

c Find the values of X and Y if $X = Y$.

15 A rectangle has a width of w units and a length of 5 units. Its perimeter, P units, is given by $P = 2(w + 5)$. Solve for w in terms of P. Create a table of values for $P = 12, 14, 16,$ and 18.

5 Solving Linear Inequalities With One Variable

Learning Objectives:
- Solve linear inequalities with one variable.
- Solve real-world problems involving linear inequalities with one variable.

 THINK

Sarah is traveling overseas and wants to leave her dog at a pet hotel. Pet hotel A charges a monthly membership fee of $430 payment plus $20 per day if the dog is left at the hotel. Pet hotel B charges a monthly membership fee of $110 payment plus $30 per day if the dog is left at the hotel. Represent this as an inequality and solve it. Hence suggest whether Sarah should leave her dog at pet hotel A or hotel B, for lower rates.

ENGAGE

Solve $x - 4 = 6 - 3x$. Discuss with your partner how you can use the method for solving the equation to solve the inequality $x - 4 > 6 - 3x$. What are the similarities and the differences in the methods and the solutions?

LEARN Solve linear inequalities with one variable

1. You can apply the techniques of solving algebraic equations with variables on both sides to solve algebraic inequalities with variables on both sides.

2. Solve the inequality $x - 7 \leq 5 - 2x$ and graph the solution set on a number line.

$$\begin{aligned}
x - 7 &\leq 5 - 2x \\
x - 7 + \mathbf{2x} &\leq 5 - 2x + \mathbf{2x} \quad &&\text{Add } 2x \text{ to both sides.} \\
3x - 7 &\leq 5 \quad &&\text{Simplify.} \\
3x - 7 + \mathbf{7} &\leq 5 + \mathbf{7} \quad &&\text{Add 7 to both sides.} \\
3x &\leq 12 \quad &&\text{Simplify.} \\
\frac{3x}{3} &\leq \frac{12}{3} \quad &&\text{Divide both sides by 3.} \\
x &\leq 4 \quad &&\text{Simplify.}
\end{aligned}$$

The solution set is represented on a number line as shown.

Math Talk

Is it possible to solve the inequality $x - 7 \leq 5 - 2x$ by subtracting x from both sides in the first step? Explain.

3. Solve the inequality $3.7x + 2.1 \geq 1.9x - 6.9$ and graph the solution set on a number line.

$$\begin{aligned}
3.7x + 2.1 &\geq 1.9x - 6.9 \\
3.7x + 2.1 - \mathbf{1.9x} &\geq 1.9x - 6.9 - \mathbf{1.9x} \quad &&\text{Subtract } 1.9x \text{ from both sides.} \\
1.8x + 2.1 &\geq -6.9 \quad &&\text{Simplify.}
\end{aligned}$$

$$1.8x + 2.1 - \mathbf{2.1} \geq -6.9 - \mathbf{2.1}$$ Subtract 2.1 from both sides.
$$1.8x \geq -9$$ Simplify.
$$\frac{1.8x}{\mathbf{1.8}} \geq \frac{-9}{\mathbf{1.8}}$$ Divide both sides by 1.8.
$$x \geq -5$$ Simplify.

The solution set is represented on a number line as shown.

4 Solve the inequality $x - 6 > 2(12 + 2x)$ and graph the solution set on a number line.

$$x - 6 > 2(12 + 2x)$$
$$x - 6 > 24 + 4x$$ Use the distributive property.
$$x - 6 - \mathbf{4x} > 24 + 4x - \mathbf{4x}$$ Subtract 4x from both sides.
$$-3x - 6 > 24$$ Simplify.
$$-3x - 6 + \mathbf{6} > 24 + \mathbf{6}$$ Add 6 to both sides.
$$-3x > 30$$ Simplify.
$$\frac{-3x}{\mathbf{-3}} < \frac{30}{\mathbf{-3}}$$ Divide both sides by −3 and reverse the inequality symbol.
$$x < -10$$ Simplify.

The solution set is represented on a number line as shown.

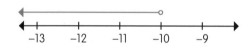

5 Solve the inequality $\frac{1}{3}x + 1 \leq \frac{1}{4}x + \frac{2}{3}$ and graph the solution set on a number line.

$$\frac{1}{3}x + 1 \leq \frac{1}{4}x + \frac{2}{3}$$
$$\frac{1}{3}x + 1 - \frac{1}{4}\mathbf{x} \leq \frac{1}{4}x + \frac{2}{3} - \frac{1}{4}\mathbf{x}$$ Subtract $\frac{1}{4}x$ from both sides.
$$\frac{4}{12}x + 1 - \frac{3}{12}x \leq \frac{2}{3}$$ Write equivalent fractions using the LCD, 12.
$$\frac{1}{12}x + 1 \leq \frac{2}{3}$$ Simplify.
$$\frac{1}{12}x + 1 - \mathbf{1} \leq \frac{2}{3} - \mathbf{1}$$ Subtract 1 from both sides.
$$\frac{1}{12}x \leq -\frac{1}{3}$$ Simplify.
$$\frac{1}{12}x \cdot \mathbf{12} \leq -\frac{1}{3} \cdot \mathbf{12}$$ Multiply both sides by 12.
$$x \leq -4$$ Simplify.

The solution set is represented on a number line as shown.

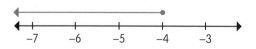

Solve each inequality and graph the solution set on a number line.

1 $x + 19 \leq 6x - 41$

2 $-0.3x + 2 \geq 14 + 0.5x$

3 $3(x - 1) > 7 + 4(x - 1)$

4 $\frac{1}{2}x - 1\frac{2}{3} < \frac{1}{3}x - 1$

ENGAGE

Antonia has a certain amount of game cards. The number of game cards Sarah has is two times the amount Antonia has minus 3. Given that Sarah has lesser game cards than Antonia, how can you represent this information using an inequality? What are the possible number of game cards Antonia has? Explain your answer.

LEARN Solve real-world problems involving linear inequalities with one variable

1 Kimberly is searching for a room to rent and found the payment plans shown offered by two landlords A and B. After how many months will renting with landlord A be cheaper than landlord B?

Landlord A	Landlord B
Initial charge: $300 Monthly charge: $450	Initial charge: $100 Monthly charge: $500

Let x be the number of months.   Define the variable.

Landlord A charges $300 + $450 · x = $300 + 450x$.
Landlord B charges $100 + $500 · x = $100 + 500x$.

$300 + 450x < 100 + 500x$	Write an inequality.
$300 + 450x - \mathbf{500x} < 100 + 500x - \mathbf{500x}$	Subtract 500x from both sides.
$300 - 50x < 100$	Simplify.
$300 - 50x - \mathbf{300} < 100 - \mathbf{300}$	Subtract 300 from both sides.
$-50x < -200$	Simplify.
$\dfrac{-50x}{-50} > \dfrac{-200}{-50}$	Divide both sides by −50 and reverse the inequality symbol.
$x > 4$	Simplify.

Renting with landlord A will be cheaper than landlord B after 4 months.

TRY Practice solving real-world problems involving linear inequalities with one variable

Solve.

1 Alexa and Jada each saves a portion of their allowances every day. The table shows the amounts.

Alexa	Jada
Initial amount of savings: $75 Daily savings: $0.50	Initial amount of savings: $32 Daily savings: $1

After how many days will Jada's savings be more than Alexa's savings?

© 2020 Marshall Cavendish Education Pte Ltd

INDEPENDENT PRACTICE

Solve each inequality and graph the solution set on a number line.

1 $2 - 3x > 8 - x$

2 $7.2 + 3.4x < 4.6x + 9.6$

3 $5(2x - 1) - 10 < 11 - 3(3x - 4)$

4 $6(3x + 4) \leq 22 + 8(2x + 1)$

5 $\frac{1}{4}x + 6 \leq \frac{3}{8}x - 2$

6 $\frac{3}{2} - \frac{2}{3}x \geq \frac{1}{6}x - \frac{1}{6}$

Solve.

7 Twenty-four minus three times an integer, x, is less than x minus four.

   a Write an inequality, in terms of x, to represent the information.

   b What is the smallest possible value of x?

8 Companies A and B provide housekeeping services. The charges are shown in the table.

Company A	Company B
First hour: $28	First hour: $20
Every subsequent half hour: $10	Every subsequent half hour: $12

After how many hours will Company A be cheaper than Company B?

Mathematical Habit 2 Use mathematical reasoning

Look at this "proof" that 2 = 0.

When $a = 1$ and $b = 1$, then
$(a - b)(a + b) = 0$
$a + b = 0$ Divide both sides by $a - b$.
$1 + 1 = 0$ Substitute for a and b.
$2 = 0$ Simplify.

What is wrong with this proof? How can a true statement lead to an inconsistent equation?

Problem Solving with Heuristics

1 **Mathematical Habit 2 Use mathematical reasoning**

Maria runs a private tutoring business. She rents a room for $500 a month, which is her only expense. She charges $50 an hour per student. She gives each student two lessons per month. Each lesson lasts 1.5 hours.

$$x^2 + x - 1 = 0$$

a Write an equation for her monthly profit, P dollars, in terms of the number of students, s, that Maria has.

b Find the monthly profit if Maria has 40 students.

c Find the minimum number of students that Maria needs if she wants to make a monthly profit of at least $4,600.

② **Mathematical Habit 8 Look for patterns**

A polygon has n sides. The sum of the measures of a polygon's interior angles is equal to the sum of the measures of r right angles. A table of r- and n-values is shown below.

n	3	4	5	6
r	2	4	6	8

Explain how you would find a linear equation involving r and n.

CHAPTER WRAP-UP

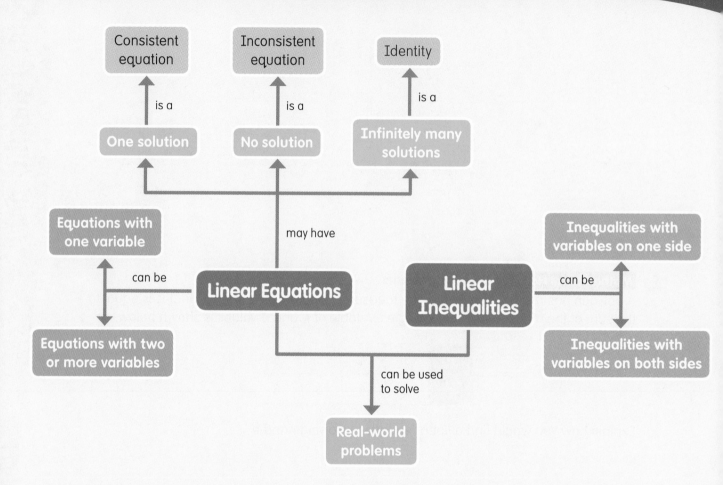

KEY CONCEPTS

- A linear equation can have one or more variables.
- A consistent equation in one variable is an equation that has one solution.
- An inconsistent equation is an equation that has no solution.
- An identity is an equation that is true for all values of the variable.
- A linear relationship between two variables can be represented with an equation or a table of values.
- Solving for a variable in a multi-variable linear equation means expressing the variable in terms of the other variable(s).
- A linear inequality can have a variable on one or both sides.
- Linear equations and inequalities can be used to represent and solve real-world problems.

Name: ______________________ Date: ______________

CHAPTER REVIEW

Solve each linear equation.

1. $2(x - 5) = 20x + 8$

2. $4x = \frac{3}{5} + \frac{5 - 2x}{5}$

Write each repeating decimal as a fraction.

3. $0.\overline{2}$

4. $0.9\overline{3}$

5. $0.2\overline{6}$

6. $0.3\overline{16}$

Determine whether each equation is a consistent equation, an inconsistent equation or an identity.

7 $2x + 4 = 2\left(\dfrac{1}{2} + x\right)$

8 $6y + (16 - 2y) = 4(4 + y)$

9 $4x + 5 = 2x - 7$

10 $2x + 5 = -4\left(-\dfrac{5}{4} - \dfrac{1}{2}x\right)$

Write a linear equation for the relationship between the given quantities.

11 kilometers, k, and meters, m

12 days, d, and hours, h

Find the value of *y* when *x* = 4.

(13) $x - 4y = 2$

(14) $y - x = \frac{1}{3}(x + 14)$

(15) $\frac{1}{7}(3x + y) = x$

(16) $\frac{3y + 1}{4} = 2x$

Express *x* in terms of *y*. Find the value of *x* when *y* = −2.

(17) $3(x - 2y) = 4x + 5y$

(18) $\frac{0.5(x - 3)}{y} = 10$

Solve each inequality and graph the solution set on a number line.

19 $3(7 - 0.3x) < 0.1x - 3$

20 $11 + \frac{1}{4}x < 25 - \frac{3}{4}x$

Solve.

21 Some students painted a design on the wall of the cafeteria using the school colors. The middle section of the design is 4.2 feet tall, and is painted white. The top section is red, and the bottom section is blue. The ratio of the height of the blue section to the height of the red section is 1 : 2. The total height of the design is 10.5 feet. Find the height of the red section of the design.

22 The company Jaden uses for Internet service charges $25 each month plus $0.04 for each minute of usage time.

a Write a linear equation for the monthly charge, *M* dollars, in terms of the usage time, *t* minutes.

© 2020 Marshall Cavendish Education Pte Ltd

b Express t in terms of M.

c Calculate Jaden's usage time in hours if he paid $49 for his Internet bill in November.

23 Madeline plans to enrol in an online course. The course offers two payment options as shown.

Option A	Option B
One time registration fee: $100 Fee per module: $275	One time registration fee: $65 Fee per module: $280

After how many modules will Option A be less expensive than Option B?

Answer each question.

24 Julian was 32 years old when his son was born. Now Julian is three times as old as his son.

Part A

Which equation could be used to determine the age, x years, of Julian's son?

Ⓐ $32 + 3x = x$

Ⓑ $32 + x = 3x$

Ⓒ $32 - 3x = x$

Ⓓ $32 - x = 3x$

Part B

What is the age of Julian's son? Write your answer and your working or explanation in the space below.

25 Which is the solution to the inequality $3x \leq 4x + 9$?

Ⓐ $x \geq 9$

Ⓑ $x \geq -9$

Ⓒ $x \leq 9$

Ⓓ $x \leq -9$

© 2020 Marshall Cavendish Education Pte Ltd

Name: _____ Date: _____

Bowling

1 Joseph and two friends want to go bowling. The bowling alley charges $3.25 for each pair of shoes they rent and $4.75 per game. All three of them need to rent shoes, and they are not sure yet how many games they will play.

a Write a linear equation for the total cost, C dollars, if they play g games.

b Find the total cost for playing 0, 1, 2, and 3 games. Fill in the table to show the total cost.

Number of Games	Total Cost
0	$9.75
1	
2	
3	

c Can you triple the cost of playing 2 games to find the cost of playing 6 games? Justify your reasoning.

d Joseph and his friends decide to spend not more than a total of $30 for the games. By writing an inequality, find the maximum number of games they can play.

Rubric

Point(s)	Level	My Performance
7–8	4	• Most of my answers are correct. • I showed complete understanding of the concepts. • I used effective and efficient strategies to solve the problems. • I explained my answers and mathematical thinking clearly and completely.
5–6	3	• Some of my answers are correct. • I showed adequate understanding of the concepts. • I used effective strategies to solve the problems. • I explained my answers and mathematical thinking clearly.
3–4	2	• A few of my answers are correct. • I showed some understanding of the concepts. • I used some effective strategies to solve the problems. • I explained some of my answers and mathematical thinking clearly.
0–2	1	• A few of my answers are correct. • I showed little understanding of the concepts. • I used limited effective strategies to solve the problems. • I did not explain my answers and mathematical thinking clearly.

Teacher's Comments

Lines and Linear Equations

How steep is that slope?

If you like to snowboard, you probably want to know how steep a mountain is before you try to go down it. You can describe how steep a mountain is by using a ratio to compare the change in elevation between two points to the horizontal distance between the two points. The greater that ratio, the steeper the mountain. In this chapter, you will learn how to find slopes of lines on coordinate planes.

How do you write an equation of a linear graph?

Interpreting direct proportion

If $\frac{y}{x} = k$ or $y = kx$, where k is a constant value, then y is said to be directly proportional to x. The constant value k in a direct proportion is called the constant of proportionality. The graph of a direct proportion is always a line through the origin (0, 0) but does not lie along the horizontal or vertical axis.

The constant of proportionality in a direct proportion is often represented by a unit rate k. In general, you can use the point (1, y) on a direct proportion graph to find a constant of proportionality. You can then use the unit rate to write a direct proportion equation $y = kx$.

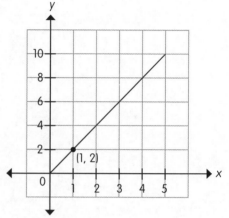

The graph shows that y is directly proportional to x. The line passes through the point (1, 2). The unit rate is 2.

So, the equation of the direct proportion is $y = 2x$.

▶ **Quick Check**

Determine whether each graph represents a direct proportion. If so, find the constant of proportionality. Then, write the direct proportion equation.

1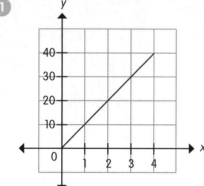

2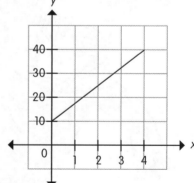

1 Finding and Interpreting Slopes of Lines

Learning Objective:
• Find slopes of lines.

THINK

Jason says that the line in Graph B has a greater slope than the line in Graph A because it is steeper. Do you agree with him? Justify your answer.

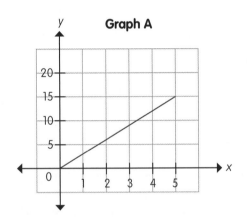

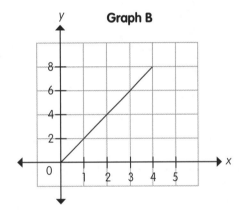

ENGAGE

The graph shows that y is directly proportional to x. The line passes through the points (2, 100) and (7, 350). A right triangle is drawn as shown. What are the lengths of the vertical and horizontal sides of the triangle? How do you find the constant of proportionality using the answers obtained? Discuss.

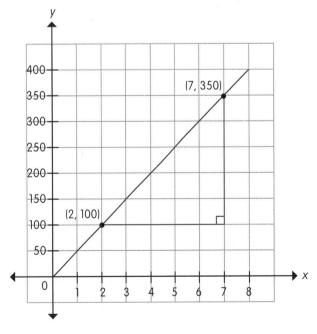

LEARN Use slopes to compare two unit rates

1. If you leave home and walk in a given direction at a steady pace, your distance from home, *d* feet, is directly proportional to the time you walk, *x* minutes. You can use a table and a graph to represent this proportional relationship.

Time (x minutes)	1	2	3	4	5
Distance from Home (d feet)	250	500	760	1,000	1,250

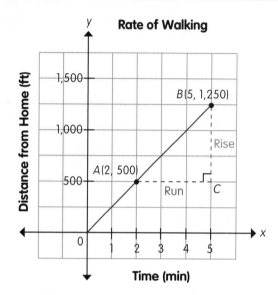

From the table, you see that the constant of proportionality is 250. You have learned that the point (1, *y*) on a direct proportion graph can be used to find the constant of proportionality. Another way to find the constant of proportionality is to find the slope of the line. You can find the slope by choosing two points and comparing the vertical change from the first point to the second, to the horizontal change from the first point to the second. The vertical change is called the rise. The horizontal change is called the run.

Suppose you choose the points *A* (2, 500) and *B* (5, 1,250) from the graph above.

Run = Horizontal change
  = 5 − 2
  = 3

Rise = Vertical change
  = 1,250 − 500
  = 750

$$\frac{\text{Rise}}{\text{Run}} = \frac{750}{3}$$
  = 250

As you can see, for this graph of a direct proportion, the slope of the line is 250, which is equal to the constant of proportionality.

2 The graphs give information about a penguin's number of heartbeats, *b*, over time, *t* minutes, during normal resting and just before diving. When is the penguin's heart rate greater, during normal resting or just before diving?

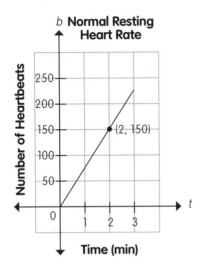

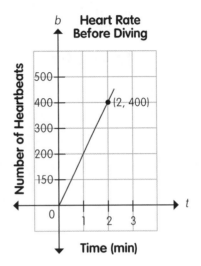

To find each heart rate, find the unit rate for each graph. To find the unit rate, you find the slope of the line. To find the slope, find the ratio $\frac{\text{Rise}}{\text{Run}}$ from the point (0, 0) to a convenient point on the graph.

Normal resting heart rate: Unit rate = $\frac{\text{Rise}}{\text{Run}}$

$= \frac{150}{2}$

$= 75$

Heart rate before diving: Unit rate = $\frac{\text{Rise}}{\text{Run}}$

$= \frac{400}{2}$

$= 200$

Math Note

Because the graphs have different scales on their vertical axes, you may not be able to tell just by seeing that the slope of one line is greater than the slope of the other line. You need to calculate the slopes of the lines to see which is greater.

The slope for the normal resting heart rate graph is 75.
So, the unit rate is 75 beats per minute.

The slope for the heart rate before diving graph is 200.
So, the unit rate is 200 beats per minute.

A penguin's heart rate before diving is greater than its normal resting heart rate.

 Practice using slopes to compare two unit rates

Solve.

1. The graphs give information about the distance, *d* miles, traveled over time, *t* hours, by cars and trucks on a highway. Which vehicle's speed is lower?

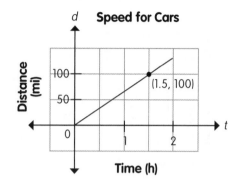
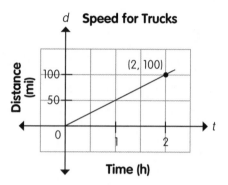

ENGAGE

Find the ratio $\frac{\text{Rise}}{\text{Run}}$, or the slope, of each line. How do the slopes compare? Explain your thinking.

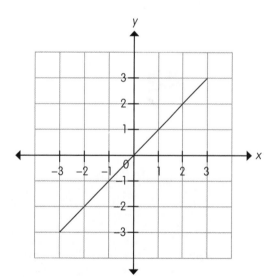
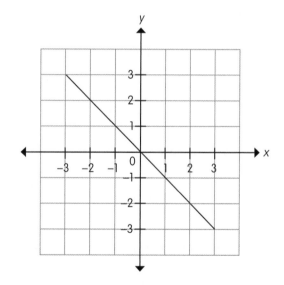

LEARN Find the slope of a line given the graph

1 Consider a line graph that goes up from left to right.

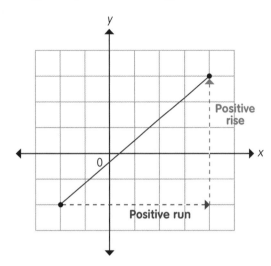

When the graph goes up from left to right, the run and the rise are both positive.

Slope = $\dfrac{\text{Positive rise}}{\text{Positive run}}$

So, the slope is positive.

Consider a line graph that goes down from left to right.

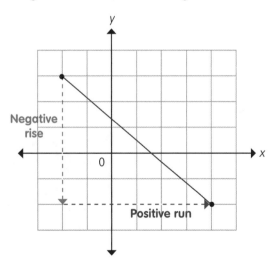

When the graph goes down from left to right, the run is positive, but the rise is negative.

Slope = $\dfrac{\text{Negative rise}}{\text{Positive run}}$

So, the slope is negative.

When you divide a negative number by a positive number, you obtain a negative quotient.

A line graph has a positive slope if it goes up from left to right. A line graph has a negative slope if it goes down from left to right.

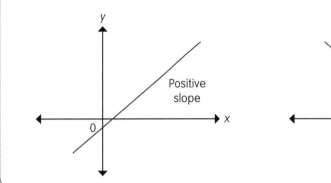

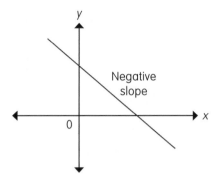

2 Find the slope of the line.

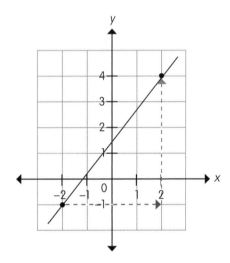

Move from (–2, –1) to (2, 4):
Vertical change = 4 – (–1)
= **5 units**

Horizontal change = 2 – (–2)
= **4 units**

So, the rise is 5 units, and the run is 4 units.

The graph passes through the points (–2, –1) and (2, 4).

Slope = $\dfrac{\text{Rise}}{\text{Run}}$

$= \dfrac{4 - (-1)}{2 - (-2)}$

$= \dfrac{5}{4}$

Math Note

It is important to remember to subtract the coordinates in the same order in both the numerator and the denominator.

The slope is $\dfrac{5}{4}$.

3 Find the slope of the line.

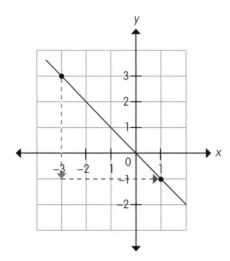

Move from (–3, 3) to (1, –1):
Vertical change = –1 –3
            = **–4 units**

Horizontal change = 1 – (–3)
            = **4 units**

So, the rise is –4 units, and the run is 4 units.

The graph passes through the points (–3, 3) and (1, –1).

$$\text{Slope} = \frac{\text{Rise}}{\text{Run}}$$

$$= \frac{-1-3}{1-(-3)}$$

$$= \frac{-4}{4}$$

$$= -1$$

The slope is –1.

TRY Practice finding the slope of a line given the graph

Find the slope of each line.

1

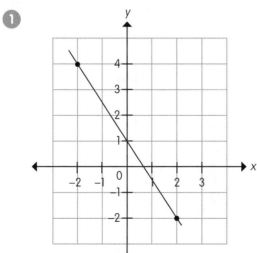

The graph passes through the points (–2, 4) and (2, –2).

$$\text{Slope} = \frac{\text{Rise}}{\text{Run}}$$

$$= \frac{-2-4}{2-(-2)}$$

$$= \frac{\quad}{\quad}$$

$$= \underline{\hspace{2cm}}$$

The slope is _____.

2

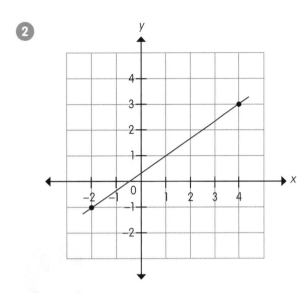

Using the coordinate plane, draw two graphs to represent the given situations: Carla is running at a constant speed of 5 miles per hour. Hayden is running at a constant speed of 6 miles per hour.

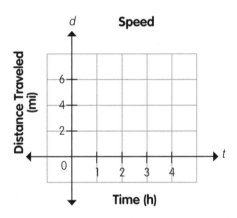

What do you notice when comparing the graphs? Share your observations.

LEARN Compare two slopes to make a conclusion about real-world situations

1 A red car and a blue car leave the same garage at the same time. Each driver drives at a steady rate. The graph represents the distance traveled by the red car, d miles, over time, t hours. The blue car traveled 140 miles over 4 hours.

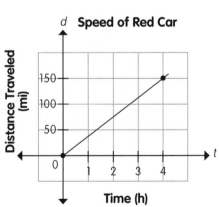

a At what speed is the red car traveling?

Find the slope of the graph and use the slope to find the rate, or speed, of the red car.

$$\text{Slope} = \frac{\text{Rise}}{\text{Run}}$$
$$= \frac{150}{4}$$
$$= 37.5 \text{ mi/h}$$

The vertical axis shows distance in miles. The horizontal axis shows time in hours. So, the rate is in miles per hour.

The red car is traveling at a speed of 37.5 miles per hour.

b At what speed is the blue car traveling?

You are told that the blue car traveled 140 miles in 4 hours.

$$\text{Speed} = \frac{\text{Distance}}{\text{Time}}$$
$$= \frac{140}{4}$$
$$= 35 \text{ mi/h}$$

The blue car is traveling at a speed of 35 miles per hour.

c Suppose you graph a line showing the distance traveled by the blue car after t hours on the same coordinate plane as the one showing the distance traveled by the red car after t hours. Would the graph of the blue car be steeper than the graph of the red car?

The speed of the blue car is 35 miles per hour, which is less than the speed of the red car. The slope of its graph will be 35, which is less than the slope of the graph of the red car.

So, the graph of the blue car will be less steep.

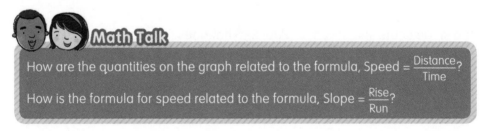

Math Talk

How are the quantities on the graph related to the formula, $\text{Speed} = \frac{\text{Distance}}{\text{Time}}$?

How is the formula for speed related to the formula, $\text{Slope} = \frac{\text{Rise}}{\text{Run}}$?

TRY Practice comparing two slopes to make a conclusion about real-world situations

Solve.

1 The graphs represent the amount of water in Pool A, w gallons, over time, t hours, and the amount of water left in Pool B, w gallons, over time, t hours.

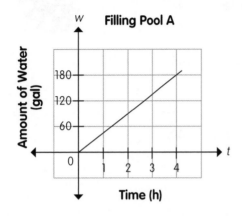

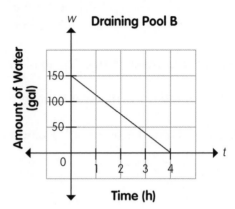

a Find the slope of the line graph for Pool A. What does it represent?

b Find the slope of the line graph for Pool B. What does it represent?

ENGAGE

Consider a horizontal line graph and a vertical line graph.

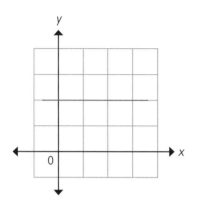
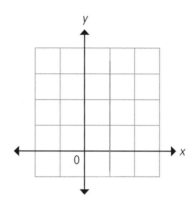

What do you think is the slope of each line? Explain your thinking.

Create a real-world situation for each line. Discuss your work.

LEARN Find slopes of horizontal and vertical lines

1 In a horizontal line graph, the run is positive.

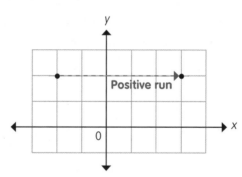

The rise is zero since the *y*-coordinates of any two points on the line are the same.

$$\text{Slope} = \frac{0}{\textbf{Positive run}}$$

So, the slope is always zero.

For a horizontal line, the vertical change (rise) from one point to another is 0. So, $\frac{\text{Rise}}{\text{Run}} = \frac{0}{\text{Run}} = 0.$

In a vertical line graph, the rise is positive.

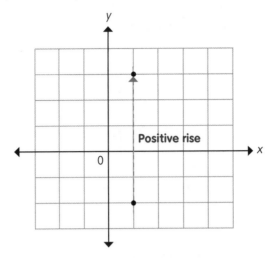

Positive rise

The run is zero since the *x*-coordinates of any two points on the line are the same.

Slope = $\dfrac{\text{Positive rise}}{0}$

So, the slope is undefined.

For a vertical line, the horizontal change (run) from one point to another is 0. So, $\dfrac{\text{Rise}}{\text{Run}} = \dfrac{\text{Rise}}{0}$ = undefined. You cannot divide by zero.

The slope of a horizontal line is zero.

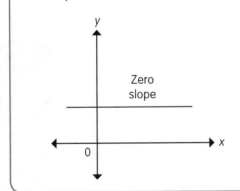

Zero slope

The slope of a vertical line is undefined.

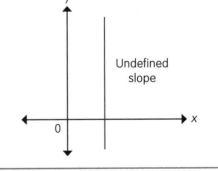

Undefined slope

2 Find the slope of the line.

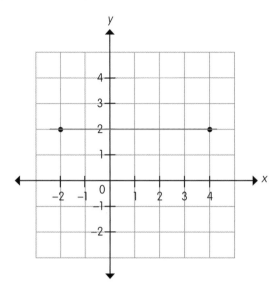

The *y*-coordinates of any two points on the line are the same. So, this means the line is a horizontal line.

The slope is 0.

TRY Practice finding slopes of horizontal and vertical lines

Find the slope of the line.

1

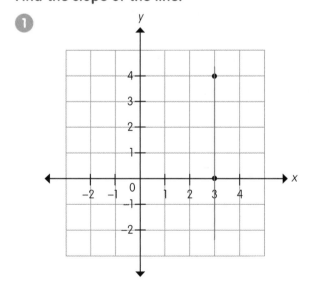

A line passes through (−2, −1) and (2, 4). Draw the line on the coordinate plane below

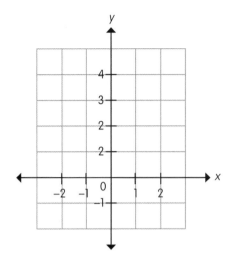

Using any two points on the line, find the rise and the run, and use them to find the slope of the line. Discuss with your partner if it is possible to be able to find the slope of the line without drawing the line. Explain your answer.

LEARN Find the slope of a line passing through two points

1 When you want to find the slope of a line, you do not need to draw the line.

Given any two points $A(x_1, y_1)$ and $B(x_2, y_2)$ on a line, you can find the rise and the run by subtracting the coordinates.

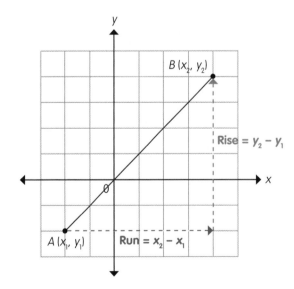

$\text{Rise} = y_2 - y_1$

$\text{Run} = x_2 - x_1$

So, slope $= \dfrac{\text{Rise}}{\text{Run}}$

$= \dfrac{y_2 - y_1}{x_2 - x_1}.$

Find the rise from point A to point B by subtracting the y-coordinate of point A from the y-coordinate of point B. Find the run from point A to point B by subtracting the x-coordinate of point A from the x-coordinate of point B.

When you find the rise or the run, it does not matter whether you subtract the coordinates of A from the coordinates of B, or the other way round. What matters is that you use the same order for both rise and run.

$\text{Rise} = y_1 - y_2$

$\text{Run} = x_1 - x_2$

So, slope $= \dfrac{\text{Rise}}{\text{Run}}$

$= \dfrac{y_1 - y_2}{x_1 - x_2}.$

Find the rise from point B to point A by subtracting the y-coordinate of point B from the y-coordinate of point A. Find the run from point B to point A by subtracting the x-coordinate of point B from the x-coordinate of point A.

The slope of a line passing through two points (x_1, y_1) and (x_2, y_2) is equal to $\dfrac{y_2 - y_1}{x_2 - x_1}$ or $\dfrac{y_1 - y_2}{x_1 - x_2}$.

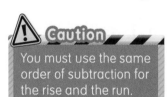

Caution

You must use the same order of subtraction for the rise and the run.

2 Find the slope of the line passing through the points A (4, 8) and B (1, 4).

Let A (4, 8) be (x_1, y_1) and B (1, 4) be (x_2, y_2).

▶ **Method 1**

Subtract the coordinates of B from the coordinates of A.

$\text{Slope} = \dfrac{y_1 - y_2}{x_1 - x_2}$

$= \dfrac{8 - 4}{4 - 1}$

$= \dfrac{4}{3}$

The slope is $\dfrac{4}{3}$.

▶ Method 2

Subtract the coordinates of A from the coordinates of B.

$$\text{Slope} = \frac{y_2 - y_1}{x_2 - x_1}$$
$$= \frac{4 - 8}{1 - 4}$$
$$= \frac{-4}{-3}$$
$$= \frac{4}{3}$$

The slope is $\frac{4}{3}$.

> You can find the slope of the line by calculating the rise and the run either from point A to point B or from point B to point A.

3 Find the slope of the line passing through the points $P(2, 5)$ and $Q(8, 2)$.

Let $P(2, 5)$ be (x_1, y_1) and $Q(8, 2)$ be (x_2, y_2).

▶ Method 1

Subtract the coordinates of Q from the coordinates of P.

$$\text{Slope} = \frac{y_1 - y_2}{x_1 - x_2}$$
$$= \frac{5 - 2}{2 - 8}$$
$$= \frac{3}{-6}$$
$$= -\frac{1}{2}$$

The slope is $-\frac{1}{2}$.

▶ Method 2

Subtract the coordinates of P from the coordinates of Q.

$$\text{Slope} = \frac{y_2 - y_1}{x_2 - x_1}$$
$$= \frac{2 - 5}{8 - 2}$$
$$= \frac{-3}{6}$$
$$= -\frac{1}{2}$$

The slope is $-\frac{1}{2}$.

Activity Exploring the slope of a line passing through two given points

Work in pairs.

① Using a geometry software, graph the line that passes through each pair of points. Then, fill in the table.

	Coordinates of Points	Slope of Line	$y_2 - y_1$	$x_2 - x_1$
a	$P(2, 1)$ and $Q(4, 7)$	Positive	$7 - 1 =$	$4 - 2 =$
b	$R(7, 6)$ and $S(4, 9)$			
c	$T(1, 1)$ and $U(4, 1)$			
d	$V(-2, 3)$ and $W(-2, 6)$			

② When the signs of $y_2 - y_1$ and $x_2 - x_1$ are the same, what do you observe about the sign of the slope?

③ When the signs of $y_2 - y_1$ and $x_2 - x_1$ are different, what do you observe about the sign of the slope?

④ When the value of $y_2 - y_1 = 0$, what do you observe about the slope?

⑤ When the value of $x_2 - x_1 = 0$, what do you observe about the slope?

TRY Practice finding the slope of a line passing through two given points

Find the slope of the line passing through each pair of points.

1 $M(-2, 0)$ and $N(0, 4)$

Let $M(-2, 0)$ be (x_1, y_1) and $N(0, 4)$ be (x_2, y_2).

▶ **Method 1**

Subtract the coordinates of N from the coordinates of M.

$\text{Slope} = \dfrac{y_1 - y_2}{x_1 - x_2}$

$= \underline{\qquad}$

$= \dfrac{}{}$

$= \underline{\qquad\qquad}$

The slope is _____.

▶ **Method 2**

Subtract the coordinates of M from the coordinates of N.

$\text{Slope} = \dfrac{y_2 - y_1}{x_2 - x_1}$

$= \underline{\qquad}$

$= \dfrac{}{}$

$= \underline{\qquad\qquad}$

The slope is _____.

2 $S(-5, 8)$ and $T(-2, 2)$

You can use either $\dfrac{y_1 - y_2}{x_1 - x_2}$ or $\dfrac{y_2 - y_1}{x_2 - x_1}$ to find the slope.

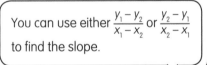

INDEPENDENT PRACTICE

Find the slope of each line.

1

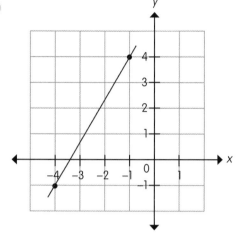

2

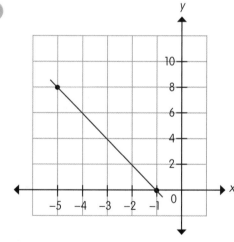

3

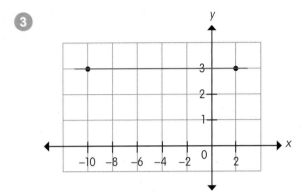

4

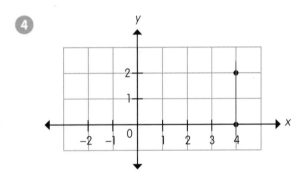

Solve.

5 **Use precise mathematical language**
Andrew graphs a vertical line through the points (5, 2) and (5, 5). He says the slope of the line is $\frac{3}{0}$. What error is he making?

Find the slope of the line passing through each pair of points.

6   A (–10, 3) and B (0, 3)

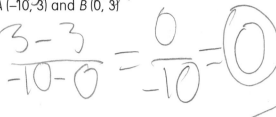

$$\frac{3-3}{-10-0} = \frac{0}{-10} = 0$$

7   S (5, –2) and T (2, –5)

$$\frac{-2-(-5)}{5-2} = \frac{3}{3}$$
$$= 3$$

8   P (0, –7) and Q (–3, 5)

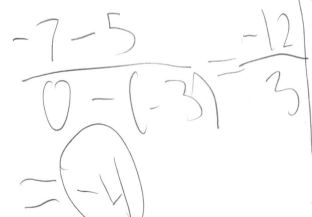

$$\frac{-7-5}{0-(-3)} = \frac{-12}{3}$$
$$= -4$$

9   X (4, 4) and Y (4, –2)

$$\frac{4-(-2)}{4-4} = \frac{6}{0}$$
$$= \text{non-defined}$$

Solve.

10 | **Mathematical Habit** 2 | **Use mathematical reasoning**

Two points have the same *x*-coordinate but different *y*-coordinates. Make a prediction about the slope of a line drawn through the points. Justify your prediction.

11 | **Mathematical Habit** 2 | **Use mathematical reasoning**

Two points have the same *y*-coordinate but different *x*-coordinates. Make a prediction about the slope of a line drawn through the points. Justify your prediction.

12 In the Fahrenheit system, water freezes at 32°F and boils at 212°F. In the Celsius system, water freezes at 0°C and boils at 100°C.

Freezes at 32°F or 0°C

Boils at 212°F or 100°C

a Translate the verbal description into a pair of points in the form (temperature in °C, temperature in °F).

$$\frac{32 - 0}{212 - 100} = \frac{32 \div 8}{112 \div 8} = \frac{4}{14} = \boxed{\frac{2}{7}}$$

b Find the slope of the line passing through the pair of points in a.

$$\frac{32 \div 8}{112 \div 8} = \frac{2}{7}$$

the slope is $2/7$

c Suppose the temperature in a room goes up by 5°C. By how much does the temperature go up in degrees Fahrenheit?

$212 = 19°F$

13 The table and the graph show the relationship between the cost, *y* dollars, of *x* gallons of gasoline purchased at each of the two stations, *A* and *B*, on a particular day.

Amount of Gasoline (x gallons)	Cost at Station A (y dollars)	Cost at Station B (y dollars)
1	3	4
3	11	10
5	19	16

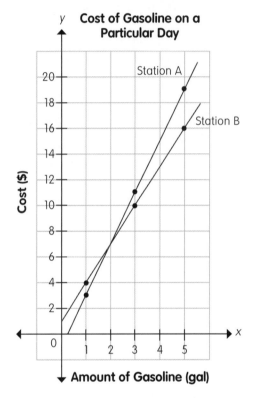

a At which station is each additional gallon of gasoline more expensive?

Station A

b Which graph is steeper?

Station A steeper

2 Understanding Slope-Intercept Form

Learning Objective:
• Write an equation of a line in the form $y = mx$ and $y = mx + b$.

> **New Vocabulary**
> y-intercept
> x-intercept
> slope-intercept form

THINK

Line A passes through the origin and has a negative slope. Line B crosses the y-axis above the origin and has a positive slope. Line C crosses the y-axis below the origin and has a negative slope. Line D crosses the x-axis to the right of the origin and is parallel to the y-axis. Give a possible equation for each line. Justify your answer.

ENGAGE

Use the graph to find the slope of Line P. You can use the equation $y = 2x + 3$ to describe Line P. How does the equation relate to what you notice about the line? Line Q has the same slope as Line P. What might be the equation of Line Q? Now draw a line that has the same slope as Line P but passes through –2 on the y-axis and label it as Line R. What might be the equation of Line R? Explain your thinking.

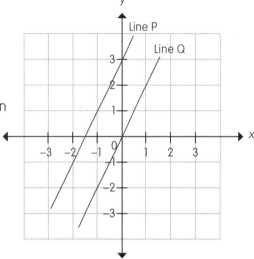

LEARN Write an equation of a line in the form $y = mx$ or $y = mx + b$

1. Jesse and his brother, Seth, walk from one end of a block to the other. Jesse starts at a curb. Seth starts 4 feet ahead of him. Both brothers walk at a rate of 4 feet per second.

   The table shows the times, x seconds, and the corresponding distances from the curb, y feet.

Time (x seconds)	0	1	2	3	4	5	6
Jesse's distance from curb (y feet)	0	4	8	12	16	20	24
Seth's distance from curb (y feet)	4	8	12	16	20	24	28

The graph shows each brother's distance from the curb after x seconds.

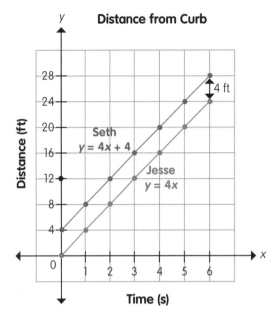

Distance from Curb

Jesse's graph represents a direct proportion. The rate, 4 feet per second, is also the slope of the red line. The equation of the red line is given by $y = 4x$. Seth is always 4 feet ahead of Jesse, but traveling at the same rate of 4 feet per second. So, for Seth's graph, the equation of the blue line is given by $y = 4x + 4$.

Jesse's graph and Seth's graph have the same slope because they walk at the same rate of 4 feet per second. So, their equations involve the same rate of change.

The graphs are different because they cross the y-axis at different points. Jesse's graph passes through the point (0, 0). Seth's graph crosses the y-axis at the point (0, 4).

The *y-intercept* of a line is the y-coordinate of the point where the line intersects the y-axis. The y-intercept of Jesse's graph is 0, hence the equation is given by $y = 4x + 0$ or $y = 4x$. The y-intercept of Seth's graph is 4, hence the equation is given by $y = 4x + 4$.

The *x-intercept* of a line is the x-coordinate of the point where the line intersects the x-axis.

A linear equation written in the form $y = mx + b$ is said to be written in slope-intercept form. The constant, m, represents the slope of the line. The constant, b, represents the y-intercept of the line.

> In the equation $y = 4x + 4$, m is 4 and b is 4.
> In the equation $y = 4x$, m is 4 and b is 0.

An equation of a line that passes through the origin, O (0, 0), is $y = mx$.

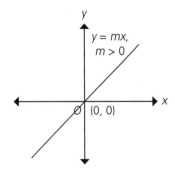

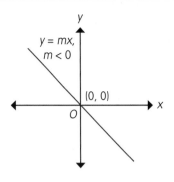

An equation of a line that intersects the y-axis at (0, b) is $y = mx + b$.

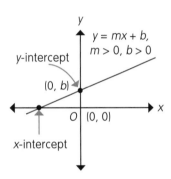

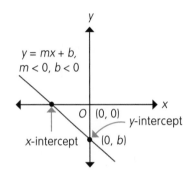

An equation of a straight line parallel to the x-axis and passing through the point (0, d) is $y = d$, where d is the y-intercept.

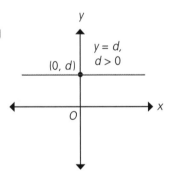

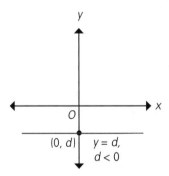

An equation of a straight line parallel to the y-axis and passing through the point (c, 0) is $x = c$, where c is the x-intercept.

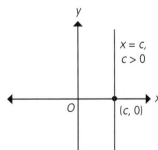

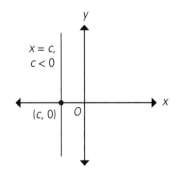

2 Write an equation in the form $y = mx$ or $y = mx + b$ for the line.

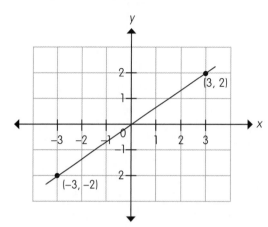

The line passes through the points (–3, –2) and (3, 2).

Slope, $m = \dfrac{2 - (-2)}{3 - (-3)}$

$\qquad = \dfrac{4}{6}$

$\qquad = \dfrac{2}{3}$

The line intersects the y-axis at the point (0, 0). So, the y-intercept, b, is 0.

Slope-intercept form: $y = \dfrac{2}{3}x + 0$ Substitute the values of m and b.

$\qquad\qquad\qquad y = \dfrac{2}{3}x$ Simplify.

The equation of the line is $y = \dfrac{2}{3}x$.

3 Write an equation in the form $y = mx$ or $y = mx + b$ for the line.

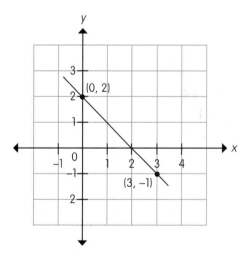

The line passes through the points (0, 2) and (3, −1).

Slope, $m = \dfrac{-1-2}{3-0}$

$\quad\quad = \dfrac{-3}{3}$

$\quad\quad = -1$

The line intersects the y-axis at the point (0, 2). So, the y-intercept, b, is 2.

Slope-intercept form: $y = (-1)x + 2$ Substitute the values of m and b.

$\quad\quad\quad\quad\quad\quad y = -x + 2$ Simplify.

The equation of the line is $y = -x + 2$.

Activity Exploring the relationship between $y = mx$ and $y = mx + b$

Work in pairs.

①   Use a graphing calculator, press `Y=` to display the $Y=$ window. Enter an equation from the table below. Then press `GRAPH` to graph the function.

②   Press `2ND` `TRACE` to select 6: dy/dx. The press `ENTER` to find the slope.

③   Press `2ND` `TRACE` to select 1: Value. Then press `0` to find the y-intercept.

④   Repeat ① to ④ for the other equations in the table. Record your results.

Equation	$y = 3x + 5$	$y = -2x + 1$	$y = 1.5x + 2$
m			
b			

⑤   **Mathematical Habit 8 Look for patterns**
The equation of another line is given by $2y = 5x - 4$. Predict the y-intercept. Use the graphing calculator to check your prediction.

Practice writing an equation of a line in the form $y = mx$ **or**
$y = mx + b$

Write an equation in the form $y = mx$ or $y = mx + b$ for each line.

①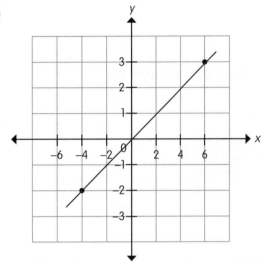

A line passes through the points $(-4, -2)$ and $(6, 3)$.

Slope, $m = \dfrac{3 - (-2)}{6 - (-4)}$

$= \dfrac{5}{10}$

$= \dfrac{1}{2}$

The line intersects the y-axis at the point $(0, 0)$.

So, the y-intercept, b, is ___0___.

Slope-intercept form:

$y = \dfrac{\frac{1}{2}x}{} + 0$

$y = \dfrac{1}{2}x$

The equation of the line is $y = \dfrac{1}{2}x$.

②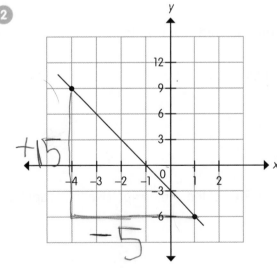

$\dfrac{15}{-5} = -3$

$y\text{-int} = -3$

$y = -3x - (-3)$

INDEPENDENT PRACTICE

Identify the *y*-intercept for each line. Then, write an equation in the form *y = mx* or
y = mx + b for each line.

1

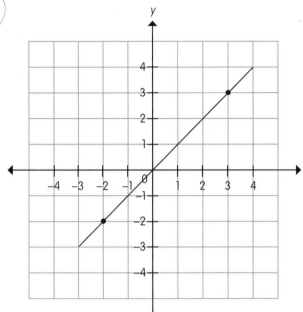

$$x_1 \quad y_1 \qquad x_2 \quad y_2$$

$$(3, 3) \quad (-2, -2)$$

$$\frac{3-(-2)}{3-(-2)} = \frac{5}{5} = 1$$

$$1 + 3 = 4$$

2

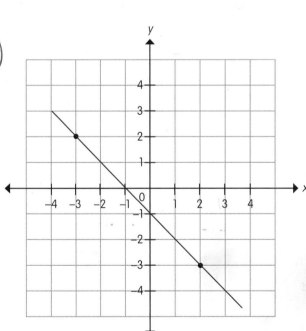

$$x_1 \quad y_1 \qquad x_2 \quad y_2$$

$$(2, -3) \quad (-3, -2)$$

$$\frac{-3-2}{2-(-3)} = \frac{-5}{-5} = 1$$

$$1 + (-3) = -2$$

3

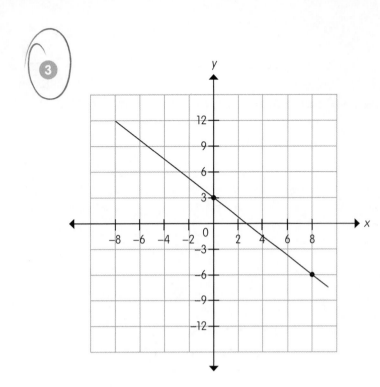

$$x_1 \quad y_1 \qquad x_2 \quad y_2$$
$$8, -6 \qquad 0, 3$$

$$\frac{-6-3}{8-0} = \frac{-9}{8}$$

$$\frac{-9}{8} + (-6) = \frac{15}{8}$$

4

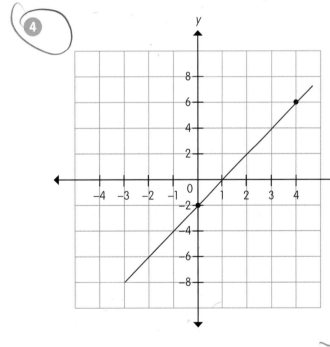

$$x_1 \quad y_1 \qquad x_2 \quad y_2$$
$$4, 6 \qquad 0, -2$$

$$\frac{6-(-2)}{4-0} = \frac{8}{4} = \frac{2}{1}$$

$$= 2$$

$$2 + 6 = 8$$

Write an equation in the form $y = mx$ or $y = mx + b$ for each line.

⑤

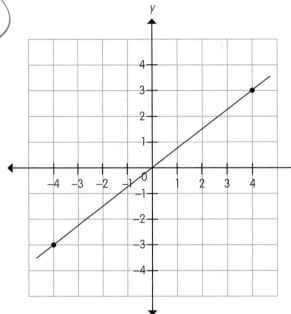

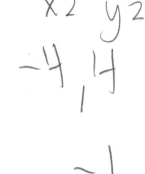

$x_1 \quad y_1 \qquad x_2 \quad y_2$

$8 \quad 3 \qquad -4 \quad 4$

$$\frac{3-4}{8-(-4)} = \frac{-1}{8}$$

$$-\frac{1}{8} 8 3 = \frac{-4}{8} - \frac{1}{2}$$

⑥

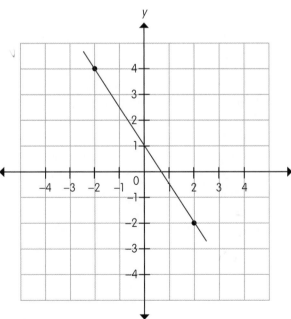

$x_1 \quad y_1 \qquad x_2 \quad y_2$

$-1 \quad 4 \qquad 2 \quad -2$

$$\frac{8-(-2)}{-1-2} = \frac{6}{-3} = \frac{2}{0}$$

$$2 + 4 = 6$$

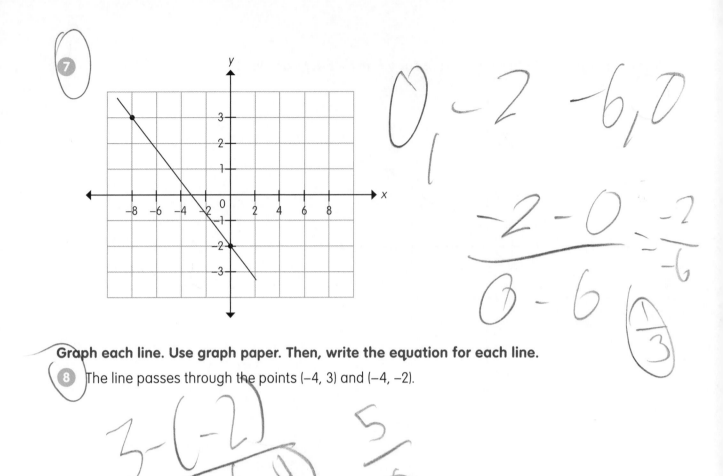

$0, -2$ $-6, 0$

$$\frac{-2-0}{0-6} = \frac{-2}{-6} \quad \left(\frac{1}{3}\right)$$

Graph each line. Use graph paper. Then, write the equation for each line.

8 The line passes through the points (–4, 3) and (–4, –2).

$$\frac{3-(-2)}{-4-(-4)} \quad \frac{5}{0}$$

9 The line passes through the points (–3, 4) and (1, 4).

$$\frac{4-4}{-3-1} \quad \frac{0}{-4}$$

Writing Linear Equations

Learning Objectives:
• Use slope-intercept form to identify slopes and *y*-intercepts.
• Write an equation of a line in slope-intercept form.
• Write an equation of a line parallel to another line.

THINK

The five items below describe part of a line. Form ten pairs of conditions using these five items. Then, for each pair, determine if the information is enough to find the equation of the line. If it is possible, describe the steps to find the equation; if it is not possible, explain why.

(a) the slope of the line
(b) the *y*-intercept
(c) a point on the line
(d) the slope of a line parallel to it
(e) the *y*-intercept of a line parallel to it

ENGAGE

Kimberly says, "If the equation $y = 2x + 5$ has a slope of 2 and a *y*-intercept of 5, then the equation $y + 3x - 4 = 0$ must have a slope of 3 and a *y*-intercept of -4." Do you agree or disagree with her? Justify your answer.

LEARN Use slope-intercept form to identify slopes and *y*-intercepts

① When given an equation, you can add, subtract, multiply, or divide both sides of the equation by the same number to write an equivalent equation in slope-intercept form.
To write an equation like $y + 2x - 6 = 0$ in slope-intercept form, you need to perform operations on both sides of the equation. What are the slope and *y*-intercept?

$$y + 2x - 6 = 0$$
$$y + 2x - 6 + \mathbf{6} = 0 + \mathbf{6} \qquad \text{Add 6 to both sides.}$$
$$y + 2x = 6 \qquad \text{Simplify.}$$
$$y + 2x - \mathbf{2x} = 6 - \mathbf{2x} \qquad \text{Subtract } 2x \text{ from both sides.}$$
$$y = -2x + 6 \qquad \text{Simplify.}$$

Compare $y = -2x + 6$ with $y = mx + b$.

Slope, $m = -2$
y-intercept, $b = 6$

Math Talk

Eve notices that the ordered pair (0, 6) is a solution of $y = -2x + 6$. Is this ordered pair also a solution of $y + 2x - 6 = 0$? Is any ordered pair (x, y) that is a solution of $y = -2x + 6$ also a solution of $y + 2x - 6 = 0$? Why or why not?

TRY Practice using slope-intercept form to identify slopes and *y*-intercepts

Find the slope and *y*-intercept of the line.

1 $5x + 4y = 8$

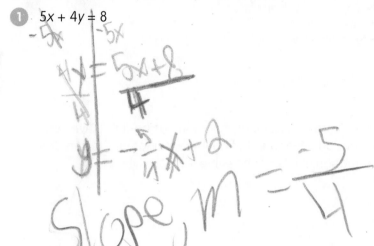

$-5x \qquad -5x$

$4y = -5x + 8$

$\dfrac{4y}{4} = \dfrac{-5x + 8}{4}$

$y = -\dfrac{5}{4}x + 2$

$\text{Slope, } m = \dfrac{-5}{4}$

ENGAGE

The slope of a line is $\dfrac{1}{3}$ and the *y*-intercept is 2. Sketch a quick graph of the line. How do you write the equation of the line? Explain your thinking.

LEARN Write the equation of a line given its slope and *y*-intercept

1 You have learned that the slope-intercept form of an equation of a line is given by $y = mx + b$. Given the slope, m, and *y*-intercept, b, of a line, you can substitute these values into $y = mx + b$ to write an equation of the line.

Use the slope, $\dfrac{1}{4}$, and the *y*-intercept of a line, 3, to write the equation of the line in slope-intercept form.

Slope, $m = \dfrac{1}{4}$

y-intercept, $b = 3$

$y = mx + b$

$y = \dfrac{1}{4}x + 3$ Substitute the given values for *m* and *b*.

The equation of the line is $y = \dfrac{1}{4}x + 3$.

2 Use the slope, –2, and the y-intercept of a line, –5, to write an equation of the line in slope-intercept form.

Slope, $m = -2$

y-intercept, $b = -5$

$y = mx + b$
$y = -2x + (-5)$ Substitute the given values for m and b.
$y = -2x - 5$ Simplify.

The equation of the line is $y = -2x - 5$.

**Math Talk**

If you graph the equations $y = \frac{1}{4}x + 3$ and $y = -2x - 5$, which line would go upward from left to right? Which line would go downward from left to right? Which line would be steeper? Explain.

TRY Practice writing the equation of a line given its slope and y-intercept

Use the given slope and y-intercept of each line to write an equation in slope-intercept form.

1 Slope, $m = -\frac{2}{3}$

y-intercept, $b = 4$
$y = mx + b$

$y = \underline{-\frac{2}{3}x + 4}$ Substitute the given values for m and b.

An equation of the line is $y = \underline{-\frac{2}{3}x + 4}$.

2 Slope, $m = 4$
y-intercept, $b = -7$

$y = 4x + (-7)$
$y = 4x - 7$

Draw two parallel lines on the coordinate plane.

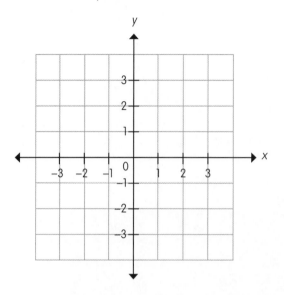

Now, write the equation of each line. How do you justify that they are parallel? Explain your thinking.

LEARN Write equations of parallel lines

① The lines shown are parallel.

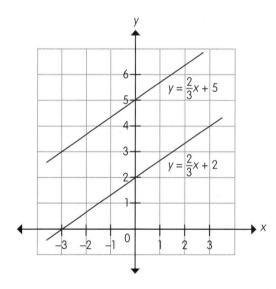

$y = \frac{2}{3}x + 5$

$y = \frac{2}{3}x + 2$

Lines on the coordinate plane that have the same slope but different y-intercepts are always parallel.

You can also use the equations of the lines to check whether the lines are parallel.

$$y = \frac{2}{3}x + 2$$

$$y = \frac{2}{3}x + 5$$

The two equations above have the same slope but different y-intercepts. So, they are parallel.

2 A line has the equation $2y = 6 - 3x$. Write the equation of a line parallel to the given line that has a y-intercept of 6.

Write the given equation in slope-intercept form.

$$2y = 6 - 3x$$

$$\frac{2y}{2} = \frac{6 - 3x}{2} \qquad \text{Divide both sides by 2.}$$

$$y = 3 - \frac{3}{2}x \qquad \text{Simplify.}$$

$$y = -\frac{3}{2}x + 3 \qquad \text{Write in slope-intercept form.}$$

The given line has a slope of $-\frac{3}{2}$ and y-intercept 3.

Write the equation for the parallel line with $m = -\frac{3}{2}$ and $b = 6$.

$$y = mx + b$$

$$y = -\frac{3}{2}x + 6 \qquad \text{Substitute the values for } m \text{ and } b.$$

The equation of a line parallel to the given line that has a y-intercept of 6 is $y = -\frac{3}{2}x + 6$.

 **Math Talk**

Give an example of another equation for a line that is parallel to $2y = 6 - 3x$ and $y = -\frac{3}{2}x + 6$.

TRY Practice writing equations of parallel lines

Solve.

1 A line has equation $3y + 6 = 10x$. Write the equation of a line parallel to the given line that has a y-intercept of 2.

You have learned to find the equation of a line by substituting the values of the given slope and y-intercept into $y = mx + b$. The line shown has a slope of $\frac{1}{6}$, but you can only estimate the y-intercept to be somewhere between 1 and 2. You also see that the line passes through the point $(3, 2)$. How do you find the equation of the line? Discuss.

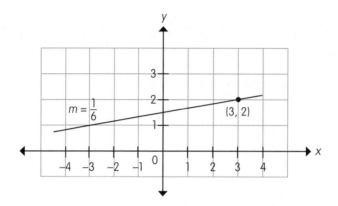

LEARN **Write the equation of a line given its slope and a point on the line**

1. The line shown has a slope of $\frac{2}{5}$ and passes through the point $(2, 3)$.

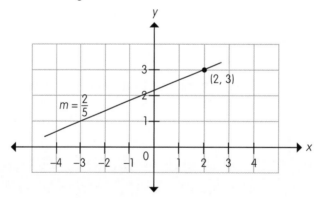

Use the given slope and the coordinates of the given point to find the y-intercept.

$y = mx + b$

$3 = \frac{2}{5}(2) + b$ Substitute the values for m, x, and y.

$3 = \frac{4}{5} + b$ Simplify.

$3 - \frac{4}{5} = \frac{4}{5} + b - \frac{4}{5}$ Subtract $\frac{4}{5}$ from both sides.

$\frac{11}{5} = b$ Simplify.

Use the given slope and the *y*-intercept to write an equation in slope-intercept form.

$y = mx + b$

$y = \frac{2}{5}x + \frac{11}{5}$ Substitute the values for *m* and *b*.

The equation of the line is $y = \frac{2}{5}x + \frac{11}{5}$.

② A line has a slope of −5 and passes through the point (1, −8). Write the equation of the line.

Use the given slope and the coordinates of the given point to find the *y*-intercept.

$y = mx + b$
$-8 = -5(1) + b$ Substitute the values for *m*, *x*, and *y*.
$-8 = -5 + b$ Simplify.
$-8 + 5 = -5 + b + 5$ Add 5 to both sides.
$-3 = b$ Simplify.

Use the given slope and the *y*-intercept to write an equation in slope-intercept form.

$y = mx + b$
$y = -5x + (-3)$ Substitute the values for *m* and *b*.
$y = -5x - 3$ Simplify.

The equation of the line is $y = -5x - 3$.

TRY **Practice writing the equation of a line given its slope and a point on the line**

Solve.

① A line has a slope of −3 and passes through the point (−6, 8). Write the equation of the line.

The equation for the red line shown in the graph is $2y = 3x + 4$. What is the slope of the red line? The blue line is parallel to the red line and passes through the point (2, 7). How do you use the equation of the red line to find the equation of the blue line? Discuss.

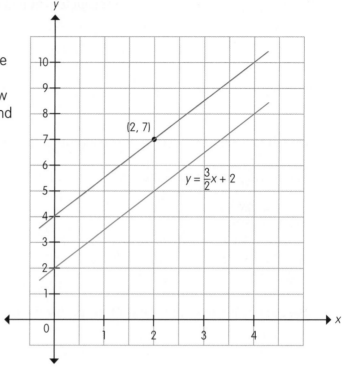

(2, 7)

$y = \frac{3}{2}x + 2$

LEARN Write the equation of a line given a point on the line and the equation of a parallel line

1 Consider the following graph.

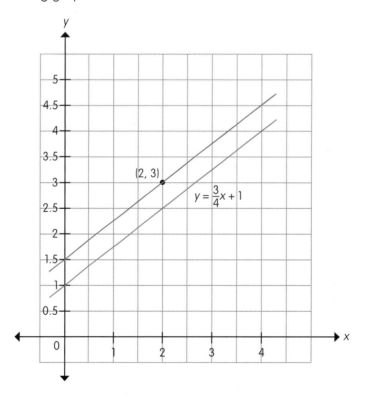

(2, 3)

$y = \frac{3}{4}x + 1$

You can use the equation of the red line to find the equation of the blue line.

Since the blue line is parallel to the red line, you know the slope of the blue line. You also know that the blue line passes through the point (2, 3). You can use the slope and the given point to write and solve an equation to find the y-intercept of the line.

$y = mx + b$

$3 = \frac{3}{4}(2) + b$ Substitute the values for m, x, and y.

$3 = \frac{3}{2} + b$ Simplify.

$3 - \dfrac{3}{2} = \dfrac{3}{2} + b - \dfrac{3}{2}$ Subtract $\frac{3}{2}$ from both sides.

$\dfrac{3}{2} = b$ Simplify.

The equation of the blue line is $y = \frac{3}{4}x + \frac{3}{2}$.

2   Write the equation of the line that passes through the point $\left(\frac{1}{4}, 8\right)$ and is parallel to $y = 2 - 4x$.

Write the equation $y = 2 - 4x$ in slope-intercept form.

$y = 2 - 4x$
$y = -4x + 2$

The line has a slope of -4. So, the line parallel to $y = 2 - 4x$ has a slope of -4.

Write the equation of the line that passes through $\left(\frac{1}{4}, 8\right)$ and has a slope of -4.

$y = mx + b$

$8 = -4\left(\dfrac{1}{4}\right) + b$ Substitute the values for m, x, and y.

$8 = -1 + b$ Simplify.

$8 + 1 = -1 + b + 1$ Add 1 to both sides.

$9 = b$ Simplify.

The equation of the line is $y = -4x + 9$.

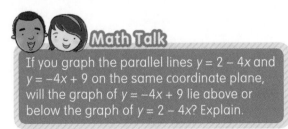
Math Talk

If you graph the parallel lines $y = 2 - 4x$ and $y = -4x + 9$ on the same coordinate plane, will the graph of $y = -4x + 9$ lie above or below the graph of $y = 2 - 4x$? Explain.

TRY Practice writing the equation of a line given a point on the line and the equation of a parallel line

Solve.

1. Write the equation of the line that passes through the point $(-2, 1)$ and is parallel to $y = 5 - 3x$.

2. Write the equation of the line that passes through the point $(0, 2)$ and is parallel to $6y = 5x - 24$.

Recall how you can use the slope of a line and a point on the line to find the equation of that line. Explain how you can extend this knowledge to find the equation of a line that passes through (4, −2) and (0, 6). Draw a quick sketch of the line to verify your answer.

LEARN Write the equation of a line given two points

1. You can find the equation of a line if any two points on the line are given. First, you use the two given points to find the slope. Then, you use this slope and either one of the given points to find the equation.

2. Write an equation of the line that passes through the points (1, 3) and (2, −4).

Use the slope formula to find the slope.

$$\text{Slope, } m = \frac{-4 - 3}{2 - 1}$$
$$= \frac{-7}{1}$$
$$= -7$$

Use $m = -7$ and (1, 3) to find the y-intercept, b.

$$y = mx + b$$
$$3 = -7(1) + b \quad \text{Substitute the values for } m, x, \text{ and } y.$$
$$3 = -7 + b \quad \text{Simplify.}$$
$$3 + 7 = -7 + b + 7 \quad \text{Add 7 to both sides.}$$
$$10 = b \quad \text{Simplify.}$$

The equation of the line is $y = -7x + 10$.

You can also use (2, −4) to find the y-intercept.

Solve.

1. Write the equation of the line that passes through the points (–2, –5) and (2, –1).

2. Write the equation of the line that passes through the points (–5, –1) and (0, 4).

INDEPENDENT PRACTICE

Find the slope and *y*-intercept of each line.

1 $y = -5x + 7$

Slope = -5
y-int = 7

2 $y = 2x + 3$

Slope = 2
y-int = 3

3 $5x + 2y = 6$

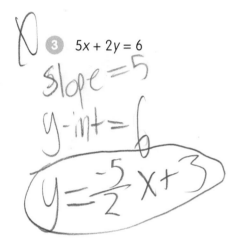

Slope = 5
y-int = 6
$y = \frac{-5}{2}x + 3$

4 $2x - 7y = 10$

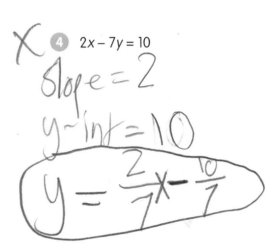

Slope = 2
y-int = 10
$y = \frac{2}{7}x - \frac{10}{7}$

Use the given slope and *y*-intercept of each line to write an equation in slope-intercept form.

5 Slope, $m = \frac{1}{2}$
   y-intercept, $b = 3$

$y = \frac{1}{2}x + 3$

6 Slope, $m = -2$
   y-intercept, $b = 5$

$y = -2x + 5$

Solve.

7 A line has the equation $4y = 3x - 8$. Write the equation of a line parallel to the given line that has a *y*-intercept of 2.

8 A line has the equation $3y = 3 - 2x$. Write an equation of a line parallel to the given line that has a *y*-intercept of 5.

9 **Mathematical Habit 3** **Construct viable arguments**
Anna says that the graphs of $y = -3x + 7$ and $y = 3x - 7$ are parallel lines. Do you agree? Explain.

10 A line has a slope of $-\frac{1}{3}$ and passes through the point (0, 4). Write the equation of the line.

11 A line has a slope of $-\frac{1}{2}$ and passes through the point (–4, –2). Write the equation of the line.

12 Write the equation of the line that passes through the point (–5, 7) and is parallel to $y = 4 - 3x$.

13 Write the equation of the line that passes through the points (–3, 2) and (–2, 5).

Sketching Graphs of Linear Equations

Learning Objective:
• Graph a linear equation by using two or more points.

 THINK

Graph the equation $y = 2 - \frac{2}{3}x$. Now draw another line parallel to the first line that passes through the point (2, 4). Explain, without measuring other points on the graph, how you can determine the equation of this new line.

ENGAGE

Use the equation $y = 2x + 1$ to fill in the table.

x	1		6
y		5	

How do you graph the equation using these values? Discuss.
How will the graph look? Explain your thinking.

LEARN Graph a linear equation using a table of values

1 A linear equation has an infinite number of solutions and each of them lies on the graph of the equation. You will learn to draw graphs of linear equations in this lesson.

To graph the equation $y = \frac{1}{2}x + 1$, you use the following steps.

STEP 1 Construct a table of values. Choose three values for x and solve to find the corresponding values for y.

x	2	4	6
y	2	3	4

Choose values of x that give integer values of y.

When $x = 2$, $y = \frac{1}{2}(2) + 1 = 2$.

When $x = 4$, $y = \frac{1}{2}(4) + 1 = 3$.

When $x = 6$, $y = \frac{1}{2}(6) + 1 = 4$.

STEP 2 Graph the equation using the table of values.

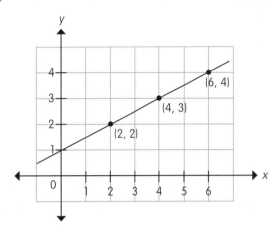

 **Math Talk**

Can you draw the graph with just two points? Why is it a good idea to include a third point when you graph an equation?

② Graph the equation $y = \frac{3}{4}x + 2$. Use 1 grid square on both axes to represent 1 unit for the x interval from −4 to 4 and the y interval from −1 to 5.

STEP 1 Construct a table of values. Choose three values for x and solve to find the corresponding values for y.

x	−4	0	4
y	−1	2	5

You may evaluate values of x that give integer values of y.

STEP 2 Graph the equation using the table of values.

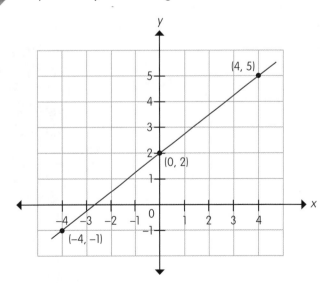

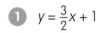
Graph the linear equation. Use graph paper. Use 1 grid square to represent 1 unit for the x **interval from –2 to 2 and the** y **interval from –2 to 4.**

1 $y = \frac{3}{2}x + 1$

ENGAGE

Consider the equation $y = 3x + 1$. Use the equation to determine two points on the line and graph the equation. Discuss with your partner if there is an easier way to graph the equation.

LEARN Graph a linear equation using m and b

1 One way to graph an equation in slope-intercept form is to use the y-intercept to plot a point on the x-axis. Then, use the slope of the line to find a second point on the line.

2 Graph the equation $y = x + 2$. Use 1 grid square on both axes to represent 1 unit for the x interval from 0 to 4 and the y interval from 0 to 6.

> **STEP 1** Plot a point on the y-axis. $y = x + 2$ has y-intercept, $b = 2$. So, it passes through the point (0, 2). Plot the point (0, 2) on the graph.

> **STEP 2** Use the slope to find another point on the graph. The slope of the line is 1. So, the ratio $\frac{\text{Rise}}{\text{Run}} = 1$. $\frac{\text{Rise}}{\text{Run}} = \frac{1}{1} = \frac{2}{2} = \frac{3}{3} = \frac{4}{4}\ldots$. Using $\frac{4}{4}$, you move up 4 units and then 4 units to the right to plot the point (4, 6).

> You can use convenient points, integer values, for the rise and the run as long as the ratio $\frac{\text{Rise}}{\text{Run}} = 1$. In this case, you use 4 for both the rise and the run.

STEP 3 Use a ruler and draw a line through the points. This line is the graph of the equation $y = x + 2$.

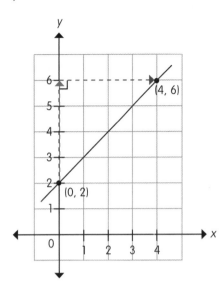

Math Note

The line graph contains all the points (x, y) with the values of x and y that make the equation true. Only some of those points can be seen on this graph. So, you can choose any convenient points of integer values for x and y.

3 Graph the equation $y = -\frac{1}{2}x - 3$. Use 1 grid square on both axes to represent 1 unit for the x interval from 0 to 4 and the y interval from 0 to −5.

STEP 1 Plot a point on the y-axis. $y = -\frac{1}{2}x - 3$ has y-intercept, $b = -3$. So, it passes through the point $(0, -3)$. Plot the point $(0, -3)$ on the graph.

STEP 2 Use the slope to find another point on the graph. The slope of the line is $-\frac{1}{2}$. So,

the ratio $\frac{\text{Rise}}{\text{Run}} = -\frac{1}{2}$. $\frac{\text{Rise}}{\text{Run}} = \frac{-1}{2} = \frac{1}{-2} = \frac{-2}{4} = \frac{2}{-4} = \dots$. Using $\frac{-2}{4}$, you move down 2 units and then 4 units to the right to plot the point $(4, -5)$.

You can use convenient points, integer values, for the rise and the run as long as the ratio $\frac{\text{Rise}}{\text{Run}} = -\frac{1}{2}$. In this case, you use −2 for the rise and 4 for the run.

STEP 3 Use a ruler and draw a line through the points. This line is the graph of the equation $y = -\frac{1}{2}x - 3$.

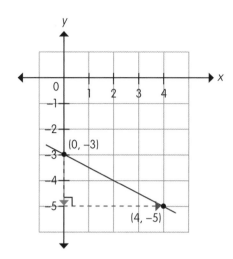

 Math Talk

Suppose that you are given the slope of a line and, instead of the y-intercept, a point on the line. For example, suppose you know a line passes through the point (4, 5) and has a slope of 3. Explain how you could graph the line.

TRY Practice graphing a linear equation using *m* and *b*

Graph each linear equation. Use graph paper. Use 1 grid square to represent 1 unit on both axes. Use suitable intervals for both axes.

1    $y = 2x + 1$

2    $y = -\frac{1}{3}x - 2$

ENGAGE

a   A line has a slope of 2 and its y-intercept is 3. Find the equation of the line and draw its graph.

b   Compare the method you used in (a) with your partner. Discuss how you would draw a line that has a slope of 2 and passes through (1, 5).

LEARN Graph a linear equation using *m* and a point

1. You can also graph a line using the information from a point on the line and the slope of the line, as shown in the following example.

2. Graph a line with a slope of 4 that passes through the point (3, 2). Use 1 grid square on both axes to represent 1 unit for the interval from 0 to 6.

STEP 1 Plot the given point (3, 2).

STEP 2 Use the slope to find another point on the graph. The slope of the line is 4. So, the ratio $\frac{\text{Rise}}{\text{Run}} = 4$. $\frac{\text{Rise}}{\text{Run}} = \frac{4}{1} = \frac{8}{2} = \frac{12}{3} = \frac{16}{4} = \dots$. Using $\frac{4}{1}$, you can move up 4 units and then 1 unit to the right to plot the point (4, 6).

STEP 3 Use a ruler and draw a line through the points. This is the line with slope 4 that passes through the point (3, 2).

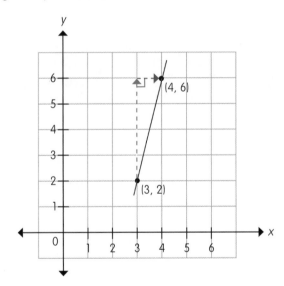

TRY Practice graphing a linear equation using *m* and a point

Graph each line. Use graph paper. Use 1 grid square on both axes to represent 1 unit for the *x* interval from –2 to 2 and the *y* interval from 0 to 10.

1. A line with a slope of –2 that passes through the point (2, 2).

2. A line with a slope of 2 that passes through the point (–2, 1).

INDEPENDENT PRACTICE

Graph each linear equation. Use graph paper. Use 1 grid square to represent 1 unit on both axes. Use suitable intervals for both axes.

1 $y = \frac{1}{3}x + 1$

2 $y = \frac{1}{6}x + 3$

3 $y = \frac{1}{2}x + 2$

4 $y = \frac{2}{3}x - 1$

5 $y = -x + 5$

6 $y = 3 - \frac{1}{4}x$

7 $y = 1 - \frac{1}{2}x$

8 $y = -\frac{1}{5}x - 2$

Solve.

9 **Mathematical Habit 2** **Use mathematical reasoning**

Maria says that the point (4, −2) lies on the graph of the equation $y = -\frac{1}{4}x - 1$. Explain how you can find out if she is right without actually graphing the equation.

Graph each line. Use graph paper. Use 1 grid square to represent 1 unit on both axes. Use suitable intervals for both axes.

10 A line with a slope of $\frac{2}{5}$ that passes through the point (5, 4).

11 A line with a slope of $\frac{2}{3}$ that passes through the point (6, 1).

12 A line with a slope of −3 that passes through the point (1, 0).

13 A line with a slope of −2 that passes through the point (−1, −2).

Name: _____   Date: _____

Real-World Problems: Linear Equations

Learning Objective:
- Explain slope and *y*-intercept in the context of real-world problems.

New Vocabulary
linear relationship

THINK

A scientist attaches a spring that is 11 inches long to a ceiling and hangs weights from the spring to see how far it will stretch. The scientist records the length of the spring, *y* inches, for different weights, *x* pounds.

Weight (*x* pounds)	0	1	2	3	4
Length of Spring (*y* inches)	11	13	15	17	19

Write an equation relating the spring length and the weights hung from the spring. Explain what information about this situation is given by the vertical intercept and the slope of the graph of the equation.

ENGAGE

A taxi service charges a $5 fixed fee plus $3 for every mile traveled. Use this information to construct a table of values comparing the distance traveled and the total charge. Then draw the graph using your table of values. What is the slope and the vertical intercept of the graph? How do they relate to the information given in the question? Will this always be the case for the slope and the vertical intercept?

LEARN Explain slope and *y*-intercept in the context of real-world problems

1. When there is a constant variation between two quantities, the relationship between the two quantities is a linear relationship. The relationship can be represented on the coordinate plane as a line. Consider the graph of the linear equation $y = 2x + 1$.

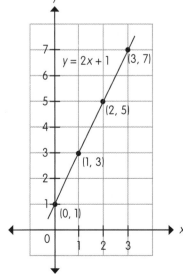

Find the rate of change for the points (0, 1) and (3, 7).

$$\frac{\text{Change in } y}{\text{Change in } x} = \frac{7-1}{3-0}$$
$$= \frac{6}{3}$$
$$= 2$$

Find the rate of change for the points (1, 3) and (2, 5).

$$\frac{\text{Change in } y}{\text{Change in } x} = \frac{5-3}{2-1}$$
$$= \frac{2}{1}$$
$$= 2$$

So, for any two points on the line, the unit rate of change, change in y per change in x, is the same as the slope of the equation.

For any linear relationship, the quantity on the horizontal axis of a graph of the relationship is the independent variable. The quantity on the vertical axis of the graph is the dependent variable.

When you graph a real-world linear relationship, the slope of the line is the rate of change in the dependent variable to the change in the independent variable.

2️⃣ A swimming pool holds a certain amount of water when full. When the drain is opened, the water in the pool drains out at a constant rate. The graph shows the amount of water in the pool, y gallons, x hours after the drain is opened.

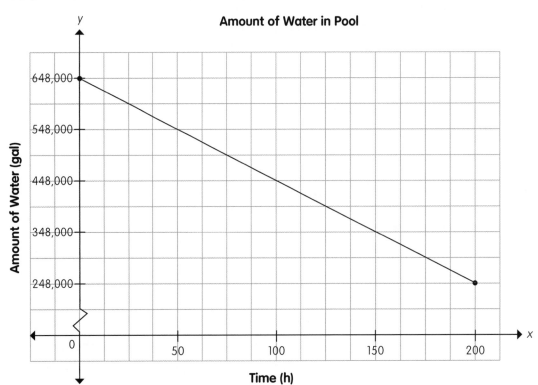

a Find the vertical intercept of the graph and explain what information it gives about the situation.

b Find the slope of the graph and explain what information it gives about the situation.

In this situation, the amount of water in the pool depends on the number of hours the pool has been draining. So, the amount of water is the dependent variable and the number of hours is the independent variable.

STEP 1 Understand the problem.

What information can I get from the graph? What do I need to find?

STEP 2 Think of a plan.

You can use the graph.

STEP 3 Carry out the plan.

a From the graph, the vertical intercept is 648,000. This is the number of gallons of water in the pool when it is full.

The vertical intercept or *y*-intercept corresponds to the initial number of gallons of water in the pool before it begins to drain.

b The graph passes through (200, 248,000) and (0, 648,000).

$$\text{Slope} = \frac{648,000 - 248,000}{0 - 200}$$
$$= \frac{400,000}{-200}$$
$$= -2,000$$

The negative slope means that as time increases, the amount of water decreases.

The graph has a slope of –2,000. The slope represents the rate, in gallons per hour, at which water is draining out of the pool. So, 2,000 gallons of water drains from the pool every hour.

STEP 4 Check the answer.

You can use another pair of points to check if your answer for the slope of the graph is correct.

> The graph passes through (50, 548,000) and (150, 348,000).
>
> $\text{Slope} = \dfrac{548,000 - 348,000}{50 - 150}$
>
> $\qquad = \dfrac{200,000}{-100}$
>
> $\qquad = -2,000$
>
> My answer is correct.

③ Lauren and Caleb are salespeople. Each of them earns a fixed monthly salary. They also earn an additional percent of the amount from their sales. So, the total monthly earnings, *y* dollars, depends on his or her sales, *x* dollars.

Total Earnings in One Month

a Find the fixed monthly salary for each person.

From the graph, the vertical intercept for Lauren's graph is 2,500. So, Lauren's fixed monthly salary is $2,500.

From the graph, the vertical intercept for Caleb's graph is 1,500. So, Caleb's fixed monthly salary is $1,500.

b Both Lauren and Caleb earn a percent commission. Who has a greater commission rate?

For each dollar a salesperson makes in sales, that person earns a certain amount of money as a commission. The person's commission rate is usually expressed as a percent. The rate is also the slope of the line graph for that person. You can see that Caleb's line is steeper. So, Caleb has a greater commission rate.

c Find each person's commission rate.

Lauren's graph passes through (0, 2,500) and (5,000, 2,750).

$$\text{Slope} = \frac{2,750 - 2,500}{5,000 - 0}$$
$$= \frac{250}{5,000}$$
$$= \frac{1}{20}$$

$$\text{Commission rate} = \frac{1}{20} \cdot 100\%$$
$$= \frac{100}{20}\%$$
$$= 5\%$$

Lauren's commission rate is 5% of her sales.

Caleb's graph passes through (0, 1,500) and (2,500, 2,000).

$$\text{Slope} = \frac{2,000 - 1,500}{2,500 - 0}$$
$$= \frac{500}{2,500}$$
$$= \frac{1}{5}$$

$$\text{Commission rate} = \frac{1}{5} \cdot 100\%$$
$$= \frac{100}{5}\%$$
$$= 20\%$$

Caleb's commission rate is 20% of his sales.

 **Math Talk**

Because Lauren's base salary is greater, she assumes that she will earn more than Caleb in any given month. Is this true? Explain.

4 Brianna and Sierra each have a coin bank. Brianna starts with a certain amount of money and adds money at regular intervals. Sierra starts with a different amount of money and takes money out over time. The amount of money in Sierra's coin bank, *y* dollars, after *x* weeks is given by the equation $y = -24x + 120$. The graph shows the amount of money in Brianna's coin bank after *x* weeks.

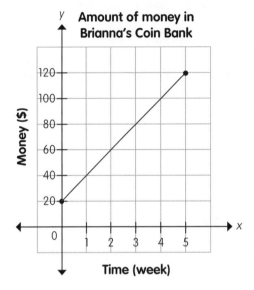

a Find the vertical intercept of Brianna's graph and explain what information it gives about the situation.

From the graph, the vertical intercept is 20. This is the amount of money that Brianna starts with.

b Find the slope of Brianna's graph and explain what information it gives about the situation.

The graph passes through (0, 20) and (5, 120).

$$\text{Slope} = \frac{120 - 20}{5 - 0}$$
$$= \frac{100}{5}$$
$$= 20$$

The graph has a slope of 20. The slope represents the rate at which Brianna is adding money. So, Brianna adds $20 every week.

c Is Brianna adding money at a faster rate or is Sierra taking out money at a faster rate? Explain.

From the equation $y = -24x + 120$, you see that each week Sierra takes out $24.

Because $24 > $20, Sierra is taking out money at a faster rate than Brianna is adding money.

TRY Practice explaining slope and *y*-intercept in the context of real-world problems

Solve.

1 Melanie rents a bike while visiting a city. She pays $7 per hour to rent the bike. She also pays $8 to rent a baby seat for the bike. She pays this amount for the baby seat no matter how many hours she rents the bike. The graph shows her total cost, *y* dollars, after *x* hours.

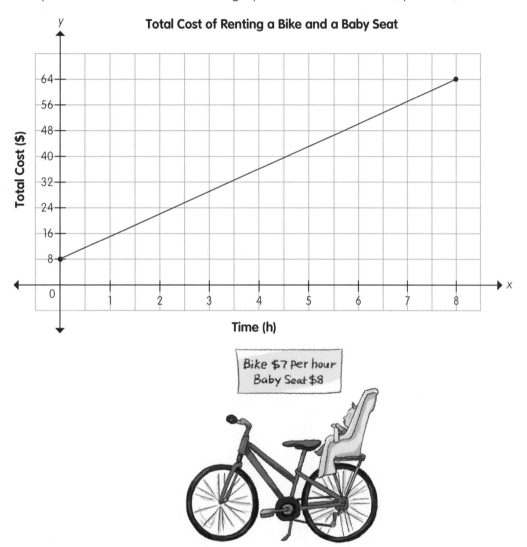

Total Cost of Renting a Bike and a Baby Seat

Bike $7 per hour
Baby Seat $8

a Find the vertical intercept of the graph and explain what information it gives about the situation.

From the graph, the vertical intercept is _____. This is the number of dollars needed to rent a baby seat.

b Find the slope of the graph and explain what information it gives about the situation.

The graph passes through (0, 8) and (8, 64).

Slope = $\dfrac{}{}$

$= \dfrac{}{}$

$= \underline{\hphantom{xxxxxx}}$

The graph has a slope of _____.

The slope represents _____.

2 Both Xavier and Nicole are salespeople. Each of them earns a fixed weekly salary and a percent commission based on the total sales he or she makes in a week. The graphs show the total earnings each person can make in one week, E dollars, based on the person's total sales, S dollars.

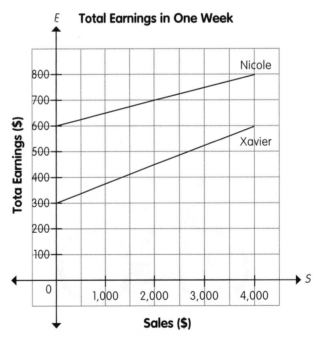

a Find the fixed weekly salary for each person.

b Both Xavier and Nicole earn a percent commission. Who earns a greater percent in commission?

c Find each person's rate of commission.

3 Sean and Timothy are brothers who live at the same house but go to different cities for vacation. When the vacation is over, they begin driving back home at the same time but at different speeds. Sean's distance from their house, D miles, x hours after he starts driving is given by the equation $D = -50x + 150$. The graph shows Timothy's distance from their house after he starts driving home.

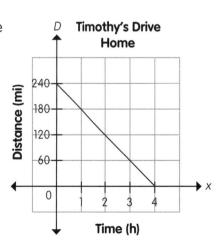

a Find the vertical intercept of Timothy's graph and explain what information it gives about the situation.

b Find the slope of Timothy's graph and explain what information it gives about the situation.

c Which brother is driving faster? How do you know?

When comparing rates of change in c, you only look at the absolute value of the slope. The sign is not taken into consideration.

INDEPENDENT PRACTICE

Solve.

1 Ang pays a fixed amount each month to use his cell phone. He also pays for each minute that he makes calls on the phone. The graph shows the amount he pays in a given month, *C* dollars, based on *x* minutes of call time.

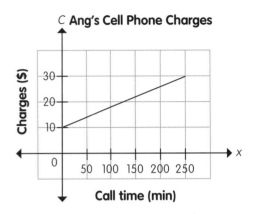

C **Ang's Cell Phone Charges**

a Find the vertical intercept of the graph and explain what information it gives about the situation.

b Find the slope of the graph and explain what information it gives about the situation.

2 Ryan and Adam are brothers. Each of them has a coin bank. In January, the boys had different amounts of money in their coin banks. Then, for each month after that, each boy added the same amount of money to his coin bank. The graphs show the savings in each coin bank, *S* dollars, after *t* months.

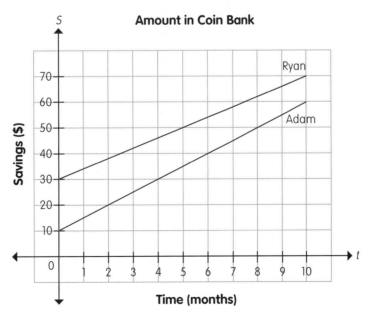

S **Amount in Coin Bank**

a Find the initial amount of money in each coin bank.

b Who added a greater amount of money each month into his coin bank?

3 Patrick and Steven drive from Town A to Town B in separate cars. The initial amount of gasoline in each car is different. The graphs show the amount of gasoline, in y gallons, in each person's car after x miles.

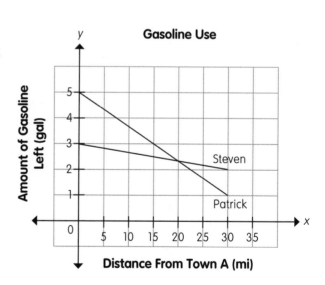

a Find the initial amount of gasoline in each car.

b Whose car uses more gasoline?

4 Mason and Zoe visit Star Café every day. They pay for the items there using a gift card. The amount on Zoe's gift card, y dollars, after x days is given by the equation $y = 100 - 19x$. The graph shows the amount left on Mason's gift card over x days.

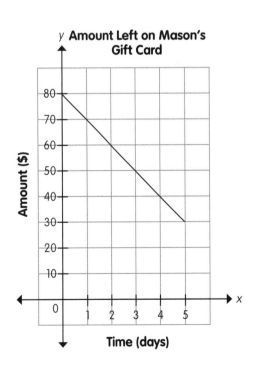

a Write the equation for the amount left on Mason's gift card.

b Using your answer in **a**, whose gift card had a higher initial amount?

c Using your answer in **a**, who spends more each day?

Mathematical Habit 3 Construct viable arguments

Suppose Gabriella shows you her homework.

Graph the equation $y = -2x + \dfrac{1}{2}$

Answer:

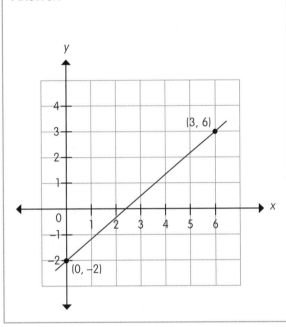

Describe Gabriella's mistakes. Graph the equation correctly.

Problem Solving with Heuristics

Mathematical Habit 4 Use mathematical models

1 Carter and Alexis are both students. Carter has $28 to spend for the whole week, and he decides to spend the same amount every day. Alexis currently does not have any savings. She is given a daily allowance and she decides to save the same amount every day. After four days, both have the same amount of money. The graph shows the amount of money Carter has, y dollars, after x days during one week.

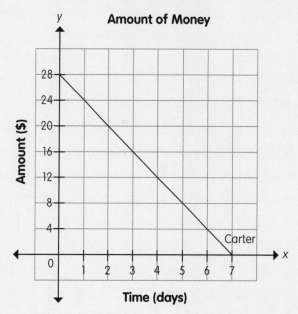

a A copy of the graph is shown below. Draw a line on the graph to represent the amount of money Alexis has after x days.

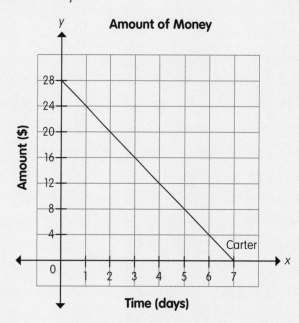

b Find the slope of Carter's graph and explain what information it gives about the situation.

c Write an equation to represent the amount of money each person has during that week.

2 Gavin left Townsville at 12 P.M. and started biking to Kingston 50 miles away. One and a half hours later, Jonathan left Kingston and started biking toward Townsville at a speed of 20 miles per hour. The graph shows Gavin's distance from Townsville, *d* miles, after *t* hours.

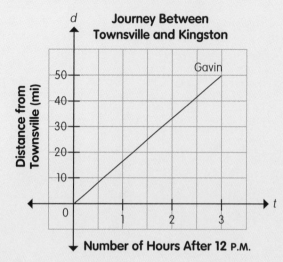

a A copy of the graph is shown below. Draw a line on the graph to represent Jonathan's distance from Kingston after *t* hours.

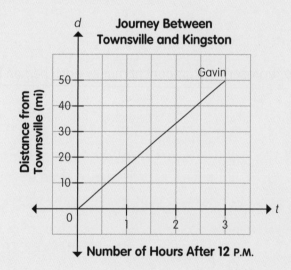

b Find the slope of Gavin's graph and explain what information it gives about this situation.

c Write an equation to represent each person's distance from Townsville after t hours.

CHAPTER WRAP-UP

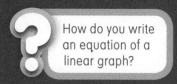
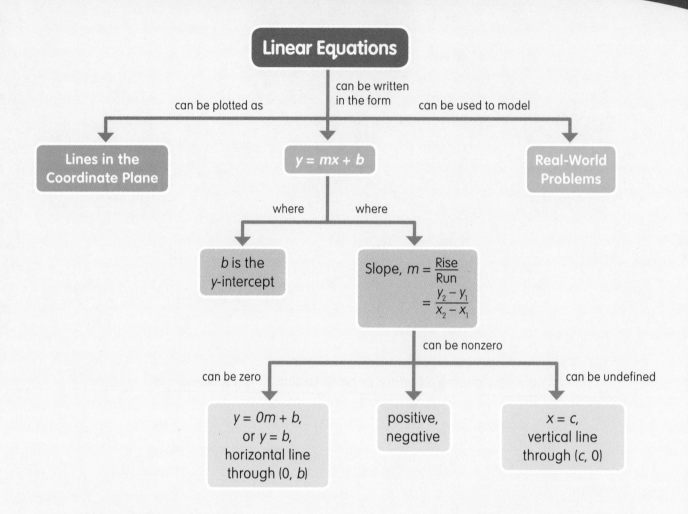

Linear Equations

can be plotted as → **Lines in the Coordinate Plane**

can be written in the form → $y = mx + b$

can be used to model → **Real-World Problems**

where → b is the y-intercept

where → Slope, $m = \dfrac{\text{Rise}}{\text{Run}}$ $= \dfrac{y_2 - y_1}{x_2 - x_1}$

can be zero → $y = 0m + b$, or $y = b$, horizontal line through $(0, b)$

can be nonzero → positive, negative

can be undefined → $x = c$, vertical line through $(c, 0)$

KEY CONCEPTS

- The slope-intercept form of a linear equation is given by $y = mx + b$, where m represents the slope and b represents the y-intercept of the graph of the equation.

- The slope of a line passing through two points (x_1, y_1) and (x_2, y_2) is equal to $\dfrac{y_2 - y_1}{x_2 - x_1}$ or $\dfrac{y_1 - y_2}{x_1 - x_2}$.

- The slope is always the same between any two distinct points on a line and can be positive, negative, zero, or undefined.

- The equation of a horizontal line through the point (c, d) is $y = d$. The equation of a vertical line through the point (c, d) is $x = c$.

- You can write the equation of a line given the slope m and the y-intercept b, the slope m and a point, or the coordinates of two points.

- You can write the equation of a line parallel to a given line if you know the y-intercept of the line you want to draw or the coordinates of a point on the line you want to draw.

- You can use linear equations and graphs to model and solve real-world problems.

Find the slope of each line using the points indicated.

1

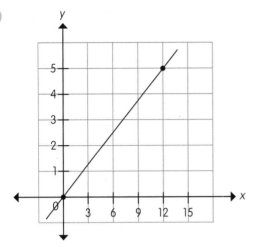

2

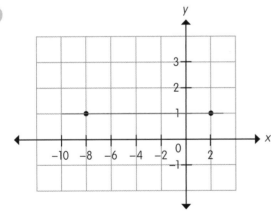

Write the equation of each line.

③

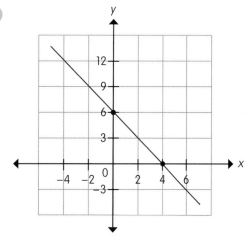

④

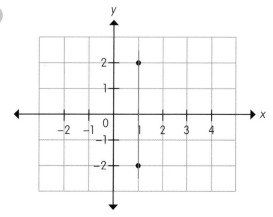

Find the slope and *y*-intercept of each line.

⑤ $y = \frac{1}{2}x - 3$

⑥ $y = -3x + 4$

Use the given slope and *y*-intercept of each line to write an equation.

7 Slope, $m = -4$

   y-intercept, $b = -\dfrac{1}{3}$

8 Slope, $m = \dfrac{2}{5}$

   y-intercept, $b = 3$

Solve.

9 A line has an equation $5y = 3x + 12$. Write the equation of a line parallel to the given line that has a *y*-intercept of 2.

10 A line has a slope of $-\dfrac{1}{2}$ and passes through the point $(-4, 5)$. Write the equation of the line.

11 Write the equation of the line that passes through the point $(-4, -4)$ and is parallel to $2y - x = -6$.

12 Write the equation of the line that passes through the point $(-4, -3)$ and is parallel to $4y - x = -16$.

13 Write the equation of the line that passes through the points $(0, 0)$ and $(7, 7)$.

14 Write the equation of the line that passes through the points $(1, 2)$ and $(4, 8)$.

Graph each linear equation. Use graph paper. Use 1 grid square to represent 1 unit on both axes. Use suitable intervals for the axes.

15 $4y = -3x - 8$

16 A line with a slope of $\frac{1}{3}$ that passes through the point $(0, -2)$.

17 Landscaping Company A and Company B each charges a certain amount as consultation fee, plus a fixed hourly charge. The graph shows the total charges, C dollars, for x hours.

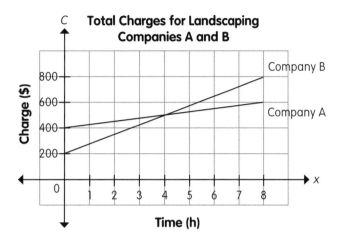

Total Charges for Landscaping Companies A and B

a Find the amount each landscaping company charges as its consultation fee.

b Which company charges a greater amount per hour?

18 The operator of a charter bus service charges a certain amount for a bus, plus per-passenger charge. The graph shows the total charges, C dollars, for carrying x passengers.

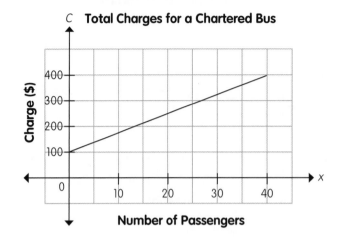

a Find the vertical intercept and explain what information it gives about the situation.

b Find the slope of the graph and explain what information it gives about the situation.

Assessment Prep
Answer the question.

19 This question has four parts.

Line P is shown on the coordinate plane.

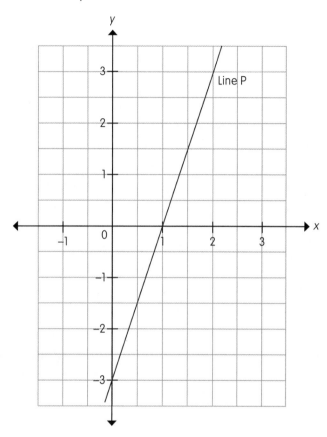

Part A

What is the slope of Line P?

Ⓐ $\frac{1}{3}$

Ⓑ 3

Ⓒ −3

Ⓓ $-\frac{1}{3}$

Part B

What is the *y*-intercept of Line P?

Ⓐ $-\dfrac{1}{3}$

Ⓑ 3

Ⓒ $-\dfrac{1}{3}$

Ⓓ −3

Part C

Line M (not shown) has the same slope and passes through the point (0, 2). Which table represents 4 points on line M?

Ⓐ

x	y
−2	−4
−1	−1
0	2
1	5

Ⓑ

x	y
−2	−5
−1	−2
0	2
1	4

Ⓒ

x	y
−2	12
−1	9
0	2
1	3

Ⓓ

x	y
−2	10
−1	8
0	2
1	1

Part D

Which equation represents Line M?

Ⓐ $y = -3x + 2$

Ⓑ $y = 3x + 2$

Ⓒ $y = \dfrac{1}{3}x + 2$

Ⓓ $y = -\dfrac{1}{3}x + 2$

Name: _____ Date: _____

Snowboarding Trails

1 The table shows the slope profiles of two snowboarding trails, A and B.

Trail	Vertical Drop (meter)	Length (meter)
A	160	625
B	87	500

a Write the linear equation for the relationship between vertical drop, y meters, and length, x meters, for Trail A.

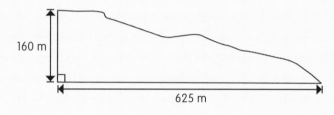

160 m

625 m

b Write a linear equation for the relationship between vertical drop, y meters, and length, x meters, for Trail B.

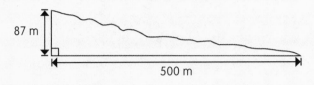

c By graphing the slope profiles of Trail A and Trail B on the same coordinate plane, state the trail that has a steeper slope.

d Using your graph, estimate the vertical drop of Trail A so that it has the same slope as Trail B with the length unchanged. Give your answer to the nearest meter.

e The difficulty level of a snowboarding trail can be measured by percent slope.

Percent slope = $\dfrac{\text{Vertical drop}}{\text{Length}} \cdot 100\%$

Level of Difficulty	Description
Easy	Percent slope ranging from 6% to 25%
Intermediate	Percent slope ranging from more than 25% to 40%
Advanced	Percent slope of more than 40%

Find the percent slopes of Trail A and Trail B. Hence, state the level of difficulty for each of the trails based on the description provided in the table.

Rubric

Point(s)	Level	My Performance
7–8	4	• Most of my answers are correct. • I showed complete understanding of the concepts. • I used effective and efficient strategies to solve the problems. • I explained my answers and mathematical thinking clearly and completely.
5–6	3	• Some of my answers are correct. • I showed adequate understanding of the concepts. • I used effective strategies to solve the problems. • I explained my answers and mathematical thinking clearly.
3–4	2	• A few of my answers are correct. • I showed some understanding of the concepts. • I used some effective strategies to solve the problems. • I explained some of my answers and mathematical thinking clearly.
0–2	1	• A few of my answers are correct. • I showed little understanding of the concepts. • I used limited effective strategies to solve the problems. • I did not explain my answers and mathematical thinking clearly.

Teacher's Comments

Have you ever planned a trip?

Suppose you stay at Town A and your uncle stays at Town B. Your family has arranged to meet your uncle at Niagara Falls during the school vacation. You know the distances from both towns to Niagara Falls. You are tasked with planning the trip so that your family and your uncle reach Niagara Falls at the same time. In this chapter, you will learn to write and solve two equations involving two variables that will help you to plan trips and solve other problems.

How do you solve two equations involving two variables?

Name: _____ Date: _____

Graphing linear equations using a table of values

To graph a linear equation, you first construct a table of x- and y-values.

For example, to construct a table of values for the equation $y = 2x + 1$, you choose values for x and solve to find the corresponding values for y.

When $x = 0$, $y = 2(0) + 1 = 1$.

When $x = 1$, $y = 2(1) + 1 = 3$.

When $x = 2$, $y = 2(2) + 1 = 5$.

When $x = 3$, $y = 2(3) + 1 = 7$.

You may evaluate values of x that give integer values of y.

x	0	1	2	3
y	1	3	5	7

From the table of values, you plot the pairs of values on a coordinate grid. Then, join the points using a straight line to graph the linear equation.

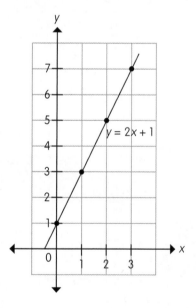

▶ **Quick Check**

Complete the table of values and graph each linear equation. Use graph paper.
Use 1 grid square to represent 1 unit on both axes. Use suitable axes for both axes.

1 $y = 5x$

x	0	1	2	3
y				

2 $y = -x + 2$

x	0	1	2	3
y				

Solving real-world problems algebraically

Real-world problems can be modeled using algebraic equations. You use algebraic reasoning to translate the problem into an algebraic expression. Then, you write an algebraic equation and solve it.

For example, Michelle has 4 more pencils than Dana. If they have 12 pencils altogether, find the number of pencils Michelle has.

You can use a letter, called a variable, to represent the unknown quantity.

Let the number of pencils that Michelle has be x.   Define the variable.

Number of pencils that Dana has: $x - 4$
Total number of pencils that the girls have: $x + x - 4 = 12$

Find the number of pencils that Michelle has.

$$x + x - 4 = 12$$
$$2x - 4 = 12$$ Add the like terms.
$$2x - 4 + 4 = 12 + 4$$ Add 4 to both sides.
$$2x = 16$$ Simplify.
$$\frac{2x}{2} = \frac{16}{2}$$ Divide both sides by 2.
$$x = 8$$ Simplify.

Michelle has 8 pencils.

▶ **Quick Check**

Solve.

3 Connor bought 30 hardcover and paperback books. Each hardcover book cost $20 and each paperback cost $8. If Connor spent a total of $480, how many paperbacks did he buy?

© 2020 Marshall Cavendish Education Pte Ltd

Introduction to Systems of Linear Equations

Learning Objective:
• Solve a system of linear equations by making tables of values.

New Vocabulary
system of linear equations
unique solution

THINK

Kaylee is 2 times as old as her cousin. Three years later, their combined age will be 27 years. The related system of linear equations is the following.

$x = 2y$
$x + 3 + y + 3 = 27$

In the above equations, what do x and y represent? How can you find Kaylee's age when her cousin was born? Discuss with your partner.

ENGAGE

Fill in the table of values that satisfies the equation $x + 5 = y$.

x	1	2	3	4	5	6
y						

Now, make a table of values that satisfies the equation $2x = y$.

x	1	2	3	4	5	6
y						

Do you see any similarities in the tables? What do you think this implies? Explain your answer.

LEARN Solve a system of linear equations by making tables of values

1. You have learned to solve linear equations with one variable. To solve an equation with two variables, you need to use two equations.

Consider the following situation.

A farmer, Dylan, has x goats and y cows. He has 9 goats and cows altogether. How many of each animal does he have?

You can represent the total number of goats and cows using the linear equation $x + y = 9$. The table shows pairs of numbers that satisfy the equation $x + y = 9$.

Number of Goats (x)	0	1	2	3	4	5	6	7	8	9
Number of Cows (y)	9	8	7	6	5	4	3	2	1	0

There are many pairs of possible values of x and y. You need more information to find the number of goats and the number of cows Dylan has.

Suppose Dylan has twice as many goats as cows. You can represent the number of goats using the linear equation $x = 2y$. The table shows some possible pairs of numbers that satisfy the equation $x = 2y$.

x	0	2	4	6	8
y	0	1	2	3	4

Again you have many possible values of x and y. Note that the values of x and y must satisfy both equations. So, the same pair of x- and y-values must appear in both tables. When you compare the two tables, you see that there is only one such pair of x- and y-values: $x = 6$ and $y = 3$. So, Dylan has 6 goats and 3 cows.

> A set of linear equations that has more than one variable is called a system of linear equations. The single pair of variables that satisfies both equations is their unique solution.

2. Logan is x years old. His younger brother is y years old. The difference between the ages is 1 year. The sum of 4 times Logan's age and his brother's age is 14 years. The related system of linear equations is the following.

$x - y = 1$
$4x + y = 14$

Solve the system of linear equations by making tables of values. Then, find Logan's age and his brother's age.

Make a table of values for each equation.

$x - y = 1$

x	2	3	4
y	1	2	3

$4x + y = 14$

x	1	2	3
y	10	6	2

> Since x and y represent ages, both will be positive integers.

© 2020 Marshall Cavendish Education Pte Ltd

Only the pair of values $x = 3$ and $y = 2$ appear in both tables. So, the solution to the system of linear equations is given by $x = 3$, $y = 2$.

Logan's age is 3 years. His brother's age is 2 years.

**Math Talk**

Why is $x \neq 1$ in the first equation?

Activity Using tables on a graphing calculator to solve a system of linear equations

Work in pairs.

You can use a graphing calculator to create tables of values and solve systems of linear equations. Use the steps in the activity to solve the system of linear equations.

$8x + y = 38$
$x - 4y = 13$

(1) Solve each equation for y in terms of x. Input the two resulting expressions for y into the equation screen.

⚠️ **Caution**
Use parentheses around fractional coefficients and the (–) key for negative coefficients.

(2) Set the table function to use values of x starting at 0, with increments of 1.

(3) Display the table. It will be in three columns as shown.

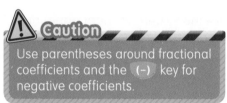

(4) Find the row where the two y-values are the same. This y-value and the corresponding x-value will be the solution to the equations.

The solution to the system of linear equations is given by $x = $ _____, $y = $ _____.

(5) **Mathematical Habit 8 Look for patterns**
How do you tell from the two columns of y-values that there is only one row where the y-values are the same?

TRY Practice making tables of values to solve a system of linear equations

Make tables of values to solve. x and y are positive integers.

① A bottle of water and a taco cost $3. The cost of 3 bottles of water is $1 more than the cost of a taco. Let x dollars be the cost of a bottle of water, and y dollars be the cost of a taco.

Cost of a bottle of water: $x

Cost of a taco: $y

The related system of linear equations is the following.

$x + y = 3$
$3x - y = 1$

Solve the system of linear equations. Then, find the cost of a bottle of water and the cost of a taco.

> For each linear equation, list in a table enough values for x and y to obtain a solution. Remember that they must be positive integers.

② $x + y = 6$
$x + 2y = 8$

③ $x + y = 8$
$x - 3y = -8$

INDEPENDENT PRACTICE

Make tables of values to solve each system of linear equations. *x* is a positive integer less than 6.

1 $2x + y = 5$
   $x - y = -2$

2 $x + 2y = 4$
   $x = 2y$

3 $3x + 2y = 10$
   $5x - 2y = 6$

4 $x - 2y = -5$
   $x = y$

5 $2y - x = -2$
   $x + y = 2$

6 $2x + y = 3$
   $x + y = 1$

Make tables of values to solve. *x* and *y* are positive integers.

7 A store selling party costumes sells a party hat at *x* dollars and a mask at *y* dollars. On a particular morning, 10 hats and 20 masks were sold for $30. In the afternoon, 8 hats and 10 masks were sold for $18. The related system of linear equations is the following.

$$10x + 20y = 30$$
$$8x + 10y = 18$$

Solve the system of linear equations. Then, find the cost of a hat and a mask.

8 Cole and Aaron start driving at the same time from Boston to Paterson. The journey is *d* kilometers. Cole drives at 100 kilometers per hour and takes *t* hours to complete the journey. Aaron, who drives at 80 kilometers per hour, is 60 kilometers away from Paterson when Cole reaches Paterson. The related system of linear equations is the following.

$$100t = d$$
$$80t = d - 60$$

Solve the system of linear equations. Then, find the distance between Boston and Paterson.

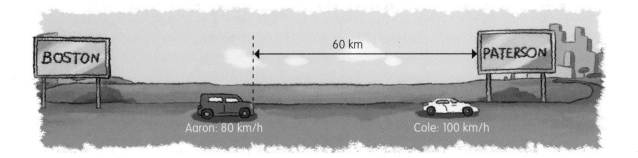

Solving Systems of Linear Equations Using Algebraic Methods

Learning Objectives:
- Solve systems of linear equations using the elimination method.
- Solve systems of linear equations using the substitution method.

New Vocabulary
common term
elimination method
substitution method

THINK

Consider the following systems of linear equations.
$2x + ay = b$
$ax - 17y = 23b$

Given that the solution is $x = 2$ and $y = -1$, find the values of a and b.

ENGAGE

Look at the following system of equations.
$p + q = 10$
$p - 2q = 8$

For each equation, express them in terms of p.
How can you use your rewritten equations to write a new equation without using p? How can you use this new equation to find the values of both p and q? Discuss.

LEARN Solve systems of linear equations with a common term using the elimination method

1. You have learned to use tables of values to solve systems of linear equations. You may have noticed that it is not always easy to find the solution. Consider the following system of linear equations.

$x + y = 8$ (Equation 1)
$x + 2y = 10$ (Equation 2)

You can use bar models to represent these equations.

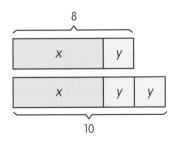

The difference in length between the two bar models is 2 units. Since the second model is one y-section longer, $y = 2$.

From the bar models, $y = 10 - 8 = 2$.

Look again at the bar model representing Equation 1.

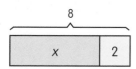

From the bar model, $x + 2 = 8$.

So, $x = 8 - 2$
$= 6$

Algebraically, you can use the same approach.

$x + y = 8$ (Equation 1)
$x + 2y = 10$ (Equation 2)

Both equations have an x term. If you subtract the two equations, both x terms will be eliminated and you will have an equation with only one variable y.

Subtract Equation 1 from Equation 2:
$x + 2y - (x + y) = 10 - 8$
   $x + 2y - x - y = 2$ Use the distributive property.
          $y = 2$ Simplify.

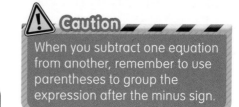

Caution

When you subtract one equation from another, remember to use parentheses to group the expression after the minus sign.

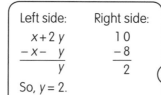

Left side: Right side:

$$\begin{array}{r} x + 2y \\ -x - y \\ \hline y \end{array} \qquad \begin{array}{r} 10 \\ -8 \\ \hline 2 \end{array}$$

So, $y = 2$.

Subtracting two equations is another form of the subtraction property of equality. You have subtracted the same number from both sides of an equation before. Now you are subtracting equal expressions from both sides of the equation.

Substitute 2 for y into Equation 1:
    $x + 2 = 8$
$x + 2 - \mathbf{2} = 8 - \mathbf{2}$ Subtract 2 from both sides.
       $x = 6$ Simplify.

So, the solution to the system of linear equations is given by $x = 6$, $y = 2$.

By adding or subtracting two equations with a common term, you obtain an equation with only one variable. This method of solving systems of linear equations is known as the elimination method.

2 Use the elimination method to solve the system of linear equations.

$4x + y = 9$ (Equation 1)
$3x - y = 5$ (Equation 2)

The common terms of a system of linear equations are two or more like terms with the same or opposite coefficients such as y and $-y$. To eliminate the y terms, add the two equations.

Add Equation 1 and Equation 2:
$(4x + y) + (3x - y) = 9 + 5$
$\quad 4x + 3x + y - y = 14$ Group the like terms.
$\qquad\qquad 7x = 14$ Simplify. y is eliminated.
$\qquad\qquad \dfrac{7x}{7} = \dfrac{14}{7}$ Divide both sides by 7.
$\qquad\qquad x = 2$ Simplify.

Substitute 2 for x into Equation 1:
$4(2) + y = 9$
$\quad 8 + y = 9$ Simplify.
$\qquad y = 1$ Subtract 8 from both sides.

You can also substitute 2 for x into Equation 2 to find y.

So, the solution to the system of linear equations is given by $x = 2$, $y = 1$.

Check

Substitute the solution into Equation 2.

$3 \cdot 2 - 1 = 5$

When $x = 2$ and $y = 1$, the equation $3x - y = 5$ is true.

So, the solution is correct.

Since the value of x was substituted into Equation 1 to find y, you use Equation 2 to check the solution.

Use the elimination method to solve the system of linear equations.

① $2a + 3b = 29$
$2a - b = 17$

② $2x - y = 2$
$3x + y = 13$

ENGAGE

Recall the methods to solve the system of linear equations $x + 3y = 8$ and $x + y = 6$. How can you use this method to solve $x + 3y = 8$ and $2x + y = 6$? Explain your answer.

LEARN Solve systems of linear equations without common terms using the elimination method

① Consider the following system of linear equations.

$2x + 3y = 7$ (Equation 1)
$x + 6y = 8$ (Equation 2)

You cannot immediately use the elimination method because the equations have no common terms. But you can modify the equations to be able to use the elimination method to solve the system.

You can represent these equations using bar models:

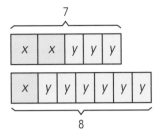

You can redraw the bar models, using two copies of the second bar model.

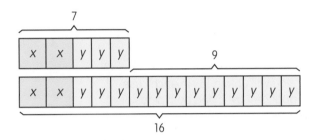

In the redrawn models, x and y still represent the same numbers because the sections are still the same size. You can see that 9y = 9, hence y = 1.

From the bar models, you see that $y = 1$.
Substituting $y = 1$ into either equation, we can get the solution $x = 2$, $y = 1$.

You can write the equation that the redrawn second bar model represents by multiplying both sides of Equation 2 by 2.

$2 \cdot (x + 6y) = 2 \cdot 8$
$\quad 2x + 12y = 16$ (Equation 3)   Use the distributive property and simplify.

Now, you have two equations with a common x term. You can use the elimination method to solve this system and the solution will be the solution to the original system.
$2x + 3y = 7$ (Equation 1)
$2x + 12y = 16$ (Equation 3)

Multiplying Equation 2 by 2 produces an equivalent equation, that is, one with exactly the same solution as Equation 2. So, the solution to the system does not change.

If the coefficients of x or y are multiples, you can rewrite equations with a common term by multiplying one of the equations.

② Use the elimination method to solve the system of linear equations.

$2x + 5y = 11$ (Equation 1)
$9x + 2y = -12$ (Equation 2)

▶ **Method 1**
Eliminate the x terms first.

Multiply Equation 1 by 9:
$9 \cdot (2x + 5y) = 9 \cdot 11$
$\quad 18x + 45y = 99$ (Equation 3)

Multiply Equation 2 by 2:
$2 \cdot (9x + 2y) = 2 \cdot (-12)$
$\quad\quad 18x + 4y = -24$ (Equation 4)

> If you multiply $2x$ by 9, and $9x$ by 2, you will obtain $18x$ in each case. So, you can multiply both sides of Equation 1 by 9, and both sides of Equation 2 by 2 to eliminate the x terms.

Subtract Equation 4 from Equation 3:
$18x + 45y - (18x + 4y) = 99 - (-24)$
$\quad 18x + 45y - 18x - 4y = 123$ Use the distributive property.
$\quad\quad\quad\quad\quad\quad 41y = 123$ Simplify. $18x$ is eliminated.
$\quad\quad\quad\quad\quad\quad \dfrac{41y}{41} = \dfrac{123}{41}$ Divide both sides by 41.
$\quad\quad\quad\quad\quad\quad\quad y = 3$ Simplify.

Substitute 3 for y into Equation 1:
$\quad 2x + 5(3) = 11$
$\quad\quad 2x + 15 = 11$
$2x + 15 - 15 = 11 - 15$ Subtract 15 from both sides.
$\quad\quad\quad\quad 2x = -4$ Simplify.
$\quad\quad\quad\quad \dfrac{2x}{2} = \dfrac{-4}{2}$ Divide both sides by 2.
$\quad\quad\quad\quad\quad x = -2$ Simplify.

The solution to the system of linear equations is given by $x = -2$, $y = 3$.

▶ **Method 2**
Eliminate the y terms first.

Multiply Equation 1 by 2:
$2 \cdot (2x + 5y) = 2 \cdot 11$
$\quad 4x + 10y = 22$ (Equation 3)

Multiply Equation 2 by 5:

$5 \cdot (9x + 2y) = 5 \cdot (-12)$

$\quad 45x + 10y = -60 \qquad$ (Equation 4)

Subtract Equation 4 from Equation 3:

$(4x + 10y) - (45x + 10y) = 22 - (-60)$

$\qquad 4x + 10y - 45x - 10y = 82 \qquad$ Use the distributive property.

$\qquad\qquad\qquad\quad -41x = 82 \qquad$ Simplify. $10y$ is eliminated.

$\qquad\qquad\qquad \dfrac{-41x}{-41} = \dfrac{82}{-41} \qquad$ Divide both sides by -41.

$\qquad\qquad\qquad\qquad x = -2 \qquad$ Simplify.

Either way, the solution to the system of linear equations is given by $x = -2$, $y = 3$.

Check

Substitute the solution into Equation 2.

$9(-2) + 2(3) = -12$

When $x = -2$ and $y = 3$, the equation $9x + 2y = -12$ is true.

So, the solution is correct.

Math Talk

In **Method 2**, does it matter which equation you substitute x into to find the value of y? Explain.

TRY **Practice using the elimination method to solve systems of linear equations without common terms**

Use the elimination method to solve the system of linear equations.

1. $7m + 2n = -8$
   $2m = 3n - 13$

You can either eliminate the m terms first or the n terms first.

Consider the following system of linear equations.

$y = 3x - 8$
$2x + 4y = 12$

In your own words, explain the meaning of the first equation. Then, think about how to solve the system of linear equations without using the elimination method.

LEARN Solve systems of linear equations using the **substitution method**

1. You have learned to use the elimination method to solve systems of linear equations.

   Look again at the system of linear equations and the bar models representing the equations.

   $x + y = 8$
   $x + 2y = 10$

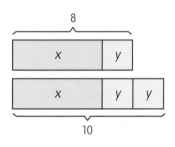

   You can redraw the bar representing x as $8 - y$.

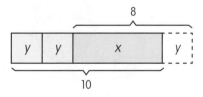

   You can redraw the bar model for $x + 2y = 10$ by replacing x with $8 - y$.

   The equation $x + 2y = 10$ becomes $(8 - y) + 2y = 10$.

Observe $8 + y = 10$ from the bar model.

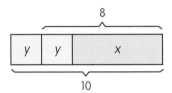

So, $y = 10 - 8$
      $= 2$.

From the bar model representing $x + y = 8$, $x + 2 = 8$. So, $x = 6$.

You can solve this system of linear equations using the same approach algebraically, that is, the substitution method.

$x + y = 8$ (Equation 1)
$x + 2y = 10$ (Equation 2)

Use Equation 1 to express x in terms of y:

$x + y = 8$
$x + y - \textbf{y} = 8 - \textbf{y}$ Subtract y from both sides.
$\quad\quad x = 8 - y$ (Equation 3) Simplify.

Substitute Equation 3 into Equation 2 to obtain an equation with only one variable:

$(8 - y) + 2y = 10$
$\quad\quad 8 + y = 10$ Simplify.
$8 + y - \textbf{8} = 10 - \textbf{8}$ Subtract 8 from both sides.
$\quad\quad\quad y = 2$ Simplify.

Substitute 2 for y into Equation 3 to obtain $x = 8 - 2 = 6$.

So, the solution to the system of linear equations is given by $x = 6$, $y = 2$.

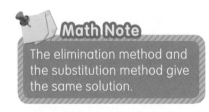

Math Note

The elimination method and the substitution method give the same solution.

Math Talk

Could you solve for y in terms of x and then solve the system of linear equations using the same method? Justify your answer.

The substitution method consists of three steps.

STEP 1 Select one equation. Express one variable in terms of the other.

STEP 2 Substitute this new equation into the second equation to find the value of one variable.

STEP 3 Substitute this value into one of the equations to find the value of the other variable.

2 Use the substitution method to solve the system of linear equations.

$3x - y = 18$ (Equation 1)
$y = x - 4$ (Equation 2)

Substitute Equation 2 into Equation 1:

$3x - (x - 4) = 18$
$3x - x + 4 = 18$ Use the distributive property.
$2x + 4 = 18$ Simplify.
$2x + 4 - 4 = 18 - 4$ Subtract 4 from both sides.
$2x = 14$ Simplify.
$\dfrac{2x}{2} = \dfrac{14}{2}$ Divide both sides by 2.
$x = 7$ Simplify.

Substitute 7 for x into Equation 2 to obtain $y = 7 - 4 = 3$.

So, the solution to the system of linear equations is given by $x = 7$, $y = 3$.

> **Check**
>
> Substitute the solution into Equation 1.
>
> $3(7) - 3 = 18$
>
> When $x = 7$ and $y = 3$, the equation $3x - y = 18$ is true.
>
> So, the solution is correct.

3 Use the substitution method to solve the system of linear equations.

$3p + 2q = 4$ (Equation 1)
$3p - 5q = \dfrac{1}{2}$ (Equation 2)

Use Equation 1 to express $3p$ in terms of q:
$3p + 2q = 4$
$3p + 2q - 2q = 4 - 2q$ Subtract $2q$ from both sides.
$3p = 4 - 2q$ (Equation 3)   Simplify.

Substitute Equation 3 into Equation 2:
$4 - 2q - 5q = \dfrac{1}{2}$
$4 - 7q = \dfrac{1}{2}$ Simplify.
$4 - 7q - 4 = \dfrac{1}{2} - 4$ Subtract 4 from both sides.
$-7q = -\dfrac{7}{2}$ Simplify.
$-7q \div (-7) = -\dfrac{7}{2} \div (-7)$ Divide both sides by –7.
$q = \dfrac{1}{2}$ Simplify.

You cannot substitute Equation 3 into Equation 1. Why?

Substitute $\frac{1}{2}$ for q into Equation 3:

$3p = 4 - 2\left(\frac{1}{2}\right)$

$3p = 3$ Simplify.

$\frac{3p}{3} = \frac{3}{3}$ Divide both sides by 3.

$p = 1$ Simplify.

You can also substitute $\frac{1}{2}$ for q into Equation 1 or Equation 2 and obtain $p = 1$. However, you obtain the value of p more quickly by substituting $\frac{1}{2}$ for q into Equation 3.

So, the solution to the system of linear equations is given by $p = 1$, $q = \frac{1}{2}$.

Check

Substitute the solution into Equation 2.

$3(1) - 5\left(\frac{1}{2}\right) = \frac{1}{2}$

When $p = 1$ and $q = \frac{1}{2}$, the equation $3p - 5q = \frac{1}{2}$ is true.

So, the solution is correct.

TRY Practice using the substitution method to solve systems of linear equations

Use the substitution method to solve each system of linear equations.

1. $2x + y = 5$
    $y = 4x - 7$

    $2x + (4x - 7) = 5$
    $6x - 7 = 5$
    $ +7 \quad +7$
    $\frac{6x}{6} = \frac{12}{6}$
    $\boxed{x = 2}$

    $y = 4(2) - 7$
    $y = 8 - 7$
    $\boxed{y = 1}$

    $(2, 1)$

    $2(2) + 1 = 5$
    $4 + 1 = 5$
    $\boxed{5 = 5}$ ✓

2. $4x + 3y = 23$
    $5x + y = 15$

Consider the following system of linear equations.

$p + 10 = r$
$3p + 4r = 12$

Would you solve them using the elimination method or the substitution method? Explain your thinking.

LEARN **Choose a method to solve a system of linear equations**

1   Use the elimination method or the substitution method to solve the system of linear equations.

$3p + 2q = 1$ (Equation 1)
$2p - 5q = -12$ (Equation 2)

Use the elimination method to solve the equations.

If you use the substitution method, you have to express p in terms of q or q in terms of p. Either way, you obtain an algebraic fraction that makes the steps complicated. So, you may want to use the elimination method instead.

Multiply Equation 1 by 2:

$\mathbf{2} \cdot (3p + 2q) = 1 \cdot \mathbf{2}$
$6p + 4q = 2$ (Equation 3) Use the distributive property and simplify.

Multiply Equation 2 by 3:
$\mathbf{3} \cdot (2p - 5q) = -12 \cdot \mathbf{3}$
$6p - 15q = -36$ (Equation 4) Use the distributive property and simplify.

Subtract Equation 4 from Equation 3:
$6p + 4q - (6p - 15q) = 2 - (-36)$
$6p + 4q - 6p + 15q = 2 + 36$ Use the distributive property.
$19q = 38$ Simplify.
$\dfrac{19q}{19} = \dfrac{38}{19}$ Divide both sides by 19.
$q = 2$ Simplify.

Substitute 2 for q into Equation 1:

$$3p + 2(2) = 1$$
$$3p + 4 = 1 \qquad \text{Simplify.}$$
$$3p + 4 - 4 = 1 - 4 \qquad \text{Subtract 4 from both sides.}$$
$$3p = -3 \qquad \text{Simplify.}$$
$$3p \div 3 = -3 \div 3 \qquad \text{Divide both sides by 3.}$$
$$p = -1 \qquad \text{Simplify.}$$

So, the solution to the system of linear equations is given by $p = -1$, $q = 2$.

Check

$$2(-1) - 5(2) = -12$$

When $p = -1$ and $q = 2$, the equation $2p - 5q = -12$ is true.

So, the solution is correct.

2 Use the elimination method or the substitution method to solve the system of linear equations.

$$5a - 2b = 8 \qquad \text{(Equation 1)}$$
$$b = 2a - 2 \qquad \text{(Equation 2)}$$

Use the substitution method to solve the equations.

In this system of linear equations, you substitute the expression for b given in Equation 2 directly into Equation 1 since b is already expressed in terms of a. So, you choose the substitution method.

Substitute Equation 2 into Equation 1:

$$5a - 2(2a - 2) = 8$$
$$5a - 4a + 4 = 8 \qquad \text{Use the distributive property.}$$
$$a + 4 - 4 = 8 - 4 \qquad \text{Subtract 4 from both sides.}$$
$$a = 4 \qquad \text{Simplify.}$$

Substitute 4 for a into Equation 2:

$$b = 2(4) - 2$$
$$= 6 \qquad \text{Simplify.}$$

So, the solution to the system of linear equations is given by $a = 4$, $b = 6$.

Check

Substitute the solution into Equation 1.

$5(4) - 2(6) = 8$

When $a = 4$ and $b = 6$, the equation $5a - 2b = 8$ is true.

So, the solution is correct.

TRY Practice choosing a method to solve a system of linear equations

Use the elimination method or substitution method to solve each system of linear equations. Explain why you choose each method.

① $2x + 3y = 29$
$2x - 17 = y$

② $3a - 2b = 5$
$2a - 5b = 51$

$2x + 3y = 29$
$2x + 3(2x - 17) = 29$
$2x + 6x - 51 = 29$
$+51 \quad +51$

$2(10) - 17 = y$ $\dfrac{8x}{8} - \dfrac{80}{8}$
$20 - 17 = y$

$\boxed{3 = y}$ $\boxed{x = 10}$

$\boxed{(10,3)}$ $2(10) + 13(3) = 29$
$20 + 3(3) = 29$
$20 + 9 = 29$
$\boxed{29 = 29}$ ✓

© 2020 Marshall Cavendish Education Pte Ltd

MATH SHARING

Mathematical Habit 2 Use mathematical reasoning

Sam wants to use the elimination method to solve the following system of linear equations without using a calculator.

$2x + 3y = 1$
$3x - 17y = 23$

He can multiply the first equation by 3 and the second equation by 2 in order to eliminate x. Or he can eliminate y by multiplying the first equation by 17 and the second equation by 3. Which way should Sam choose? What other way can he use to get the solution? Discuss.

INDEPENDENT PRACTICE

Use the elimination method to solve each system of linear equations.

1 $3x - y = 9$
$+ 2x + y = 7$

$5x + 0 = 2$ $(2, -3)$

$\boxed{x = 2}$

$3(2) - y = 9$
$6 - y = 9$
$-6 \quad -6$

$\boxed{y = 3}$

2 $5s - t = 12$
$3s + t = 12$

3 $2b + c = 10$
$+ 2b - c = 6$

$4b + 0 = 16$

$\dfrac{4b}{4} = \dfrac{16}{4}$ $(4, 2)$

$B = 4$

$2(4) + c = 10$
$8 + c = 10$
$-8 \quad -8$

$c = 2$

4 $3m - n = 7$
$21m + 6n = -29$

5 $7a + b = 10$
$+2a + 3b = -8$

$\overline{9a + 4b = 2}$
$-9a \quad\quad -9a$

$\dfrac{4b}{4} = \dfrac{-9a + 2}{4}$

$7(2) + b = 16$

$14 + b = 16$

$-14 \quad -14$

$\boxed{b = -4}$

$7(2) + (-4) = 16$

$14 - 4 = 16$

$\boxed{0 = 16}$

$5 = \dfrac{-9}{4}a + \dfrac{2}{4}$

$\left(\dfrac{-9a + 2}{a}\right) = 16 \, (2, 9)$

$4\tfrac{3}{4}a + \dfrac{2}{4} = 16$

$-\dfrac{2}{4} \quad\quad -\dfrac{2}{4}$

$\dfrac{4\tfrac{3}{4}a}{4\tfrac{3}{4}} = \dfrac{9.5}{4\tfrac{3}{4}}$: $\boxed{a = 2}$

6 $2p + 5q = 4$
$7p + 15q = 9$

Use the substitution method to solve each system of linear equations.

7 $3h - k = 10$
$+h - k = 2$

$\overline{4h - 2k = 12}$
$-4h + 2k - 4h$
$-4h \quad\quad -4h$

$-8 + k = 2$
$+8 \quad\quad +8$

$\dfrac{-k}{-1} = \dfrac{-10}{-1}$

8 $3s - t = 5$
$s + 2t = 4$

9 $2x + y = 20$
$3x + 4y = 40$

10 $3x + 2y = 0$
$5x - 2y = 32$

11 $5x - y = 20$
$4x + 3y = 16$

12 $3p + 4q = 3$
$\dfrac{1}{2} + q = 3p$

Use the elimination method or substitution method to solve each system of linear equations. Explain why you choose each method.

◎ $7m + 2n = 20$
$2m = 3m - 5$

14 $3h - 4k = 35$
$k = 2h - 20$

◐ $2h + 7k = 32$
$3h - 2k = -2$

16 $2m + 4 = 3n$
$5m - 3n = -1$

Name: ______________________ Date: ______________

3 Real-World Problems: Systems of Linear Equations

Learning Objective:
- Solve real-world problems using systems of linear equations.

New Vocabulary
standard form

THINK

In an experiment, James was given two saline (salt) solutions with the concentrations shown below.

	Volume of Solution (fl oz)	Concentration of Solution (%)
Saline Solution A	x	30
Saline Solution B	y	18

He had to prepare 10 fluid ounces of a new saline solution at a concentration of 27% from the two solutions. Calculate the volume of each solution used to prepare the new solution.

ENGAGE

Mr. Smith buys a total of 15 apples and grapefruits for \$24. Each apple costs \$1 and each grapefruit costs \$2. If a represents the number of apples and g represents the number of grapefruits, what are the two equations you can write to find how many of each fruit he bought? Explain your thinking.

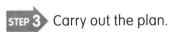

LEARN Solve real-world problems using a systems of linear equations

1 At a carnival, 700 tickets were sold for a total amount of \$5,500. An adult ticket cost \$10. A child ticket cost \$5. Find the number of adult tickets and the number of child tickets sold.

STEP 1 Understand the problem.

How many tickets were sold altogether? What were the costs of an adult ticket and a child ticket? What do I need to find?

STEP 2 Think of a plan.
I can write two algebraic equations.

STEP 3 Carry out the plan.

This problem gives us data about the numbers of tickets and the prices of tickets, so the given information can be organized into a table. Use two variables to represent the number of adult tickets sold and the number of child tickets sold, because this is what you are asked to find.

Let a be the number of adult tickets sold and c be the number of child tickets sold.

	Number of Tickets	Ticket Sales (dollars)
Adult Tickets	a	$10a$
Child Tickets	c	$5c$
Total	$a + c$	$10a + 5c$

Use the algebraic expressions to write two algebraic equations. Remember, you know the total number of tickets sold (700) and the total sales of these tickets ($5,500).

Relate the sales of the tickets:

$10a$	+	$5c$	=	$5,500$
Sales of adult tickets		Sales of child tickets		Total sales

Relate the number of tickets:

a	+	c	=	700
Number of adult tickets sold		Number of child tickets sold		Total tickets sold

> **Math Note**
>
> The linear equations in a system of equations are usually written in the form $px + qy = r$, where p, q, and r are constants. This is called the standard form of a linear equation. When solving a system of linear equations by elimination, both equations may be in standard form.

Solve the system of linear equations.
$10a + 5c = 5,500$ (Equation 1)
$a + c = 700$ (Equation 2)

> You can choose the elimination method or the substitution method to solve a system of linear equations. The elimination method is used here.

Multiply Equation 2 by 10:
$\mathbf{10} \cdot (a + c) = \mathbf{10} \cdot 700$
$10a + 10c = 7,000$ (Equation 3)   Use the distributive property.

Subtract Equation 1 from Equation 3:
$10a + 10c - (10a + 5c) = 7,000 - 5,500$
$10a + 10c - 10a - 5c = 1,500$ Use the distributive property.
$5c = 1,500$ Simplify.
$\dfrac{5c}{5} = \dfrac{1,500}{5}$ Divide both sides by 5
$c = 300$ Simplify.

Substitute 300 for c into Equation 2:
$a + 300 = 700$
$a + 300 - \mathbf{300} = 700 - \mathbf{300}$ Subtract 300 from both sides.
$a = 400$ Simplify.

400 adult tickets and 300 child tickets were sold.

STEP 4 Check the answer.
I can use the values obtained to substitute into
Equation 1 to check if they make the equation true.

$(10 \cdot 400) + (5 \cdot 300) = 5,500$
My answer is correct.

2 The difference between the length, ℓ inches, and the
width, w inches, of the shaded face of the box is 4 inches.
The face has a perimeter of 52 inches. Find the length
and the width.

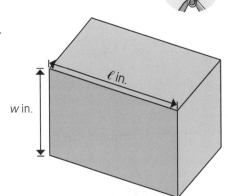
ℓ in.

w in.

Length: $\ell = w + 4$ (Equation 1)
Perimeter: $2\ell + 2w = 52$ (Equation 2)

Divide Equation 2 by 2:
$$\frac{2\ell + 2w}{2} = \frac{52}{2}$$
$\ell + w = 26$ (Equation 3)   Simplify.

Substitute Equation 1 into Equation 3:
$(w + 4) + w = 26$
$\quad\quad 2w + 4 = 26$ Simplify.
$2w + 4 - 4 = 26 - 4$ Subtract 4 from both sides.
$\quad\quad\quad 2w = 22$ Simplify.
$\quad\quad\quad \frac{2w}{2} = \frac{22}{2}$ Divide both sides by 2.
$\quad\quad\quad\quad w = 11$ Simplify.

Substitute 11 for w into Equation 1:
$\ell = 11 + 4$
$ = 15$

The length is 15 inches and the width is 11 inches.

 Math Talk

There is often more than one way to solve a problem. To solve this system using elimination,
how would you rewrite Equation 1? How can you solve this problem using one equation with
one variable?

3 Katherine gave the following riddle to her friend to solve. There are two numbers. The sum of
the first number and twice the second number is 14. When the second number is subtracted
from the first number, the result is 2. What are the two numbers?

Let the first number be x and the second number be y.

Sum of the first number and twice the second number:
$x + 2y = 14$ Equation 1

Second number subtracted from first number:
$x - y = 2$ Equation 2

Subtract Equation 2 from Equation 1:

$x + 2y - (x - y) = 14 - 2$

$x + 2y - x + y = 12$ Use the distributive property.

         $3y = 12$ Simplify.

        $\dfrac{3y}{3} = \dfrac{12}{3}$ Divide both sides by 3.

         $y = 4$ Simplify.

The elimination method is used here to solve the system of linear equations. Practice using the substitution method to solve.

Substitute 4 for y into Equation 2:

     $x - 4 = 2$

$x - 4 + 4 = 2 + 4$ Add both sides by 4.

       $x = 6$ Simplify.

The two numbers are 6 and 4.

TRY Practice solving real-world problems using a systems of linear equations

Use systems of linear equations.

① Two bowls and one cup have a mass of 800 grams. One bowl and two cups have a mass of 700 grams. Find the mass of a bowl and the mass of a cup.

You can let the mass of a bowl be b grams and the mass of a cup be c grams.

② Jennifer is thinking of a 2-digit number. When the tens digit is subtracted from the ones digit, the difference is 2. One-fifth of the number is 1 less than the sum of the digits. What is the number?

A 2-digit number can be written as $10x + y$, where x is the first digit and y is the second digit.

INDEPENDENT PRACTICE

Use systems of linear equations to solve.

1. Morgan stocked her aquarium with 36 freshwater fish, which cost $212. Each male fish cost $5, while each female fish cost $7. Find the number of male fish and the number of female fish.

2. Isaac paid $2.75 for 4 granola bars and 1 apple. Amelia paid $2.25 for 2 granola bars and 3 apples. Find the cost of a granola bar and an apple.

3. 4 USB sticks and 1 compact disk have a total capacity of 9 gigabytes. 5 USB sticks have 9 gigabytes more capacity than 1 compact disk. Find the capacity of 1 USB stick and the capacity of 1 compact disk.

4 The length and width (in inches) of a notebook are shown in the diagram.

   a Find the values of a and b.

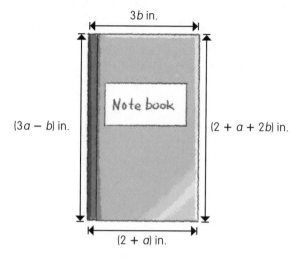

3b in.

$(3a - b)$ in.

Note book

$(2 + a + 2b)$ in.

$(2 + a)$ in.

   b Find the perimeter of the notebook.

5 Jasmine saves some dimes and quarters. She has 40 coins in her coin bank, which total up to $6.55.
How many of each coin does she have?

6 Melissa gave three riddles to her class to solve.

a The sum of the digits of a two-digit number is 11. Twice the tens digit plus 2 equals ten times the ones digit. What is the number?

b There are two numbers. The first number minus the second number is 15. One-third of the sum of the numbers is one-quarter of the first number. What are the two numbers?

c A 2-digit number is 1 more than eight times the sum of the digits. The ones digit is 3 less than the tens digit. What is the number?

7　On Saturday, $585 was collected from the sale of 55 tickets for a performance. The table below shows the information about the sale of the tickets.

	Number of Tickets	Cost of Each Ticket ($)
Adult Tickets	a	12
Student Tickets	s	25% discount

Find the number of adult tickets and the number of student tickets sold on that day.

8　Eight years ago, Elijah was six times as old as his son. In twelve years' time, he will be twice as old as his son. How old are they now?

	Elijah's Age (yr)	His Son's Age (yr)
Eight Years Ago	$f - 8$	$s - 8$
In Twelve Years' Time	$f + 12$	$s + 12$

9 A restaurant sells four combo meals. The Jolly Meal, which costs $12.60, consists of 2 yogurt cups and 1 sandwich. The Special Meal, which is made up of 2 sandwiches and 1 yogurt cup, costs $13.50. Calculate the cost of the following combo meals if the charges for the sandwiches and the yogurt cups are the same for all combo meals.

a Children's Meal: 1 sandwich and 1 yogurt cup

b Family Meal: 2 sandwiches and 3 yogurt cups

10 In a boat race, Arianna's team rowed their boat from point A to point B and back to point A. Points A and B are 30 miles apart. During the race, there was a constant current flowing from A to B. They took 2 hours to travel from A to B and 2.5 hours to travel from B to A.

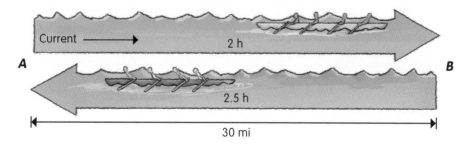

a Calculate the average speed of the boat from *A* to *B* and the average speed from *B* to *A*.

b Find the speed of the boat from *A* to *B* if there was no current.

c Find the speed of the current.

4 Solving Systems of Linear Equations by Graphing

Learning Objective:
• Solve systems of linear equations using the graphical method.

> **New Vocabulary**
> graphical method
> point of intersection

THINK

Taxi company A charges $8 for the flag-down fare and $0.75 for each mile of distance traveled. Taxi company B charges $3 for the flag-down fare and $1.25 for each mile of distance traveled. By forming two linear equations and drawing the graphs, decide which taxi company offers better value based on the distance you wish to travel.

ENGAGE

The graph of $y = x + 3$ is shown. On the same coordinate plane, draw the graph of $x + y = -1$.

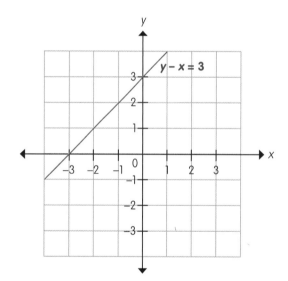

What do you think is the solution to the system of linear equations $y - x = 3$ and $x + y = -1$? Explain your thinking.

LEARN Solve systems of linear equations using the graphical method

Activity Exploring the graphical method of solving systems of linear equations

Work in pairs.

① Use the elimination method or substitution method to solve the system of linear equations.

$$x + 2y = 4$$
$$x - y = 1$$

② To solve this system of linear equations using a graphing calculator, solve each equation for *y* and enter each expression for *y* into the calculator.

> ⚠️ **Caution**
> Be sure to use parentheses around any fractional coefficients, and use the (−) key if the coefficient is negative.

③ Press the GRAPH key. Use the 2ND TRACE function and select "5: Intersect" to find where the two graphs intersect.

④ Repeat ① to ③ for the system of linear equations.
$$6x - 5y = -3$$
$$x + y = 5$$

⑤ **Mathematical Habit 7 Make use of structure**
How is the solution found in ① related to the coordinates of the point of intersection in ③? Why do you think this happens?

1 You can use the graphical method to solve systems of linear equations.

Consider the system of linear equations.

$y - x = 3$ Equation 1
$x + y = -1$ Equation 2

First, rewrite Equation 1 in slope-intercept form as $y = x + 3$. Then, graph the linear equation $y - x = 3$ on a coordinate plane.

> The graph has a slope of 1, and intersects the y-axis at (0, 3).

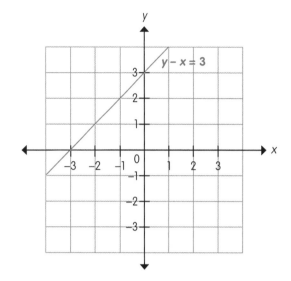

The point $(-3, 0)$ lies on the graph. It corresponds to values, $x = -3$, $y = 0$, which satisfy the equation $y - x = 3$. All pairs of values of x and y, which satisfy the equation $y - x = 3$, are represented by the points on the graph.

Next, rewrite Equation 2 in slope-intercept form as $y = -x - 1$ and graph the linear equation $x + y = -1$ on the same coordinate plane. All pairs of values of x and y that satisfy the equation $x + y = -1$ are represented by the points on the graph.

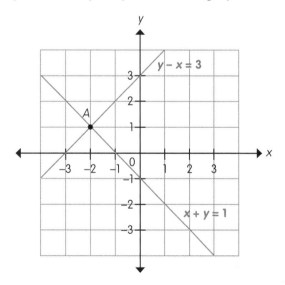

The two graphs intersect at $A(-2, 1)$. You say that A is the **point of intersection** of $y - x = 3$ and $x + y = -1$.

A is the only point that lies on both graphs.
This means that the corresponding values, $x = -2$
and $y = 1$, is the only pair of values that satisfy
both equations.

So, the system of linear equations has a unique solution
$x = -2$, $y = 1$.

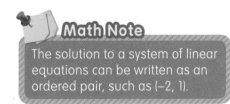

Math Note

The solution to a system of linear
equations can be written as an
ordered pair, such as (–2, 1).

Check

Substitute the solution into both equations.

For $y - x = 3$, $1 - (-2) = 3$.

For $x + y = -1$, $-2 + 1 = -1$.

When $x = -2$ and $y = 1$, both equations are true.

So, the solution is correct.

This method of solving systems of linear equations is called the graphical method.

The coordinates of the point of intersection may not be integers. In that case, you have to
estimate the coordinates, and the solution is approximate.

② Use the graphical method to solve the system of linear equations. Use 1 grid square on both
axes to represent 1 unit for the *x* interval from –1 to 4 and the *y* interval from 0 to 7.

$2x + y = 7$
$y - 3x = -3$

$2x + y = 7$

x	1	2	3
y	5	3	1

$y - 3x = -3$

x	1	2	3
y	0	3	6

Math Note

You only need to plot two points
to draw a linear graph. However,
using a third point will ensure
that your calculations are correct.

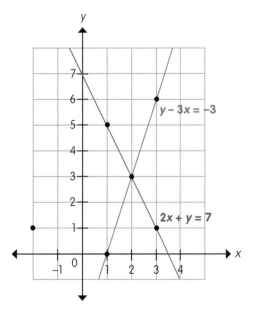

From the diagram, the coordinates of the point of intersection are (2, 3).

So, the solution to the system of linear equations is given by $x = 2$, $y = 3$.

Two intersecting lines can have only one point of intersection. So, a system whose graphs are two intersecting lines has a unique solution.

3 Two cars are traveling along a highway in the same direction. They take x hours to travel y miles from a point on the highway. Their motions are described by the following linear equations.

$y = 60x$
$y = 50x + 20$

Solve the system of linear equations graphically. When will the cars meet?

Draw the graphs of the two equations using the slope and y-intercept values.

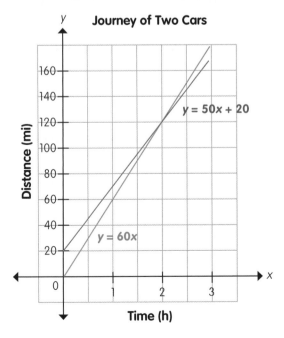

The point of intersection of the graphs is (2, 120).

So, the solution to the system of linear equations is given by $x = 2$, $y = 120$.

The cars will meet 2 hours later.

Because Distance = Rate · Time, the two equations tell many things about the journey of each car. For example, the speed of each car, whether they start at the same time and whether they start at the same place.

TRY Practice using the graphical method solving systems of linear equations

Use the graphical method to solve the system of linear equations.

1. $2x + y = 5$
   $x - y = -2$

$2x + y = 5$

x	0	1	2
y			

$x - y = -2$

x	0	1	2
y			

The coordinates of the point of intersection are (_____ , _____).

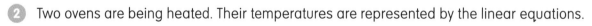

So, the solution to the system of linear equations is given by $x =$ _____ , $y =$ _____ .

Solve.

2. Two ovens are being heated. Their temperatures are represented by the linear equations.

   Oven 1: $T = t + 200$
   Oven 2: $T = 2t + 80$

   T is the temperature of the oven in °F and t is the time in seconds. Solve the system of linear equations graphically. When will the temperatures of the ovens be the same?

INDEPENDENT PRACTICE

Use the graphical method to solve each system of linear equations.

1 $x + y = 6$
$2x + y = 8$

2 $x + y = 5$
$x - y = 2$

3 $x + 2y = 5$
$2x - 2y = 1$

4 $2x + 3y = -1$
$x - 2y = 3$

5 $x = 2y$
$y = x + 2$

6 $y = 3$
$y = 2x + 1$

7 $x = 2$
$y = 2x - 8$

8 $3x - 2y = 19$
$3y = 2x - 21$

Solve.

9 Mary jogged from Point P to Point Q while Wyatt jogged from Point Q to Point P. Point P and point Q are 7.5 kilometers apart. Mary's motion is represented by $d = 8t$ and Wyatt's motion is represented by $2d + 14t = 15$, where t hours is the time and d kilometers is the distance from point P.

Wyatt
$2d + 14t = 15$

Mary
$d = 8t$

P ◄———————————————► Q

7.5 km

a Use the graphical method to solve the system of linear equations.

b When did Mary and Wyatt meet? How far from point Q did they meet?

10 Two cyclists are traveling along a track in the same direction. Their motions are described by the linear equations $d = 10t$ and $d - 8t = 2$, where t hours is the time and d miles is the distance from a point on the track.

a Use a graphing calculator to solve the system of linear equations.

b When will the cyclists meet?

5 Inconsistent and Dependent Systems of Linear Equations

Learning Objective:
• Identify inconsistent systems and dependent systems of linear equations.

> **New Vocabulary**
> inconsistent system of linear equations
> dependent system of linear equations

THINK

Consider the following systems of linear equations.

A $y = 2x + 4$
   $y = 2x - 3$

B $y = 2x + 4$
   $y = 2(x + 2)$

C $y = 2x + 4$
   $y = 4x + 1$

Solve each system. If the system does not have a solution, explain why.

ENGAGE

Try solving the system of linear equations $y = 2x + 10$ and $y - 2x = 4$ using any of the methods you have learned. What can you say about the solution? Discuss.

LEARN Identify inconsistent systems of linear equations

1. You have learned to find the unique solution to a system of linear equations, when it exists. However, not every system of linear equations has a unique solution. Consider this system of linear equations.

   $2x + y = 1$ (Equation 1)
   $4x + 2y = 4$ (Equation 2)

   Look at what happens when you try to solve the system of linear equations using the elimination method.

   Multiply Equation 1 by 2:
   $2 \cdot (2x + y) = 2 \cdot 1$
   $\quad 4x + 2y = 2$ (Equation 3)   Use the distributive property.

   Subtract Equation 3 from Equation 2:
   $(4x + 2y) - (4x + 2y) = 4 - 2$
   $\quad 4x + 2y - 4x - 2y = 2$ Use the distributive property.
   $\quad\quad\quad\quad\quad 0 = 2$ Simplify. False statement.

   Because $0 \neq 2$, the system of linear equations has no solution.

A system of linear equations with no solution is an inconsistent system of equations.

Sometimes when you try to eliminate a variable, you end up eliminating both variables instead. Then, you cannot have a unique solution.

Look what happens when you try to use the graphical method to solve the system of linear equations. Make a table of values for each equation.

$2x + y = 1$

x	0	1	2
y	1	−1	−3

$4x + 2y = 4$

x	0	1	2
y	2	0	−2

Use the tables of values to graph the system of linear equations on the same coordinate plane.

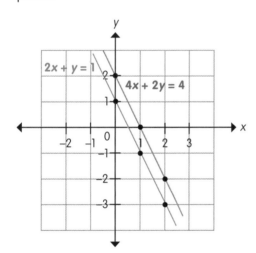

The linear graphs have the same slope, hence they are parallel.

The graphs of the equations are parallel lines, hence there is no point of intersection. Since there are no common point that lies on both graphs, the system of linear equations has no solution.

Write each linear equation in the form $y = mx + b$ to find the slope and y–intercept of its graph.

$$2x + y = 1$$
$$2x + y - \mathbf{2x} = 1 - \mathbf{2x} \quad \text{Subtract } 2x \text{ from both sides.}$$
$$y = -2x + 1 \quad \text{Simplify and write in slope-intercept form.}$$

So, the graph of Equation 1 has a slope of −2 and y-intercept 1.

$$4x + 2y = 4$$
$$(4x + 2y) \div \mathbf{2} = 4 \div \mathbf{2} \quad \text{Divide both sides by 2.}$$
$$2x + y = 2 \quad \text{Simplify.}$$
$$2x + y - \mathbf{2x} = 2 - \mathbf{2x} \quad \text{Subtract } 2x \text{ from both sides.}$$
$$y = -2x + 2 \quad \text{Simplify and write in slope-intercept form.}$$

So, the graph of Equation 2 has a slope of −2 and y-intercept 2.

When two graphs have the same slope and different *y*-intercepts, they are parallel.

This system of linear equations has no solution.

> A system of linear equations is inconsistent when the graphs of the equations have the same slope but different *y*-intercepts.

2 Consider another system of linear equations.

$$-3x + 2y = 2 \quad \text{Equation 1}$$
$$-6x + 4y = 6 \quad \text{Equation 2}$$

Use tables of values to graph the system of linear equations on the same coordinate plane.

$$-3x + 2y = 2$$

x	0	1	2
y	1	2.5	4

$$-6x + 4y = 6$$

x	−1	0	1
y	0	1.5	3

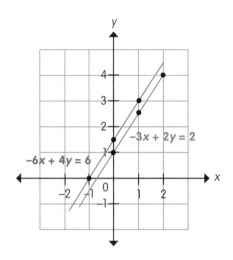

The graphs of the equations are parallel lines. So, this system of linear equations has no solution.

3 The two systems of linear equations that you have seen have no solutions and are inconsistent systems of linear equations.

$$2x + y = 1 \quad \text{Equation 1} \qquad -3x + 2y = 2 \quad \text{Equation 3}$$
$$4x + 2y = 4 \quad \text{Equation 2} \qquad -6x + 4y = 6 \quad \text{Equation 4}$$

Compare the coefficients and constants of Equation 2 with Equation 1 in the first system of linear equations.

	Coefficient of *x*	Coefficient of *y*	Constant
Equation 1	2	1	1
Equation 2	4	2	4
Ratio	$\frac{4}{2} = 2$	$\frac{2}{1} = 2$	$\frac{4}{1} = 4$

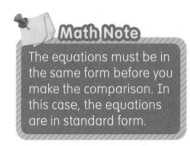

Math Note

The equations must be in the same form before you make the comparison. In this case, the equations are in standard form.

Observe that the coefficients of *x* and the coefficients of *y* have the same ratio and the constants have a different ratio.

You can make the same observation in the second system of linear equations when you compare the coefficients and constants of Equation 4 with Equation 3.

	Coefficient of x	Coefficient of y	Constant
Equation 3	–3	2	2
Equation 4	–6	4	6
Ratio	$\frac{-6}{-2} = 2$	$\frac{4}{2} = 2$	$\frac{6}{2} = 3$

If the coefficients of one equation are multiples of the coefficients of the other equation and the constants are in a different ratio, the system of linear equations is inconsistent.

4 Determine whether the system of linear equations is inconsistent or has a unique solution.

$2x + 2y = 3$ (Equation 1)
$x + y = 5$ (Equation 2)

▶ **Method 1**

Rewrite each linear equation in slope-intercept form, $y = mx + b$.

Equation 1

$$2x + 2y = 3$$
$2x + y - \mathbf{2x} = 3 - \mathbf{2x}$ Subtract $2x$ from both sides.
$\qquad 2y = 3 - 2x$ Simplify.
$\qquad \frac{2y}{2} = \frac{3 - 2x}{2}$ Divide both sides by 2.
$\qquad y = \frac{3}{2} - x$ Simplify.
$\qquad y = -x + \frac{3}{2}$ Write in slope-intercept form.

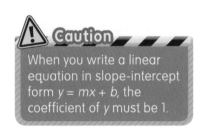
Caution
When you write a linear equation in slope-intercept form $y = mx + b$, the coefficient of y must be 1.

Equation 2

$$x + y = 5$$
$x + y - \mathbf{x} = 5 - \mathbf{x}$ Subtract x from both sides.
$\qquad y = 5 - x$ Simplify.
$\qquad y = -x + 5$ Write in slope-intercept form.

The slope of the graph of Equation 1 is –1 and the y-intercept is $\frac{3}{2}$. The slope of the graph of Equation 2 is –1 and the y-intercept is 5.

The graphs of the linear equations have the same slope and different y-intercepts. So, the system of linear equations is inconsistent.

▶ **Method 2**

Compare the coefficients and constants of Equation 2 to Equation 1.

	Coefficient of x	Coefficient of y	Constant
Equation 1	2	2	3
Equation 2	1	1	5
Ratio	$\frac{1}{2}$	$\frac{1}{2}$	$\frac{5}{3}$

The coefficients of x and y in Equation 1 are twice those of Equation 2. But the constant in Equation 1 is not twice the constant term in Equation 2.

So, the system of linear equations is inconsistent.

5 Determine whether the system of linear equations is inconsistent or has a unique solution.

$2x - 2y = 3$ (Equation 1)
$x + 4y = 20$ (Equation 2)

Rewrite each linear equation in slope-intercept form, $y = mx + b$.

Equation 1

$$2x - 2y = 3$$
$$2x - 2y - \textbf{2x} = 3 - \textbf{2x} \quad \text{Subtract } 2x \text{ from both sides.}$$
$$-2y = 3 - 2x \quad \text{Simplify.}$$
$$\frac{-2y}{-2} = \frac{3 - 2x}{-2} \quad \text{Divide both sides by 2.}$$
$$y = x - \frac{3}{2} \quad \text{Simplify and write in slope-intercept form.}$$

Equation 2

$$x + 4y = 20$$
$$x + 4y - \textbf{x} = 20 - \textbf{x} \quad \text{Subtract } x \text{ from both sides.}$$
$$4y = 20 - x \quad \text{Simplify.}$$
$$\frac{4y}{4} = \frac{20 - x}{4} \quad \text{Divide both sides by 4.}$$
$$y = -\frac{x}{4} + 5 \quad \text{Simplify and write in slope-intercept form.}$$

The slope of the graph of Equation 1 is 1 and the y-intercept is $-\frac{3}{2}$.
The slope of the graph of Equation 2 is $-\frac{1}{4}$ and the y-intercept is 5.

The graphs of the linear equations have different slopes and different y-intercepts. So, the system of linear equations has a unique solution.

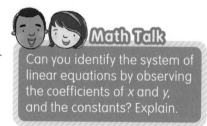

Math Talk

Can you identify the system of linear equations by observing the coefficients of x and y, and the constants? Explain.

Determine whether each system of linear equations is inconsistent or has a unique solution.

1 $11x + y = 2$
$22x + 2y = 3$

Rewrite each linear equation in slope-intercept form, $y = mx + b$.

Equation 1

$$11x + y = 2$$

$11x + y -$ _____ $= 2 -$ _____   Subtract _____ from both sides.

$y =$ _____ $+$ _____   Simplify.

Equation 2

$$22x + 2y = 3$$
$22x + 2y -$ _____ $= 3 -$ _____   Subtract _____ from both sides.
$2y = -22x + 3$ Simplify.
$\dfrac{2y}{\boxed{}} = \dfrac{-22x + 3}{\boxed{}}$ Divide both sides by _____.

$y =$ _____ $+$ _____ Simplify.

The slope of the graph of Equation 1 is _____ and the y-intercept is _____.

The slope of the graph of Equation 2 is _____ and the y-intercept is _____.

The graphs of the linear equations have the same _____ and different _____.

So, the system of linear equations _____.

2 $\dfrac{1}{2}x + y = 4$
$3x + 8y = 16$

ENGAGE

Try solving the system of linear equations $3x - 3y = 7$ and $6x - 6y = 14$ using any of the methods you have learned. What can you say about the solution? Discuss.

LEARN Identify dependent systems of linear equations

1 Consider the following system of linear equations.

$x + 2y = 2$ (Equation 1)
$2x + 4y = 4$ (Equation 2)

Look what happens when you try to solve the system of linear equations use the substitution method.

Use Equation 1 to express x in terms of y:

$x + 2y = 2$
$x + 2y - \mathbf{2y} = 2 - \mathbf{2y}$ Subtract 2 from both sides.
$x = 2 - 2y$ (Equation 3)   Simplify.

Substitute Equation 3 into Equation 2:

$2(2 - 2y) + 4y = 4$
$4 - 4y + 4y = 4$ Use the distributive property.
$4 = 4$ Simplify.

Since $4 = 4$ is always true regardless of the values of x and y, the system of linear equations has an infinite number of solutions.

> A system of linear equations with an infinite number of solutions is a dependent system of equations.

Look what happens when you solve the system of linear equations graphically. Make a table of values for each equation. Use the tables of values to graph the system of linear equations on the same coordinate plane.

$x + 2y = 2$

x	−1	0	1
y	1.5	1	0.5

$2x + 4y = 4$

x	−1	0	1
y	1.5	1	0.5

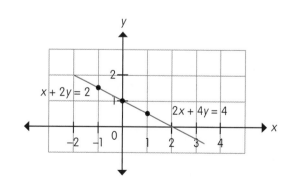

The two graphs form a single line. Since there are an infinite number of common points on the two graphs, the system of linear equations has an infinite number of solutions. Write each linear equation in slope-intercept form, $y = mx + b$.

Equation 1

$$x + 2y = 2$$
$$x + 2y - x = 2 - x \qquad \text{Subtract } x \text{ from both sides.}$$
$$2y = -x + 2 \qquad \text{Simplify.}$$
$$\frac{2y}{2} = \frac{-x + 2}{2} \qquad \text{Divide both sides by 2.}$$
$$y = -0.5x + 1 \qquad \text{Simplify.}$$

So, the slope of the graph of Equation 1 is –0.5 and the y-intercept is 1.

Equation 2

$$2x + 4y = 4$$
$$2x + 4y - 2x = 4 - 2x \qquad \text{Subtract } x \text{ from both sides.}$$
$$4y = -2x + 4 \qquad \text{Simplify.}$$
$$\frac{4y}{4} = \frac{-2x + 4}{4} \qquad \text{Divide both sides by 4.}$$
$$y = -0.5x + 1 \qquad \text{Simplify.}$$

So, the slope of the graph of Equation 2 is –0.5 and the y-intercept is 1.

When two linear graphs have the same slope and y-intercept, the graphs are the same. This system of linear equations has an infinite number of solutions.

You may notice that Equation 1 and Equation 2 are equivalent if you multiply Equation 1 by 2.

$$2 \cdot (x + 2y) = 2 \cdot 2$$
$$2x + 4y = 4$$

You may need to rewrite the equations in a system in the same form in order to tell whether one is a multiple of the other.

Checking to see if one equation is a multiple of the other is another way to check for dependent systems of equations.

2 Consider the following system of linear equations.

$$-3x + 2y = 2 \qquad \text{(Equation 1)}$$
$$-6x + 4y = 4 \qquad \text{(Equation 2)}$$

Make a table of values for each equation.

$$-3x + 2y = 2 \qquad\qquad -6x + 4y = 4$$

x	0	1	2
y	1	2.5	4

x	0	1	2
y	1	2.5	4

Use the tables of values to graph the system of linear equations on the same coordinate plane.

The graphs of the equations are the same. So, this system of linear equations has an infinite number of solutions.

A system of linear equations is dependent when the graphs of the equations have the same slope and y-intercept or if one equation is a multiple of the other.

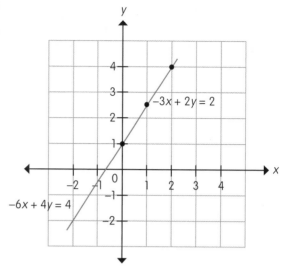

3 Determine whether the following system of linear equations is dependent.

$3x = 3 - 3y$ (Equation 1)
$x + y = 1$ (Equation 2)

Divide Equation 1 by 3 and write the equation in standard form:

$\dfrac{3x}{3} = \dfrac{3 - 3y}{3}$

$x = 1 - y$ Simplify.
$x + y = 1 - y + y$ Add y to both sides.
$x + y = 1$ Simplify.

Equation 1 and Equation 2 are equivalent. So, the system of linear equations is dependent.

4 Determine whether the following system of linear equations is dependent.

$4x + y = 2$ (Equation 1)
$x + y = 20$ (Equation 2)

Solve for y in both Equations 1 and 2:

$4x + y = 2$
$4x + y - 4x = 2 - 4x$ Subtract $4x$ from both sides.
$y = -4x + 2$ Simplify.

$x + y = 20$
$x + y - x = 20 - x$ Subtract x from both sides.
$y = -x + 20$ Simplify.

The graphs of the linear equations have different slopes and different y-intercepts. So, the system of linear equations is not dependent.

There is no number you can multiply Equation 2 by to obtain Equation 1, so these equations cannot be equivalent.

TRY Practice identifying dependent systems of linear equations

Identify whether each system of linear equations is inconsistent, dependent or has a unique solution.

1. $5x + 2y = 4$
   $20x + 8y = 30$

2. $7x + y = 14$
   $10x + 4y = 32$

3. $12x + 4y = 16$
   $9x + 3y = 12$

LET'S EXPLORE

Charles uses a cell phone plan that charges 2¢ per minute for local calls and 3.5¢ per minute for long distance calls. He made x minutes of local calls and y minutes of long distance calls in June. In July, he made 2x minutes of local calls and 2y minutes of long distance calls. His bill was $12 in June and $24 in July. Can he find the call duration of each type of call he made each month using these information? Why?

INDEPENDENT PRACTICE

Use a graphing calculator to graph each system of linear equations. Determine whether each system of linear equations is inconsistent or has a unique solution.

1 $3x + y = 4$
$6x + 2y = 14$

2 $10x + 5y = 15$
$x + y = 3$

3 $x - 2y = 14$
$4y = 5 + 2x$

Determine whether each system of linear equations is inconsistent, dependent or has a unique solution. Solve the system of linear equations if it has a unique solution.

4 $x + y = 3$
$8x + 8y = 32$

5 $6x + 2y = 12$
$3x + y = 21$

6 $3x - 6y = 12$
   $x - 2y = 4$
   $+2y \quad +2y$

   $x = 2y + 4$

   $x = 2(0) + 4$
   $x = 0 + 4$
   $x = 4$

   $3(2y + 4) - 6y = 12$
   $6y + 12 - 6y = 12$

   $y + 12 = 12$
   $\quad -12 \quad -12$
   $y = 0$

   $(4, 0)$

   infinite
   Solution

7 $-15x + 3y = 3$
   $-5x + y = 21$

8 $2x + y = 8$
   $4x - 2y = 24$

9 $8x + 7y = 9$
$40x + 35y = 45$

$\dfrac{40x}{40} = \dfrac{16}{40}$

$\boxed{x = 0.5}$

$8x + 7y = 9 \quad -8x$
$\dfrac{-8x \quad -7y}{7y} = 1$

$\dfrac{7y}{7} = \dfrac{1}{7}$

$\boxed{y = 8.14}$

$8(0.5) + 7(8.14) = 9$

$4 + 0.98 = 9$

$4.98 = 9$

infinite
Solution

Solve.

10 Jeremiah bought 9 apples and 6 apricots for $8.50 yesterday. He bought 3 apples and 2 apricots for $7.40 today.

a Write a system of linear equations to find the cost of an apple and the cost of an apricot.

Yesterday Today

9 apples and 6 apricots for $8.50   3 apples and 2 apricots for $7.40

b Determine whether the system of linear equations is inconsistent, dependent or has a unique solution.

c What does this tell you about the costs of apples and apricots on those two days?

⑪ Amanda gave the following riddle to her friend to solve. A string is 2 meters longer than a rod. Half of the rod is 1 meter shorter than half of the string. Is this true or false?

a Write a system of linear equations to find the length of the string and the length of the rod.

b Determine whether the system of linear equations is inconsistent, dependent or has a unique solution.

c Comment on Amanda's riddle.

Mathematical Habit 3 **Construct viable arguments**

Explain when it is convenient to use each method of solving a system of linear equations: elimination or substitution. Give an example for each method.

Problem Solving with Heuristics

1 **Mathematical Habit 1** **Persevere in solving problems**

In their bank accounts, Lillian has $110 and Jenna has $600. Lillian's account balance increases by $30 every year. Her account balance will be C dollars in x years. Jenna's account balance decreases by $40 every year. Her account balance will also be C dollars in x years.

a Write two equations of C in terms of x.

b Solve this system of linear equations to find the amounts in the girls' account balances when they are equal.

2 **Mathematical Habit 2** **Use mathematical reasoning**

Each block of Metal A and Metal B is a cube of side 1 centimeter. Five blocks of A and two blocks of B have a total mass of 44 grams. Three blocks of A and five blocks of B have a total mass of 34 grams. An alloy is made by melting and mixing two blocks of metal A and one block of metal B. Using the density formula, Density $= \dfrac{\text{Mass}}{\text{Volume}}$, find the density of the alloy.

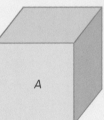

CHAPTER WRAP-UP

Real-world problems

can be translated to

Two Linear Equations in Two Variables

make up

Systems of Equations

can be solved using

Graphical Method

Substitution Method

Elimination Method

may be

Dependent Equations

are graphed as

The same line. The coordinates of any point on the line solve both equations.

Inconsistent Equations

are graphed as

Two parallel lines. No ordered pair satisfies both equations.

Equations with Unique Solution

are graphed as

Two intersecting lines. The coordinates of the point of intersection represent the unique solution.

KEY CONCEPTS

- A set of linear equations with more than one variable is called a system of linear equations.

- A system of linear equations can have a unique solution, no solution, or infinitely many solutions.

- A system of linear equations can be solved algebraically by using
  - the elimination method: eliminate one variable by adding or subtracting two equations with a common term, or
  - the substitution method: solve one equation for one variable and substitute the expression into the other equation.

- A system of linear equations can be solved graphically by graphing the equations and finding a point (or points) that both graphs have in common. If the coordinates of the points are not integers, the solution may only be an estimate.

- A system of linear equations is
  - inconsistent if the graphs of the equations have the same slope and different y-intercepts. The graphs of the two equations are parallel lines. Since the graphs have no points in common, the system has no solution.

  - dependent if the graphs of the equations have the same slope and the same y-intercept. The graphs of the two equations coincide, so every point on the line satisfies both equations.

  - solvable with a unique solution if the two equations have different slopes. The graphs of the two equations are two intersecting lines and the coordinates of the point of intersection represent the solution to the system.

- When the equations of a linear system are written in standard form, the two equations
  - are dependent if one equation is a multiple of the other,

  - are inconsistent if only the coefficients of x and y in one equation are multiples of the coefficients of the other equation, or

  - have a unique solution for all other cases.

- Real-world problems can be solved by writing and solving systems of linear equations.

Name: _____   Date: _____

Solve each system of linear equations by making tables of values. x **and** y **are positive integers.**

1 $x + y = 6$
   $x + 2y = 8$

2 $x + y = 8$
   $x - 3y = -8$

Use the elimination method to solve each system of linear equations.

3 $3x + 2y = 18$
   $2x + 3y = 22$

4 $5x + y = 8$
   $x + 3y = 10$

Use the substitution method to solve each system of linear equations.

⑤ $a + 2b = 1$
$2a + b = 8$

⑥ $\frac{1}{2}x + \frac{1}{2}y = 7$
$3x - y = 22 \quad -3x$

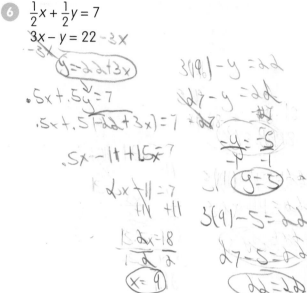

Use the graphical method to solve each system of linear equations.

⑦ $2x + 3y = 24$
$2x + y = 12$

⑧ $2x + 5y = 1$
$3x - y = -7$

Solve each system of linear equations. Explain your choice of method.

⑨ $x = 4y - 1$
$2x - 6y = -1$

⑩ $3x - 14y = -49$
$5x + 2y = 45$

Determine whether each system of linear equations is inconsistent, dependent or has a unique solution. Solve the system of linear equations if it has a unique solution.

11. $3x + 2y = 8$
    $6x + 4y = 16$

12. $\frac{x}{3} + y = 8$
    $x + 3y = 10$

13. $\frac{1}{2}x + y = 7$
    $x + 2y = 14$

14. $2x - 5y = -21$
    $4x + 3y = 23$

Solve

15 Adrian and Bryan both worked a total of 88 hours in a week. Bryan worked 8 hours more than Adrian. Find the number of hours each man had worked.

16 In 3 years' time, Cody will be 3 times as old as his daughter. Six years ago, he was 6 times as old as she was. How old are they now?

17 The shape *ABC* in the quilt block shown is an isosceles triangle, where *AB* = *AC*. The perimeter of the triangle is 27.3 inches. Find the values of *x* and *y*. Then, find the length of each side of the triangle.

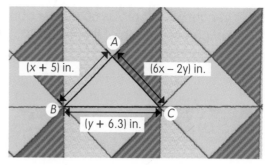

18 A bus company requires 4 buses and 8 vans to take 240 school children to the library. It requires 2 buses and 9 vans to take 170 children to the museum. Calculate the number of children a bus can carry and the number of children a van can carry.

19 At noon, Balloon *M* is 60 meters above ground and Balloon *N* is 50 meters above ground. Balloon *M* is rising at the rate of 10 meters per second, while Balloon *N* is rising at the rate of 15 meters per second.

a Write a system of two linear equations in which each equation gives the height, *h* meters, of a balloon *t* seconds after noon. Then, solve the system using a graphing calculator.

b How many seconds after noon will the two balloons be at the same height? How do you know?

20 The water levels in two identical tanks rise at a rate of 4 inches per second. The water level in Tank A is 3 inches at 0 seconds. The water level in Tank B is 16 inches after 3 seconds.

a Write a linear equation for the water level, *h* inches, in each of the tanks after *t* seconds.

b Graph the two equations on the same coordinate plane.

c When will the two tanks have the same water level? How do you know?

Assessment Prep
Answer each question.

21 A system of equations is shown.

$$x = 2$$
$$2x + 3y = 10$$

In the system of equations, what is the value of y?

Ⓐ $\dfrac{5}{6}$ Ⓑ $1\dfrac{1}{4}$

Ⓒ 1 Ⓓ 2

22 Consider the system of equations.

$$y = 3x + 5$$
$$y - 6x = 5$$

Which statements are true about the system of equations? Choose all that apply.

Ⓐ The graph of the system consists of lines that have more than one point of intersection.

Ⓑ The graph of the system consists of lines that have exactly one point of intersection.

Ⓒ The graph of the system consists of lines that have no points of intersection.

Ⓓ The system has more than one solution.

Ⓔ The system has exactly one solution.

Ⓕ The system has no solution.

23 The equations of the lines $y = 2x + 3$ and $y = 6 - x$ form a system of equations. The solution to the system of equations is located at point S. Which graph correctly shows the lines and point S?

Ⓐ

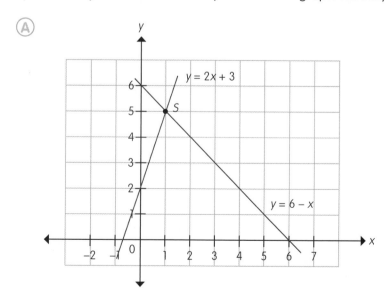

(B)

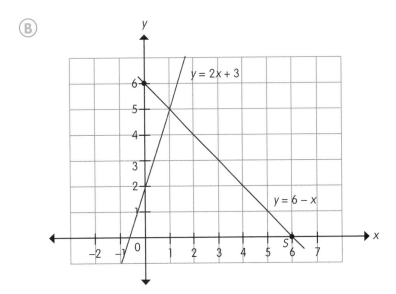

(C)

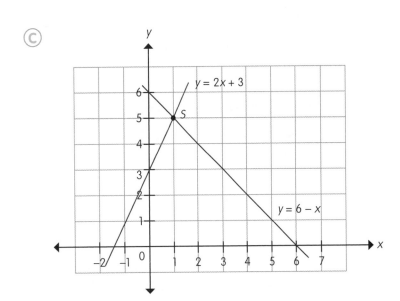

(D)

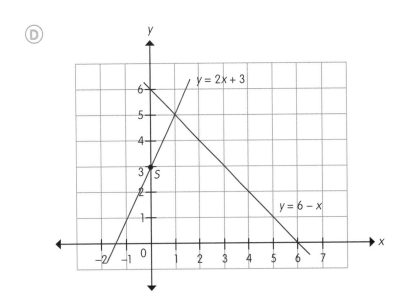

Name: _____   Date: _____

Trip to Niagara Falls

1 Aidan and Brandon are planning to drive to Niagara Falls during the school vacation. Aidan lives in Detroit and Brandon lives in Pittsburgh. They plan to meet in Cleveland before traveling to Niagara Falls. The distance from Detroit to Cleveland is 200 miles. The distance from Pittsburgh to Cleveland is 140 miles.

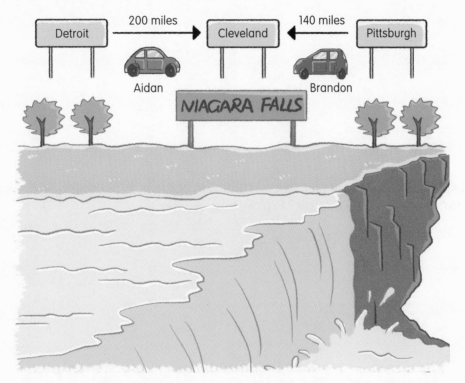

a Aidan wants to meet Brandon at 11 30 in Cleveland. If he travels at an average speed of 50 miles per hour, find his departure time from Detroit.

b If Brandon plans to leave his home at 09 30, what would his required average speed be?

c The speed limit is 70 miles per hour. If Brandon adheres to the speed limit, would his average speed in b be realistic? Explain your answer.

d Aidan and Brandon reach Cleveland as planned. Immediately, Aidan travels at an average speed of 40 miles per hour all the way to the Niagara Falls. If he reaches Niagara Falls at 17 00, find the distance from Cleveland to Niagara Falls.

e Brandon sets off from Cleveland at the same time as Aidan, traveling along the same route. He travels at an average speed of 50 miles per hour for part of the journey from Cleveland to Erie and rests for an hour. After that, he continues the remaining journey at an average speed of 48 miles per hour. If he reaches the Niagara Falls at the same time as Aidan, find the distance from Cleveland to Erie.

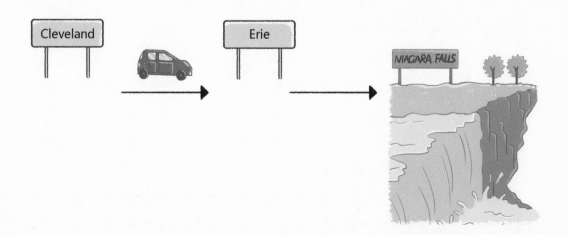

Rubric

Point(s)	Level	My Performance
7–8	4	• Most of my answers are correct. • I showed complete understanding of the concepts. • I used effective and efficient strategies to solve the problems. • I explained my answers and mathematical thinking clearly and completely.
5–6.5	3	• Some of my answers are correct. • I showed adequate understanding of the concepts. • I used effective strategies to solve the problems. • I explained my answers and mathematical thinking clearly.
3–4.5	2	• A few of my answers are correct. • I showed some understanding of the concepts. • I used some effective strategies to solve the problems. • I explained some of my answers and mathematical thinking clearly.
0–2.5	1	• A few of my answers are correct. • I showed little understanding of the concepts. • I used limited effective strategies to solve the problems. • I did not explain my answers and mathematical thinking clearly.

Teacher's Comments

Glossary

C

- **common term**

  The same term that appears more than once in a system of equations.

- **consistent equation**

  An equation with only one solution

  Example:

  $$3(x - 4) = 2(x - 1)$$
  $$3x - 12 = 2x - 2$$
  $$3x - 12 - \mathbf{2}x = 2x - 2 - \mathbf{2}x$$
  $$x - 12 = -2$$
  $$x - 12 + \mathbf{12} = -2 + \mathbf{12}$$
  $$x = 10$$

  The equation has one solution. The equation is a consistent equation.

- **cube root**

  The cube root of a number, when multiplied by itself twice, gives the number.

  Example: $4 \cdot 4 \cdot 4 = 64$

  4 is the cube root of 64.

D

- **dependent system of equations**

  A system of equations with an infinite number of solutions

  Example:

  $$3x = 3 - 3y \quad \text{Equation 1}$$
  $$x + y = 1 \quad \text{Equation 2}$$

  Divide Equation 1 by 3 and write the equation in standard form:

  $$\frac{3x}{3} = \frac{3 - 3y}{3}$$
  $$x = 1 - y$$
  $$x + y = 1 - y + y$$
  $$x + y = 1$$

  Equation 1 and Equation 2 are equivalent. So, the system of linear equations is dependent.

E

- **elimination method**

  A method for solving a system of equations in which equations are added or subtracted to eliminate one variable.

  Example:

  $$4x + y = 9 \quad \text{Equation 1}$$
  $$3x - y = 5 \quad \text{Equation 2}$$

  Add Equation 1 and Equation 2:
  $$(4x + y) + (3x - y) = 9 + 5$$
  $$4x + 3x + y - y = 14$$
  $$7x = 14$$
  $$\frac{7x}{7} = \frac{14}{7}$$
  $$x = 2$$

  Substitute 2 for x into Equation 1:
  $$4(2) + y = 9$$
  $$8 + y = 9$$
  $$y = 1$$

  So, the solution to the system of linear equations is given by $x = 2$, $y = 1$.

- **exponential notation**

  Notation used to write a number as a base raised to an exponent.

  Example: 2^3, 3^5, and 6^9 are numbers in exponential notation.

G

- **graphical method**

  A method in which equations are graphed to find the point (or points) of intersection.

I

- **identity**

  An equation that is true for all values of the variable.

  Example:

  $$3x + 5 = x + 2x + 5$$
  $$3x + 5 = 3x + 5$$
  $$3x + 5 - \mathbf{3x} = 3x + 5 - \mathbf{3x}$$
  $$5 = 5$$

- **inconsistent equation**

  An equation with no solution

  Example:

  $$5(x + 3) = 5x + 3$$
  $$5x + 15 = 5x + 3$$
  $$5x + 15 - \mathbf{5x} = 5x + 3 - \mathbf{5x}$$
  $$15 = 3$$

  The equation has no solution. The equation is an inconsistent equation.

- **inconsistent system of equations**

  A system of equations with no solution

  Example:

  $$2x + y = 1 \qquad \text{Equation 1}$$
  $$4x + 2y = 4 \qquad \text{Equation 2}$$

  Multiply Equation 1 by 2:
  $$2 \cdot (2x + y) = 2 \cdot 1$$
  $$4x + 2y = 2 \qquad \text{Equation 3}$$
  Subtract Equation 3 from Equation 2:
  $$(4x + 2y) - (4x + 2y) = 4 - 2$$
  $$4x + 2y - 4x - 2y = 2$$
  $$0 = 2$$

Because $0 \neq 2$, the system of linear equations has no solution.

- **irrational number**

  A number that cannot be written as $\frac{m}{n}$, where m and n are integers with $n \neq 0$.

  Examples: π and $\sqrt{2}$ are irrational numbers.

L

- **linear relationship**

  A relationship between two quantities in which there is a constant variation between the two quantities.

P

- **point of intersection**

  A point where two (or more) graphs meet each other and whose coordinates are the solution to a system of equations.

R

- **real number**

  A number that is either rational or irrational.

  Example: 3, $-\frac{2}{3}$, and π are real numbers.

- **rise**

  The vertical change from one point to a second point on a coordinate plane

Examples:

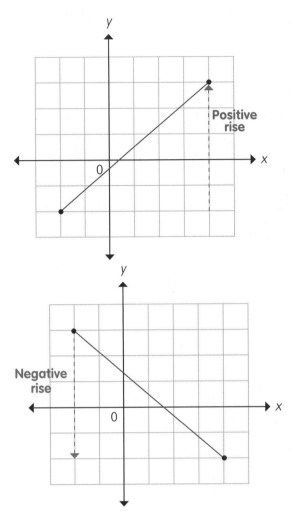

Positive rise

Negative rise

S

- **scientific notation**

  A way of expressing a large or small number in the form $A \cdot 10n$, where $1 \leq A < 10$ and n is an integer.

  Example: $1.38 \cdot 10^{-2}$ and $5.59 \cdot 10^{12}$ are numbers in scientific notation.

- **significant digit**

  The digit that is certain or that is estimated in a number.
  The number of significant digits shows the precision of the estimation.

  Examples: 2.506 has 4 significant digits.
  2.560 has 4 significant digits.
  0.256 has 3 significant digits.

- **slope**

  The ratio of the rise, or vertical change, to the run, or horizontal change, between any two points on a nonvertical line on the coordinate plane

  Example:

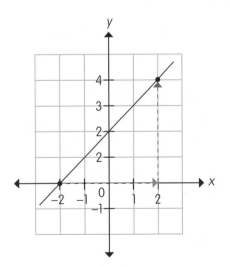

- **run**

  The horizontal change from one point to a second point on a coordinate plane

  Example:

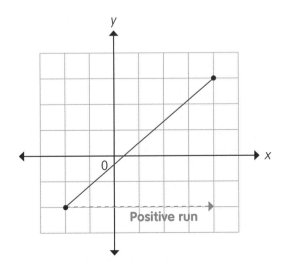

Positive run

$$\text{Slope} = \frac{\text{Rise}}{\text{Run}}$$

$$= \frac{4-0}{2-(-2)}$$

$$= \frac{4}{4}$$

$$= 1$$

- **slope-intercept form**

  A form of a linear equation, $y = mx + b$, where m is the slope and b is the y-intercept of the graph of the equation.

  Example: $y = \frac{5}{4}x - 3$ is a linear equation written in slope-intercept form.

- **square root**

  The square root of a number, when multiplied by itself, gives the number.

  Example: 3 is the positive square root of 9.
  $3 \cdot 3 = 9$
  -3 is the negative square root of 9.
  $-3 \cdot (-3) = 9$

- **standard form (of a linear equation)**

  A linear equation in the form $ax + by = c$.

  Example: $2x + 4y = 3$ is an example of a linear equation written in standard form.

- **standard form (of numbers)**

  A way of expressing a number using the ten digits 0 to 9 and place value notation.

  Example: -0.005, 9, and 2,158 are numbers in standard form.

- **substitution method**

  A method for solving a system of equations in which one variable is expressed in terms of the other to eliminate one variable

- **system of linear equations**

  A set of linear equations that has more than one variable

- **unique solution**

  The single set of values that satisfies a system of linear equations

- ***x*-intercept**

  The x-coordinate of the point where a line intersects the x-axis

  Example:

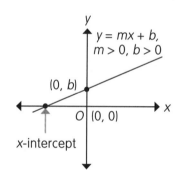

  x-intercept

- ***y*-intercept**

  The y-coordinate of the point where a line intersects the y-axis

  Example:

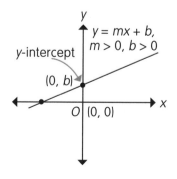

Index

Pages in **boldface** type show where a term is introduced.

Dependent
  systems of linear equations, **363**–364, 366,
    see also, Equations, Linear equations,
    System of linear equations
  variables, 280

Direct proportion, 220–222, 246

Division
  rules, 49
  decimals by positive powers of 10, 112
  expressions in exponential notation, 57–58
  of integers, 43
  in scientific notation, 135, 137–138

E

Elimination method, **321**–326

Equations
  adding, 323
  algebraic, 313
  consistent, **172**, 208
  direct proportion, 220
  equivalent, 158
  inconsistent, **171**, 208
  linear, 157
    graphing, 271–276, 312
    real-world problems, 167–168, 279
    relationship between two quantities, 159
    solving with one variable, 163–164
    systems of linear equations, 315–343
    using
      m and a point, 276
      m and b, 273–275
      a table of values, 271–273, 312
    variable in a two-variable, 191–192, 194
    with infinitely many solutions, 173–174
    with no solution, 171–172
    with one variable, 163–164, 208
  lines
    given two points, 264–265
    of parallel, 258–259, 262, 264
    point and slope on line, 260–261
    slope and y-intercept, 256–257
  solving algebraic, 160, 199
  involving variables that is squared or cubed, 91–92
  subtracting, 322–323
  equivalent, 158

Exponential notations, **45**
  expressions
    divide, 57–58
    expand
      evaluate, 47–48
    multiply, 57–58, 100
  write numbers in, 45–46

Exponents, 41, 99
  negative, 82, 84, 99
  positive, 114
  prime factorization of a number, 49–50
  properties of, 64, 66, 75–79, 146
  zero, 79–81, 99

Expressions
  in exponential notation
    multiplying and dividing, 57–58
  simplifying
    negative exponents, 82, 84, 99
    properties of exponents, 64, 66, 75–76
    zero exponent, 79–81, 99

F

Formula, *throughout, see for example*, 47–52, 108, 191–194, 229–264, 372

Fractions
  as repeating decimals, 161, 166

G

Giga, 129

Graphical method, **349**–350, 352, 354, 373

Graphing calculator
  systems of linear equations, 317, 350
  table of values, 185

Graphs
  direct proportion, 220
  of linear equations, 271
    using m and a point, 276
    using m and b, 273–275
    using slope and y-intercept, 358
    using table of values, 271–273, 358
  slope of line, 225–227
  systems of linear equations, 349–350, 352, 354
  x-intercept, **246**
  y-intercept, **246**

Measurement
and the prefix system, 129

Mega, 129

Micro, 129

Milli, 129

Multiplication
decimals by positive powers of 10, 112
expressions in exponential notation,
57–58
integers, 43
scientific notation, 135–136

Nano, 129

Negative exponents, 82, 84, 99, 114

Notations
exponential, *see* Exponential notation
scientific, *see* Scientific notation

Number lines, *throughout, see for example*, 2–3, 16,
42, 162, 199–201
irrational numbers on
using area of squares, 7–8, 10
using calculator, 11–12
rational numbers on, 2
comparing, 5

Numbers
comparing
irrational, 42
in scientific notation, 116, 118
cube roots, **90**–91
different powers of 10, 126–127
divisibility rules, 49
irrational, *see* Irrational numbers
rational, *see* rational numbers
real, **15**, 32, 42
rounding, 6

same power of 10, 123–124
of significant digits, **19**–32
square roots, **89**–90, 95
writing
in exponential notation, **45**–46
in scientific notation, **113**–115
in standard form **115**–116

One-variable
linear equations with, 163–164, 208
real-world problems, 167–168
linear inequalities with, 199–200
real-world problems, 202

Ordering real numbers, 15–16

Parallel lines, 258–259, 262, 264

Perfect square, 44

Pico, 129

Pictorial representations
bar models, *see* Bar models
number lines, *see* Number lines
line graphs, *see* Line graphs

Point of intersection, **351**–354

Positive exponents, 84

Power, 45
of 10
adding and subtracting, 123–127
multiplying and dividing decimals, 112
power of, 61–62, 64, 99
of product, 71–72, 99
product of, 53–54, 99
of quotient, 73–74, 99
quotient of, 55–56, 99

Prefix system, 129–130, 146

Prime factorization, 49–50

Problem solving
real-world problems, *see* Real-world problems

Product
> power of a, 71–72, 99
> of powers property, 53–54, 99

Properties
> of exponents, 64, 66, 75–76
> product of powers, 53–54, 99
> quotient of powers, 55–56, 99

Proportions
> direct, 220

Quotient
> power of a, 73–74, 99, *see also*, Power
> of powers property, 55–56, 99

Rational numbers, 8, 32, 42
> in $\frac{m}{n}$ form, 2
> on a number line, 2
> > comparing, 5
> repeating decimals, 3, 32, 42
> terminating decimals, 3, 32, 42

Real numbers, **15**, 32, 42, *see also*, Numbers
> ordering, 15–16

Real-world linear relationship, 280

Real-world problems, 208, 298, 373
> algebraic equations for, 313
> compare two slopes, 228, 230
> interpreting slopes and *y*-intercepts, 279–280, 282, 284–285
> linear equations, 208, 279
> > with one variable, 167–168, 208
> linear inequalities, 208
> > with one variable, 202, 208
> squares or cubes, 89, 93–94
> systems of linear equations for, 339–340, 342

Repeating decimals, **42**
> fractions as, 161, 166
> writing rational numbers as, 3, 32

Rise, **222**

Rounding
> decimals to significant digits, 22–23
> numbers, 6
> whole numbers to significant digits, 21–22

Rules
> divisibility, 49

Run, **222**

Scientific notation, **113**
> adding
> > with different power of 10, 126–127
> > with same power of 10, 123–124
> comparing numbers in, 116, 118
> dividing in, 135, 137–138
> multiplying in, 135–136
> subtracting
> > with different power of 10, 126–127
> > with same power of 10, 123–124
> understanding, 113
> writing numbers in, 113–115

Significant digits, **19**, 32
> number of, 19–20
> rounding decimals, 22–23
> rounding whole numbers, 21–22

Signs
> adding and subtracting integers, 43
> multiplying and dividing integers, 43

Simplify expressions
> negative exponents, 82, 84
> > power property, 64
> > product property, 72
> > properties of exponents, 64, 66

Slopes, **222**, 298
> comparing two, 228, 230
> comparing two unit rates using, 222, 224
> of line
> > given graph, 225–227
> > horizontal, 231–233, 298
> > passing through two points, 234, 236–238
> > vertical, 231–233, 298
> negative, 225, 298
> and point on line form, 260–261
> positive, 225, 298
> undefined, 232

Writing
    numbers in exponential notation, **45**–46
    prime factorization using exponents, 49–50

Writing equations, *see also*, Equations
    line given two points, 265
    of parallel lines, 258–259, 262, 264
    slope and point on line, 260–261

x-intercept, **246**

y-intercept, **246**, 255–257
    real-world problem solving, 279–280, 282,
        284–285

Zero
    exponent, 79–81, 99
    slope, 231

Photo Credits

1: © Thomas Trompeter/Shutter Stock, 29: Created by Fwstudio - Freepik.com, 40tr: © Viacheslav Dyachkov/Dreamstime.com, 40mr: © Eugene_Sim/Think Stock/iStock, 41: © dwphotos/Think Stock/iStock, 97: Created by Fwstudio - Freepik.com, 107b: © Khunaspix/Dreamstime.com, 108b: © dwphotos/Think Stock/iStock, 110mr: © msymons/Think Stock/iStock, 111: © Meinzahn/Dreamstime.com, 111mr: © greenleaf123/Think Stock/iStock, 143: Created by Fwstudio - Freepik.com, 157: © Irochka/Dreamstime.com, 205: Created by Fwstudio - Freepik.com, 207b: © Monkey Business Images/Dreamstime.com, 215: © Irochka/Dreamstime.com, 219: © Dmitry Molchanov/Dreamstime.com, 293: Created by Fwstudio - Freepik.com, 309b: © Svitlana Imnadze/Dreamstime.com, 311: © palette7/123rf.com, 371: Created by Fwstudio - Freepik.com

NOTES

© 2020 Marshall Cavendish Education Pte Ltd

Published by Marshall Cavendish Education
Times Centre, 1 New Industrial Road, Singapore 536196
Customer Service Hotline: (65) 6213 9688
US Office Tel: (1-914) 332 8888 | Fax: (1-914) 332 8882
E-mail: cs@mceducation.com
Website: www.mceducation.com

Distributed by
Houghton Mifflin Harcourt
125 High Street
Boston, MA 02110
Tel: 617-351-5000
Website: www.hmhco.com/programs/math-in-focus

First published 2020

ISBN 978-0-358-10194-9

Printed in Singapore

2 3 4 5 6 7 8   1401   25 24 23 22
4500839429   B C D E F

The cover image shows a rockhopper penguin.
Rockhopper penguins live in the cold waters of South America, South Africa, and Antarctica. They feed on small fish, krill, or squid. A unique characteristic is the yellow crest on their heads. They are amazing swimmers, but are also very agile on land, getting their name from the way they leap effortlessly over rocks. There are no distinct differences in physical characteristics between the males and females so a DNA test is required to check the gender of a rockhopper penguin.